Meaningful And Manageable Assessment Through Cooperative Learning

David W. Johnson And Roger T. Johnson

Interaction Book Company
7208 Cornelia Drive
Edina, Minnesota 55435
(612) 831-9500, FAX (612) 831-9332

This book is dedicated to the teachers who build cooperative learning groups in which members (a) strive for academic excellence and (b) are committed to each other and each other's learning.

ISBN 0-0939603-25-X

Table Of Contents

Preface

The purpose of this book is to provide you with a practical guide to (a) make your assessments more meaningful and manageable and (b) help you use cooperative learning as an inherent part of the assessment process. Read this book carefully and apply its content immediately and often in the classes you teach.

With the call for increased accountability of schools there has been an emphasis on assessment. In this book we have presented a wide range of procedures for assessment in a meaningful and practical format that makes them easy to understand. Most of the more powerful and interesting assessment procedures require considerable time and effort to implement and use. Teachers simply do not have the time and energy to use them. Cooperative learning groups provide the setting in which the new assessment procedures can be integrated with instruction so that students provide the assistance teachers need. With the use of cooperative learning, you can link what is taught with what is measured. The more skillfully instruction and assessment are interwoven in cooperative learning groups, the more students will learn and the more successful the teacher will be.

This book will be most useful when you read it with one or more colleagues. In reading and discussing this book with colleagues, you are then in position to help each other implement new assessment procedures with real fidelity in your classrooms. Implementing new assessment procedures, as with all teaching, is like being in love--it always goes better with two.

We would like to thank Linda Johnson for editing and preparing the graphics for this book and Catherine Mulholland and Laurie Stevahn for their help in editing. Their creativity and hard work are deeply appreciated.

Chapter One: Making Assessment Manageable And Meaningful

What Is Assessment?

Education is not filling a pail. It is lighting a fire.

W. B. Yeats

Aesop tells of two travelers who were walking along the seashore. Far out they saw something riding on the waves. "*Look*," said one, "*a great ship rides in from distant lands, bearing rich treasures!*" As the object came closer, the other said, "*That is not a great treasure ship. It is a fisherman's skiff, with the day's catch of savory fish!*" Still nearer came the object and the waves washed it up on shore. "*It's a chest of gold lost from some wreck*," they cried. Both travelers rushed to the beach, but there they found nothing but a water-soaked log. The moral of the story is, **Before you reach a conclusion, do a careful assessment**.

Doing careful assessments is an inherent responsibility of being an educator. Instruction, learning, assessment, and evaluation are all interrelated. Teachers are responsible for instructing students to create learning, which is assessed in order to (a) verify learning is taking place and (b) improve the effectiveness of instruction. Periodically, the assessment is used to judge the quality and quantity of learning and award grades. Instruction, learning, assessment and evaluation are so intertwined that it is hard to separate them. In the table below, match the definition with the appropriate concept. Compare your answers with the answers of a partner, and then explain to him or her how instruction, learning, assessment, and evaluation are interrelated.

Concept	Definition
_____ 1. Instruction	a. Change within a student that is brought about by instruction.
_____ 2. Learning	b. Judging the merit, value, or desirability of a measured performance.
_____ 3. Assessment	c. Structuring of situations in ways that help students change, through learning.
_____ 4. Evaluation	d. Collecting information about the quality or quantity of a change in a student, group, teacher, or administrator.

(1: c, 2: a, 3: d, 4: b)

Meaningful And Manageable Assessment Through Cooperative Learning, Interaction Book Company, 7208 Cornelia Drive, Edina, MN 55435, (612) 831-9500, FAX (612) 831-9332

Assessment And Evaluation

You can have assessment without evaluation, but you cannot have evaluation without assessment. Ideally, you assess continually while only occasionally evaluating. You can use the information provided by assessments to (a) evaluate students to award grades, honors (such as National Honor Society, Honor's lists, Valedictorian), and graduation based on exit criteria (knowledge and skills students need to be graduated from a program, grade, or school), (b) evaluate the instructional program to award teachers recognition and merit salary increases, and (c) evaluate schools and districts to compare their effectiveness with that of other districts, states, and countries (in order to make such comparisons, schools have to use the same assessment procedures). The quality of the assessment largely determines the quality of the evaluation. If the assessment is faulty, the evaluation will be faulty. A valid judgment can only be made if an accurate and complete assessment has taken place.

Assessment Issues

In order to plan, conduct, and manage meaningful assessments, you need to answer the following questions:

1. What are the student performances that may be assessed?
2. What are the assessment procedures that may be used?
3. What is the purpose of the assessment?
4. What is the focus of the assessment?
5. In what setting will the assessment be conducted?
6. How will these questions be answered so a meaningful assessment results?
7. How will these questions be answered so the assessment is manageable?
8. How will cooperative learning make the assessment more meaningful and manageable?

What Is Assessed?

In understanding what is to be assessed, you must select the student performances that you want to assess and the procedures you will use. In doing so, you must understand the purpose of the assessment, its focus, the setting in which the assessment will take place, what is at stake, and who are the relevant stakeholders.

Meaningful And Manageable Assessment Through Cooperative Learning, Interaction Book Company, 7208 Cornelia Drive, Edina, MN 55435, (612) 831-9500, FAX (612) 831-9332

Student Performances Assessed

There is an old saying, "*What gets measured gets done.*" What teachers assess may be the single most powerful message as to what teachers value and wish to accomplish. There are so many indices of student learning that all cannot be discussed in any one book. Given below, however, are some of the most common indices of student learning:

1. **Academic Learning**: What students know, understand, and retain over time.

2. **Reasoning**: The quality of students' reasoning, conceptual frameworks, use of the scientific method and problem-solving, and construction of academic arguments.

3. **Skills And Competencies**: Examples are oral and written communication skills, teamwork skills, research skills, skills of organizing and analyzing information, technology skills, skills of coping with stress and adversity, conflict resolution skills.

4. **Attitudes**: The attitudes students develop, such as a love of learning, commitment to being a responsible citizen, desire to read, liking scientific reasoning, self-respect, liking of diversity, commitment to making the world a better place, and many others.

5. **Work Habits**: The work habits students develop, such as completing work on time, using time wisely, meeting responsibilities, striving for quality work, continuously improving one's work, striving to add value to each job one does, and so forth.

Assessment Procedures

After deciding which student performances to assess, you need to decide which procedures you will use. The procedures you can use include:

Goal Setting Conferences

Standardized Tests

Teacher-Made Tests, Quizzes, Exams

Written Compositions

Oral Presentations

Projects, Experiments,

Portfolios

Observations

Simulations

Questionnaires

Interviews

Learning Logs & Journals

Student Management Teams

Total Quality Learning Procedures

Teacher Assessment Teams

Student-Led Parent Conferences

Record Keeping (Attendance, Participation, Homework, Extra-Credit)

Each of the above procedures is discussed in some detail in this book. Each chapter introduces one or more tools to assess students' learning and addresses the questions:

1. What is the procedure/tool?
2. Why should you use it?
3. How should you use it?
4. How do you adapt (customize) it to your needs?

To decide which student performances are to be assessed by what procedures, you will wish to clarify the purpose of your assessment, whether it will focus on processes or outcomes, the setting in which the assessment will take place, and whether the assessment will be of high or low stakes to which stakeholders.

Assessment Issues

Purpose	Focus	Setting	Stakes	Stakeholders
Diagnostic	Process Of Learning	Artificial (Classroom)	Low	Students-Parents
Formative	Process Of Instruction	Authentic (Real-World)	High	Teachers
Summative	Outcomes Of Learning			Administrators
	Outcomes Of Instruction			Policy-Makers
				Colleges, Employers

Purpose Of Assessment

To achieve your purposes, you match the student performances you can assess with the appropriate assessment method. The purposes for assessing may be to (a) diagnose students' present level of knowledge and skills, (b) monitor progress toward learning goals to help form the instructional program, and (c) provide data to judge the final level of students' learning.

1. **Diagnostic assessments** are conducted at the beginning of an instructional unit, course, semester, or year to determine the present level of knowledge, skill, interest, and attitudes of a student, group, or class. Diagnostic assessments are never used for giving grades. Information about the student's entry level characteristics enables the teacher and student to set realistic but challenging learning goals. The better the diagnosis, the more clear and specific the learning goals will be.

2. **Formative assessments** are conducted periodically throughout the instructional unit, course, semester, or year to monitor progress and provide feedback concerning

Meaningful And Manageable Assessment Through Cooperative Learning, Interaction Book Company, 7208 Cornelia Drive, Edina, MN 55435, (612) 831-9500, FAX (612) 831-9332

progress toward learning goals. Its intention is to facilitate or form learning. Formative assessments are an integral part of the ongoing learning process for two reasons. **First**, they provide students with feedback concerning the progress they are making toward achieving their learning goals. On the basis of that feedback, students can plan what they need to do next to advance their learning. **Second**, formative assessments provide teachers with feedback concerning their progress in providing effective instruction. Teachers can then plan what to do next to help students achieve their learning goals. Formative evaluations are not used to evaluate either the student or the teacher.

3. **Summative assessments** are conducted at the end of an instructional unit or semester to judge the final quality and quantity of student achievement and/or the success of the instructional program. They sum up performance and provide the data for giving grades and determining the extent to which goals and objectives have been met and desired outcomes achieved. The judgments about student achievement are then communicated to interested audiences such as students, parents, administrators, post-secondary educational institutions, and potential employers.

Focus Of Assessment

Diagnostic, formative, and summative assessments may take place to improve the process of learning or to determine the outcomes of learning. In conducting formative assessments, you may focus on both the process of learning and the outcomes of learning. In conducting summative assessments, you focus primarily on outcomes.

1. **The Processes Of Learning:** To improve continuously the quality of students' efforts to learn, you must engineer a system whereby the processes students use to learn are identified and assessed. Instead of only conducting summative assessments, formative assessments are conducted. The assumption is that if you continuously improve the processes of learning, the quality and quantity of student learning will also continuously improve. To implement **total quality learning**, you assign students to cooperative learning groups. Each group takes charge of the quality of the work of its members. The group (a) defines and organizes the process members are going to use to learn, (b) assesses the quality of members' engagement of each step of the process, (c) places the data on a quality chart, and (d) plans how to improve the effectiveness of the learning process.

2. **The Processes Of Instruction:** To improve continuously the quality of instruction colleagial teaching teams (a) define the instructional process, (b) assess the quality of members' engagement in each step of the process, (c) place the data on a quality chart, and (d) plan how to improve the effectiveness of the instructional process.

Meaningful And Manageable Assessment Through Cooperative Learning, Interaction Book Company, 7208 Cornelia Drive, Edina, MN 55435, (612) 831-9500, FAX (612) 831-9332

Accountability For What?

Schools are under increasing accountability pressures to reexamine the outcomes they are trying to achieve.

1. **The definitions of achievement have expanded.** In addition to doing well on standardized tests, students are expected to be able to demonstrate (a) achievement related behaviors (ability to communicate, cooperate, perform certain motor activities, and solve complex problems, (b) achievement-related products (writing themes or project reports, art products, craft products), or (c) achievement-related attitudes and dispositions (pride in work, desire to improve continuously one's competencies, commitment to quality, internal locus of control, self-esteem).

2. **The organizational structure of the school is changing.** With the change to a team-based, high-performance organizational structure (that emphasizes cooperative learning in the classroom and colleagial teaching teams in the building), teachers are expected to work in teams to assess (a) the quality of students' teamwork skills and (b) the quality of the instructional program.

3. **High school and college graduates often lack the competencies necessary to be citizens in our society and live a high-quality life.** Schools are being held accountable to teach successfully what students need to (a) advance educationally, (b) get and hold a job, (c) be a responsible citizen, and (d) have a high quality of life. Many graduates are unemployable, uninformed on current issues, and unmotivated to vote or participate in the political process. They fail to build and maintain stable friendships and family relationships. A fourth-grade teacher may think primarily in terms of getting students ready for the fifth-grade, and a high-school teacher may think primarily in terms of getting students ready for college instead of preparing students to live productive lives in society.

4. **Many schools are blind to the need to prepare students to compete with graduates of schools in other countries for jobs and promotions.** The internationalization of the economy has resulted in an internationalization of schools. It is no longer enough to be one of the best schools in a local area, in a state, or even in the nation. The quality of a school in America has to be compared with the quality of schools in Japan, Germany, Finland, Thailand, and every other country in the world. Schools in America have to be educating "*world-class workers*" and individuals who are able to work for and be successful in international companies that have branches and employees from all over the world.

3. **The Outcomes Of Learning:** To assess the quality and quantity of student learning, you need (a) an appropriate method of sampling the desired student performances and (b) a clearly articulated set of criteria to judge their quality and

Meaningful And Manageable Assessment Through Cooperative Learning, Interaction Book Company, 7208 Cornelia Drive, Edina, MN 55435, (612) 831-9500, FAX (612) 831-9332

quantity. You can use paper-and-pencil tests or you can have students perform a procedure or skill, such as writing a composition or conducting a science experiment.

4. **The Outcomes Of Instruction:** You assess the effectiveness of instruction by measuring whether the instructional program actually motivated students to strive to learn above and beyond their usual level.

Setting Of Assessments

Assessments may take place in artificial situations (such as the classroom) or in authentic or "real life" settings. **Authentic assessment** requires students to demonstrate desired skills or procedures in "real-life" contexts. Since it is difficult to place students in many real-life situations, you may wish to have students complete simulated real-life tasks or solve simulated real-life problems. To conduct an authentic assessment in science, for example, you may assign students to research teams working on a cure for cancer who must (a) conduct an experiment, (b) write a lab report summarizing results, (c) write a journal article, and (d) make an oral presentation at a simulated convention. Like performance-based assessment, to conduct an authentic assessment you need procedures for (a) sampling performances and (b) developing criteria for evaluation. You also need the imagination to find real-life situations or create simulations of them.

List three examples of authentic assessment you have used in your classes:

1. ______________________________
2. ______________________________
3. ______________________________

Stakes And Stakeholders

There are at least four audiences for the results of assessments of students' learning, instructional programs, and the effectiveness of a school: Students and their parents, teachers, administrators, and policy makers. For each of these audiences, assessments can be of high or low importance. In designing and conducting assessments, you must determine who the audiences for the assessment will be and what kind of stake they have in its results.

1. **Low Stake Assessments**: Formative assessments of student learning and classroom instruction tend to be low stake as they are designed and administered by teachers for the purpose of giving students feedback and guiding instructional decisions. Students are not adversely affected if they perform poorly on low-stake assessments and teachers are not penalized if a lesson does not go well.

Meaningful And Manageable Assessment Through Cooperative Learning, Interaction Book Company, 7208 Cornelia Drive, Edina, MN 55435, (612) 831-9500, FAX (612) 831-9332

2. **High Stake Assessments**: Summative assessments that may partially determine students' futures or whether teachers receive merit raises tend to be high stake. College admission tests such as the SAT or the ACT are high-stakes assessments for students because admission to colleges and universities is affected by these scores. Statewide assessments or some standardized tests are typically high-stakes assessments for teachers, schools, or districts but not students. In some districts, the average scores of different schools or districts within the state are published in the newspaper, which can influence real estate values and are, therefore, of high stake for many interested audiences.

The Stake You Have In Assessments

1. List the assessment procedures you use.
2. Divide your list into two categories: High Stake and Low Stake.
3. Repeat Step 2 for each of the major stakeholders in your school.

Stakeholders In Assessment

Students-Parents	Teachers	Administrators	Policy-Makers
Determine Student Progress	Diagnose Students' Strengths And Weaknesses	Monitor Effectiveness Of Teachers	Set Standards
Diagnose Student's Strengths And Weaknesses	Give Students Feedback	Monitor Effectiveness Of Instructional Programs	Monitor The Quality Of Education
Plan How To Improve Students' Achievement	Determine Students' Grades	Identify Program Strengths And Weaknesses	Formulate Policies
Understand What Is Expected Of Them In School	Make Grouping Decisions	Designate Priorities	
Make Informed Decisions About College And Careers	Determine Effectiveness Of Instruction And Curriculum		
	Decide How To Modify & Improve Instructional Program		

The danger of low-stake assessments is that students and faculty may not take them seriously. The danger of high-stake assessments is that students and faculty may be tempted to cheat in some manner.

Meaningful And Manageable Assessment Through Cooperative Learning, Interaction Book Company, 7208 Cornelia Drive, Edina, MN 55435, (612) 831-9500, FAX (612) 831-9332

Making Assessments Meaningful

Just because an assessment is conducted does not mean that it will achieve its purpose or be perceived as meaningful by relevant stakeholders. Assessments have meaning when they (a) achieve a significant purpose, (b) provide clear and useful information to stakeholders, and (c) provide clear direction for increasing the quality of learning and instruction. **First, to be meaningful, assessment has to have a purpose that is significant.** Significant purposes include (a) giving students and other stakeholders accurate and detailed feedback on the process students are using to learn and the quality and quantity of their learning and (b) improving learning and instruction. The more assessment focuses on actual student performances in authentic settings, reflects the breadth and depth of the instructional goals and curricula, and reflects shared goals, the more meaningful it becomes. **Meaningless assessment** is assessment conducted with no specific purpose that results in information that is too general and ambiguous to be used to improve learning or instruction.

Second, assessments are meaningful when students are involved in conducting the assessment. In meaningful assessments students (a) understand the assessment procedures, (b) invest their own time and energy in making the assessment process work, (c) take ownership of assessing the quality and quantity of their work, and (d) want to share their work and talk about it with others. **Meaningless assessment** results when students do not understand the procedures, are uninvolved, feel the assessment is being forced on them, and do not want to share the results with anyone else. Conducting the assessment in an authentic context may help assessment be meaningful by catching students' attention, holding their interest, and involving them in the process. For parents, assessments tend to be meaningful when parents understand the procedures used to assess student learning and they obtain a clear picture of their children's academic performance.

Third, meaningful assessments provide a direction and road map for future efforts to learn. Assessments should give a direction for correcting misunderstandings, filling in gaps in learning, and advancing to the next level of knowledge and skill. Assessments are more meaningful as the results are used to improve learning and instruction. **Meaningless assessments** may provide achievement scores with no implications for what the student should do to correct and advance his or her learning.

The meaning of the assessment is part of the overall meaning contained in the learning process. **Meaning is created through involvement which leads to commitment and ownership.** There are five steps in making assessment meaningful. You must ensure students are involved in (a) setting learning goals, (b) planning how to achieve their learning goals, and (c) the assessment process to determine progress and success in achieving their goals. The assessment results are used for students to (d) take pride and satisfaction from their efforts to learn and (e) set new learning goals and repeat the first four steps.

What Makes Assessments Meaningful?

Rank order from most important ("1") to least important ("8") the following ways that assessments can be meaningful.

_____ Parents understanding the assessment procedures and process and having a clear picture of how well their children are doing academically.

_____ Giving teachers and other stakeholders accurate and detailed feedback on the quality of instruction.

_____ Students wanting to share their work and talk about it with others.

_____ Students investing their own time and energy in conducting the assessment.

_____ Making assessment procedures and process easily understandable.

_____ Conducting the assessment in an authentic context.

_____ Students feeling ownership of the assessment procedures and process.

_____ Giving students and other stakeholders accurate and detailed feedback on the quality and quantity of student learning.

Step One: Involve students in setting their own learning goals (see Chapter 2). People strive to achieve goals they set for themselves, but resist and resent goals imposed on them by others. Involvement in setting goals comes from (a) participation (b) with others (c) to contribute to the common good (d) leads to doing one's best.

a. **Participation**: By participating in setting their own learning goals students (1) can ensure that the goals relate to their central needs and values and (2) develop ownership of the goals.

b. **With Others:** More involvement comes from being part of a group effort than from working alone. A student's peer group and classmates often have considerable influence on the student's academic aspirations. The more learning goals reflect group aspirations as well as personal aspirations, the more significant the goals will be and the more committed students will be to achieving them.

c. **To Contribute To The Common Good:** Meaning increases as students go beyond self-interest and adopt the goals of contributing to the others' well-being and the common good. The more one wants to achieve a higher purpose beyond one's own success, the more significant the goals will be. Children are natural collaborators whose highest involvement and joys may be (a) the natural joy of mastering new knowledge and competencies and (b) the joy of using what is

Meaningful And Manageable Assessment Through Cooperative Learning, Interaction Book Company, 7208 Cornelia Drive, Edina, MN 55435, (612) 831-9500, FAX (612) 831-9332

learned to benefit others. The more group members' learning goals are interdependent (so efforts to achieve one's own goals contribute to others' success and the overall group productivity), the more meaningful and significant are the learning goals.

d. **Leads To Striving To Do One's Best**: Involvement comes from adopting goals that represent a realistic but challenging level of aspiration. The greater the achievement of each individual, the greater the contribution to the common good. The harder each group member works, the greater the benefit for all members.

Step Two: Involve students in planning the path to be taken to achieve their learning goals. Again, involvement tends to lead to commitment and ownership. People follow the paths they have planned for themselves while deviating from and subverting the paths imposed on them by others. The involvement in planning the path to achieve learning groups increases as students plan in cooperative learning groups, especially when the plan (a) utilizes each student's talents and competencies and (b) gives each student the support and assistance of other members.

Step Three: Involve students in assessing the progress they and their classmates are making in achieving their goals. Assessment becomes more meaningful when students are involved in planning the assessment process. The involvement includes (a) discussing and clarifying the assessment process with groupmates (a shared mental model results), (b) assessing one's own and groupmates' learning (clearer understanding of quality work results), and (c) sharing their work and progress with each other.

Step Four: Help students take satisfaction from and pride in achieving their goals and helping groupmates achieve their goals. Joint celebrations in cooperative learning groups result in greater pride and satisfaction than does a solitary reflection on one's achievement. Students need to (a) share the joy and satisfaction of achieving their goals with others and (b) take pride in the help they have provided to others.

Step Five: Involve students in using the results of the assessment to set new goals and repeat steps one through four. Students need to plan how to correct misunderstandings, fill in gaps in learning, and advance to the next level of knowledge and skill.

Making Assessment Manageable

Meaningful assessments are hard to manage. Many assessment procedures are labor intensive, involve more than one modality, examine more diverse outcomes, require multi-sources of information, require more authentic settings, and are aimed at more complex procedures. One teacher can no longer manage the assessment system. It takes

Meaningful And Manageable Assessment Through Cooperative Learning, Interaction Book Company, 7208 Cornelia Drive, Edina, MN 55435, (612) 831-9500, FAX (612) 831-9332

the involvement of students, working in cooperative learning groups. **Cooperative learning groups provide**:

Problems In Conducting Fair & Complete Assessments

Rank the following problems in conducting good assessment from most important to you ("1") to least important to you ("12"). Add any other problems you can think of. Then explain how having students working together in cooperative learning groups creates possible solutions to the problems.

______ Amount of time and effort required to implement the assessment process.

______ Limited primarily to reading and writing as modalities.

______ Outcomes most commonly assessed are subject matter knowledge and recognition of facts.

______ Sources of information limited to teacher assessments.

______ Results biased by making reading and writing a prerequisite for demonstrating knowledge and skill.

______ Most individual students lack the resources necessary to implement continuous improvement process.

______ Many individual students will not learn the criteria and rubrics used to assess their work.

______ Assessment process is not a learning experience for most individual students.

______ Teacher bias can effect the assessment and evaluation process.

______ Many individual students are not able to learn from assessments, make improvement plans, and implement plans on their own.

______ Only individual outcomes can be assessed.

______ Assessing individual students in isolation is incongruent with ideal instructional experiences.

______ Other:

______ Other:

1. **Additional sources of labor to conduct assessments and communicate the results**. Traditionally, only the teacher conducted assessments. The teacher and only the teacher administered tests and graded compositions. Many of the most important assessment procedures are labor intensive. Teachers simply do not have the time to use them without help and assistance. The most natural sources of help for teachers are students and colleagues. Students are involved because they are always present in the classroom. Student commitment to implement the results of an assessment is greater when they collect, analyze, and interpret the data themselves. Students, therefore, need to learn the assessment rubrics and use them to reflect on and assess their own and their classmates' work.

2. **More modalities to be used in assessing students' work**. In addition to reading and writing, learning in cooperative groups allows for assessment procedures such as observing students speaking and listening, performing cognitive and social skills, demonstrating higher-level reasoning procedures, using visuals such as graphs and illustrations, and even acting out or role playing aspects of the content being learned. These modalities are unavailable when students work alone, individualistically or competitively.

3. **More diverse outcomes to be assessed**. Besides subject matter knowledge and expertise, cooperative learning groups enable teachers to assess a wide variety of other outcomes:

   a. The verbal interaction required in cooperative learning groups gives teachers a "*window in each student's mind*" that enables teachers to assess students' critical thinking and level of reasoning. The processes of reasoning and problem-solving are made public so that they can be assessed and improved.

   b. In cooperative learning groups, students can perform academic skills (conducting a science experiment), cognitive skills (ability to give clear explanations), and social skills.

   c. It is within cooperative learning groups that the intellectual challenge, disagreement, and controversy takes place that fuels higher-level reasoning, divergent thinking, creativity, and long-term retention (Johnson & Johnson, 1995c). Without cooperative learning groups, academic controversies cannot be structured and their processes and outcomes cannot be assessed and improved.

   d. The interaction among group members can reflect attitudes toward the subject area and learning. Learning in cooperative groups not only creates more positive attitudes, but it provides a setting in which they can be assessed and improved.

Management Problems With Assessment

Problem	Solution
Amount of time and effort required to implement the assessment process.	Have cooperative groups manage the assessment process for their members.
Limited primarily to reading and writing as modalities.	Expand modalities by having students work in groups where they can be observed, perform cognitive and social skills, demonstrate higher-level reasoning, and so forth.
Outcomes most commonly assessed are subject matter knowledge and recognition of facts.	Have students work in cooperative groups where more diverse outcomes can be assessed, such as critical thinking, academic, cognitive, and social skills.
Sources of information limited to teacher assessments.	Have students work in cooperative groups to include self and peer assessments in addition to teacher assessments.
Results biased by making reading and writing a prerequisite for demonstrating knowledge and skill.	Use cooperative groups so students can exchange and reveal knowledge orally and demonstrate skills.
Most individual students lack the resources necessary to implement the continuous improvement process.	Use cooperative groups so that continuous improvement process can be implemented.
Many individual students will not learn the criteria and rubrics used to assess their work.	Use cooperative groups to ensure that all group members learn the criteria and rubrics used to assess their work.
Assessment process is not a learning experience for most individual students.	Use cooperative groups to involve students in assessing each others' work thereby learn from the assessment process.
Teacher bias can effect the assessment and evaluation process.	Reduce possibility of teacher bias by using cooperative learning groups and involving members in assessing each other's work.
Many individual students are not able to learn from assessments, make improvement plans, and implement plans on their own.	Use cooperative learning groups to provide students a support system for creating and implementing improvement plans.
Only individual outcomes can be assessed.	Use cooperative learning groups so group outcomes can be assessed in addition to individual outcomes.
Assessing individual students in isolation is incongruent with ideal instructional experiences.	Use cooperative learning groups so that assessment process is congruent with ideal instructional methods.

4. **More sources of information**. Cooperative learning makes self and peer assessments available as well as teacher assessments. Self, peer, and teacher assessments can then be coordinated and integrated. Students and classmates as well as teachers can be involved in communicating the results of assessments to interested audiences.

5. **A way to avoid the bias present when reading and writing are made a prerequisite for revealing knowledge or engaging in a performance**. In cooperative learning groups, students can learn subject matter orally and reveal their understanding of what was learned orally. Other group members can read questions to a student who cannot read or write well, and the student can explain to groupmates step-by-step how the answer may be derived or what the answer is.

6. **A way to avoid the possibility of teacher bias impacting the assessment and evaluation process**. There are numerous ways that bias may be introduced into teachers' assessments. Even characteristics such as neatness of handwriting (Sweedler-Brown, 1992) and teachers' perceptions of students' behavior (Bennett et al., 1993; Hills, 1991) can influence a teacher's judgment of a student's achievement.

7. **A setting in which students may best learn the rubrics used to assess and communicate about each student's work**. Understanding the rubrics help students produce higher quality work, understand feedback, and assess their classmates work.

8. **A setting in which assessment can promote academic learning**. When the assessment requires group members to discuss the accuracy, quality, and quantity of their own and each other's work, learning is enhanced while the assessment and reporting are taking place.

9. **For group outcomes to be assessed as well as individual outcomes**. There are times when groups' scientific, dramatic, or creative projects need to be assessed.

10. **The support system necessary to implement the improvement plan resulting from the assessment**. Communication of results must directly point towards what needs to be improved and what the students do next.

11. **For the continuous improvement process to be an ongoing part of classroom life**. Cooperative learning groups provide the resources for making the continuous improvement of learning part of every lesson. **Total quality learning** requires that students be organized into teams working to continuously improve the process of learning. Continuous improvement requires continuous assessment.

12. **The means to make assessment procedures congruent with ideal instructional methods**. Instructional and assessment procedures need to be aligned so they work for, not against, each other. Since cooperative learning tends to promote higher achievement and a variety of other outcomes (Johnson & Johnson, 1989), it is used

increasingly as the dominant instructional method in most classes and, therefore, ways to use the new assessment procedures with cooperative learning need to be identified.

What gets measured gets noticed and, in turn, influences what is taught. To overcome the simplistic view of education as textbook driven lectures, assessment procedures must focus on higher-level reasoning, problem solving, and meta-cognitive thinking. To do so, assessment must take place in a group setting.

Demonstrate your understanding of the different types of groups by matching the definitions with the appropriate group. Check your answers with your partner and explain why you believe your answers to be correct.

Type Of Group	Definition
_____ **Pseudo Group**	a. A group in which students work together to accomplish shared goals. Students perceive they can reach their learning goals if and only if the other group members also reach their goals.
_____ **Traditional Learning Group**	b. A group whose members have been assigned to work together but they have no interest in doing so. The structure promotes competition at close quarters.
_____ **Cooperative Learning Groups**	c. A group whose members agree to work together, but see little benefit from doing so. The structure promotes individualistic work with talking.
_____ **High-Performance Cooperative Learning Group**	d. A group that meets all the criteria for being a cooperative group and outperforms all reasonable expectations, given its membership.

Meaningful And Manageable Assessment Through Cooperative Learning, Interaction Book Company, 7208 Cornelia Drive, Edina, MN 55435, (612) 831-9500, FAX (612) 831-9332

Understanding Cooperative Learning

Together we stand, divided we fall.

Watchword Of The American Revolution

Sandy Koufax was one of the greatest pitchers in the history of baseball. Although he was naturally talented, he was also unusually well trained and disciplined. He was perhaps the only major-league pitcher whose fastball could be heard to hum. Opposing batters, instead of talking and joking around in the dugout, would sit quietly and listen for Koufax's fastball to hum. When it was their turn to bat, they were already intimidated. There was, however, a simple way for Koufax's genius to have been negated. By making the first author of this book his catcher. To be great, a pitcher needs an outstanding catcher (his great partner was Johnny Roseboro). David is such an unskilled catcher that Koufax would have had to throw the ball much slower in order for David to catch it. This would have deprived Koufax of his greatest weapon. Placing Roger and Edythe at key defensive positions in the infield or outfield, furthermore, would have seriously affected Koufax's success. Sandy Koufax was not a great pitcher on his own. Only as part of a team could Koufax achieve greatness. In baseball and in the classroom it takes a cooperative effort. Extraordinary achievement comes from a cooperative group, not from the individualistic or competitive efforts of an isolated individual.

Types Of Groups	Cooperative Groups	Essential Elements	Outcomes
Psuedo Groups	Formal Cooperative Learning	Positive Interdependence	Effort To Achieve
Traditional Groups	Informal Cooperative Learning	Individual Accountability	Positive Relationships
Cooperative Groups	Cooperative Base Groups	Promotive Interaction	Psychological Health
High-Performance Cooperative Groups		Interpersonal And Small Group Skills	
		Group Processing	

Often in the past, all learning groups were assumed to be the same. There is much more to cooperative learning than seating students together. There is nothing magical about being in a group. Many groups are ineffective and counter-productive. Pseudo and traditional learning groups, for example, provide little if any advantage over individual instruction. Assessment is only enhanced if the groups are truly cooperative. To use the new assessment procedures, students must work in cooperative learning groups. Teachers need to understand what cooperative learning is, the different types of cooperative learning groups, the essential elements of cooperation, and the outcomes resulting from cooperation among students.

Cooperative learning groups exist when students work together to accomplish shared goals. Students perceive that they can reach their learning goals if and only if the other students in the learning group also reach their goals. Thus, students seek outcomes that are beneficial to all those with whom they are cooperatively linked. Students are given two responsibilities: to complete the assignment and to ensure that all other group members complete the assignment. Students discuss material with each other, help one another understand it, and encourage each other to work hard. Individual performance is checked regularly to ensure that all students are contributing and learning. A criteria-referenced evaluation system is used. The result is that the group is more than a sum of its parts and all students perform higher academically than they would if they worked alone.

There are three types of cooperative learning groups. **Formal cooperative learning** groups last from one class period to several weeks. Formal cooperative learning groups ensure that students are actively involved in the intellectual work of organizing material, explaining it, summarizing it, and integrating it into existing conceptual structures. They are the heart of using cooperative learning. **Informal cooperative learning** groups are ad-hoc groups that last from a few minutes to one class period. You use them during direct teaching (lectures, demonstrations, films, videos) to focus students' attention on the material they are to learn, set a mood conducive to learning, help set expectations as to what the lesson will cover, ensure that students cognitively process the material you are teaching, and provide closure to an instructional session. **Cooperative base groups** are long-term (lasting for at least a year), heterogeneous groups with stable membership whose primary purpose is for members to give each other the support, help, encouragement, and assistance each needs to progress academically. Base groups provide students with long-term, committed relationships.

To structure instructional units so students do in fact work cooperatively with each other, you must understand the basic elements that make cooperation work. Mastering the basic elements of cooperation allows you to:

1. Take your existing instructional units, curricula, and courses and structure them cooperatively.

2. Tailor cooperative learning instructional units to your unique instructional needs, circumstances, curricula, subject areas, and students.

3. Diagnose the problems some students may have in working together and intervene to increase the effectiveness of the student learning groups.

For cooperation to work well, you must structure five essential elements in each lesson (Johnson & Johnson, 1989). **The first and most important element is positive interdependence.** You must give a clear task and a group goal so that students believe they "*sink or swim together.*" You have successfully structured positive interdependence when group members perceive that they are linked with each other in a way that one cannot succeed unless everyone succeeds. The work of any member benefits all members. If one fails, all fail. Positive interdependence may be structured through common goals, joint rewards, division of resources, complementary roles, a division of labor, and a joint identity.

The second essential element of cooperative learning is individual (and group) accountability. Each member must be accountable for contributing his or her share of the work (which ensures that no one can "hitch-hike" on the work of others). **Individual accountability** exists when the performance of each individual student is assessed and the results given back to the group and the individual. The purpose of cooperative learning groups is to make each member a stronger individual in his or her right. Students learn together so that they can subsequently perform higher as individuals.

The third essential component of cooperative learning is promotive interaction, preferably face-to-face. Students need to do real work together in which they promote each other's success by orally explaining to each other how to solve problems, discussing with each other the nature of the concepts being learned, teaching their knowledge to classmates, and explaining to each other the connections between present and past learning. Cooperative learning groups are both an academic support system (every student has someone who is committed to helping him or her learn) and a personal support system (every student has someone who is committed to him or her as a person).

The fourth essential element of cooperative learning is teaching students the required interpersonal and small group skills. In cooperative learning groups students are required to learn academic subject matter (taskwork) and also to learn the interpersonal and small group skills required to work together effectively (teamwork). Cooperative learning is inherently more complex than competitive or individualistic learning because students have to engage simultaneously in taskwork and teamwork. Group members must know how to provide effective leadership, decision-making, trust-building, communication, and conflict-management. Procedures and strategies for teaching students social skills may be found in Johnson (1991, 1993) and Johnson and F. Johnson (1994).

The fifth essential component of cooperative learning is group processing. Group processing occurs when group members discuss how well they are achieving their goals and maintaining effective working relationships. Groups need to describe what member actions are helpful and unhelpful and make decisions about what behaviors to continue or change. Continuous improvement of the process of learning results from the

Meaningful And Manageable Assessment Through Cooperative Learning, Interaction Book Company, 7208 Cornelia Drive, Edina, MN 55435, (612) 831-9500, FAX (612) 831-9332

careful analysis of how members are working together and determining how group effectiveness can be enhanced.

Your use of cooperative learning becomes effective through disciplined action. The five basic elements are not just characteristics of good cooperative learning groups. They are a discipline that you have to apply rigorously (much like a diet has to be adhered to) to produce the conditions for effective cooperative action.

Over the past 100 years, hundreds of research studies have been conducted on social interdependence. Cooperation, compared with competitive and individualistic efforts, results in (Johnson & Johnson, 1989):

1. **Higher achievement**. The superiority of cooperation (over competitive and individualistic efforts) increases: the more the task is complex and conceptual, the more problem solving and creativity required, the more higher-level reasoning and critical thinking required, and the more transfer to the "real world" required.

2. **More positive relationships among students and between students and faculty**. This was true even when students were from different ethnic and cultural backgrounds, social classes, and language groups. It was also true for students who were and were not handicapped. Individuals tend to like others with whom they have worked cooperatively.

3. **More positive psychological well-being**. Working with classmates cooperatively has been found to promote greater self-esteem, self-efficacy, social competencies, coping skills, and general psychological health. Included in this area are also students' attitudes toward schooling and subject areas. Working cooperatively tends to result in students developing more positive attitudes toward school, learning, and subject areas and being more interested in taking advance courses and continuing one's education.

4. **A more constructive classroom and school learning environment** (Johnson & Johnson, 1991). The more frequently cooperative learning is used, the more students perceive the classroom climate as being both academically and personally supportive and enhancing. The more positive the attitudes toward cooperative learning, (a) the more students report peer and teacher encouragement to exert effort to achieve, (b) the more students perceive themselves to be involved in positive and supportive personal relationships with classmates and teachers, (c) the higher students' academic self-esteem, and (d) the more fair the grading procedures are perceived to be.

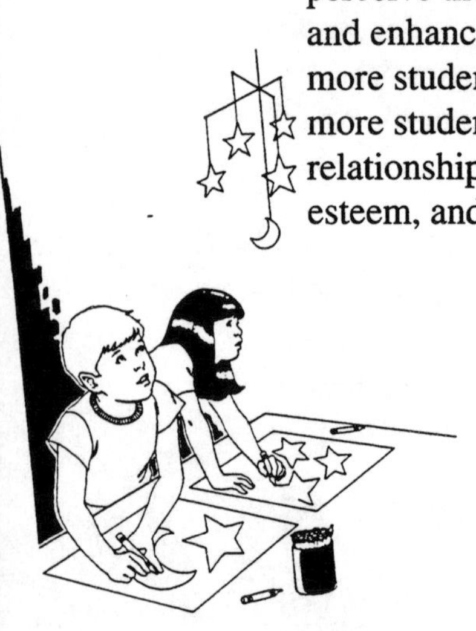

Cooperative Learning And "Whose Work Is It?

When students work in cooperative groups, they provide each other with help and support. This raises the question, "*Whose work is it?*" It may be unclear what they can do individually. This same questions may be asked about a student's work after a teacher has provided academic help or support. Additional complications arise when class work merges with homework. The amount of help students get from family and friends becomes an additional threat to the validity of interpretations about individual scores. Many assessment procedures put students who do not receive help from family and peers at a disadvantage. Communities in which parents are highly educated professionals, furthermore, may produce student work superior to those produced by students in districts with less educated and wealthy parents. This problem is avoided when assessment procedures lead to individual performances on demand. A student, for example, can write a series of compositions during a school year, all of which go through a peer editing process. While these compositions reflect what the student is capable of (given the editing and feedback from classmates, parents, and teachers), it does not reflect how well the student can write on demand. The teacher, therefore, may wish to give a test in which students are given a certain amount of class time (such as 30 minutes) to write an essay. The extent to which the writing skills learned transfer to new writing demands can then be assessed.

Assessment With Cooperative Learning Groups

In every instructional unit, teachers are responsible for ensuring that instruction, assessment and the communication of the results take place and are connected. The steps in doing so include (a) specifying instructional objectives, helping students set learning goals, making an assessment plan, and structuring the instructional unit, (b) conducting the instructional unit and monitoring and assessing students' efforts to learn, and (c) assessing student learning, judging its quality and quantity, and communicating the results following instruction.

Structure Objectives, Assessment, And Instruction

Communicating the results of an assessment begins with (Johnson, Johnson, & Holubec, 1993):

1. Specifying objectives: The objectives provide clear guidelines for conducting the instructional unit and assessing and evaluating student progress. In any cooperative lesson, there are both academic and social skills objectives. The **academic objectives** need to be specified at the correct level for the students and matched to the right level of instruction according to a conceptual or task

Meaningful And Manageable Assessment Through Cooperative Learning, Interaction Book Company, 7208 Cornelia Drive, Edina, MN 55435, (612) 831-9500, FAX (612) 831-9332

analysis. The **social skills objective** details what interpersonal and small group skills are going to be emphasized during the instructional unit.

2. Setting individual learning goals for each student. This is best done through a goal-setting conference (see Chapter 2).

3. Designing a sequence of instructional tasks aimed at achieving the objectives specified for the instructional unit.

4. Establishing the criteria for success to be used to evaluate student performance (involving students in developing the criteria when it is appropriate).

5. Defining the process of learning through which students are to reach the criteria.

6. Establishing the plan for collecting the information needed to assess students' learning and the success of the instructional unit.

Conduct Instruction And Assess Students' Efforts To Learn

Once you have laid your plans you are ready to conduct the instructional unit. Much of the assessment information needed to communicate to interested audiences must be collected during the instructional unit. **First**, each lesson may begin with assessing the quality of students' homework. **Second**, the teacher communicates to students (a) the learning tasks to be completed, (b) the criteria for success, (c) they are to work cooperatively, (d) the ways each student will be individually accountable for both learning the assigned material and helping their groupmates, and (e) the behaviors the teacher expects to see while the students work together. **Third**, after the students begin working, the teacher systematically monitors each learning group and intervenes when necessary to ensure that students correctly understand the academic content of the assignment. The monitoring and intervening provide opportunities for assessing student learning by (a) observing the students at work in their cooperative learning groups and (b) interviewing members of each cooperative learning group. **Fourth**, special attention is spent on assessing students' use of the interpersonal and small group skills required to work together effectively.

Assess Student Learning And Communicate The Results

Once the instructional unit is over outcomes may be assessed and the results communicated to students, cooperative groups, parents, and other interested parties. The traditional assessment measures are paper-and-pencil achievement tests. Teachers may also wish to examine actual performances of students. Students, for example, may present for assessment compositions, class presentations, and samples of their work in a portfolio. Students' critical thinking may be assessed during the academic controversy

Meaningful And Manageable Assessment Through Cooperative Learning, Interaction Book Company, 7208 Cornelia Drive, Edina, MN 55435, (612) 831-9500, FAX (612) 831-9332

procedure. Students can assess themselves and their groupmates with rating scales. Group products can be used in the assessment and reporting process. In communicating the results of assessments, the most important audience may be the students themselves and the cooperative learning groups in which they are members. The groups use the assessment information in their group processing. Finally, students and cooperative learning groups may be involved in conferences with teachers, parents, and other interested audiences in which the assessment results are reported and communicated.

Summary

Assessment is the collecting of information about the quality and quantity of a change in a student or group. The student performances assessed can be academic learning, reasoning, skills and competencies, attitudes, and work habits. The purpose of assessments may be to diagnose the level of student knowledge and skills before an instructional unit is implemented, to form the instructional program by periodically checking on its progress, and to sum up the information needed to judge the quality and quantity of student learning. The focus of assessment can be on the processes of learning and instruction or on their outcomes. The more the assessments are conducted in authentic settings, the better. The results of the assessments can be of high or low importance to students and their parents, teachers, administrators, policy-makers, and colleges and employers.

Many of the most valued and needed outcomes cannot be assessed by standardized tests or other paper-and-pencil measures. The challenge is to find assessment procedures that can be used to measure a broad array of valued outcomes. The more assessment procedures available, the easier it is to get a more complete picture of learning and instructional quality. These assessment options require that both teachers and students become directly involved in gathering, analyzing, and interpreting data about the instructional process in the classroom.

Assessment has traditionally focused on individual-to-individual transfer of learning. Students worked in isolation from classmates (in either competitive or individualistic learning situations) and were given individual achievement tests to assess their achievement. There are two assumptions underlying this practice. One is that individual assessment requires individual learning. This is a misconception. Group-to-individual transfer has been repeatedly demonstrated to be superior to individual-to-individual transfer (Johnson & Johnson, 1989). The purpose of cooperative learning groups is to ensure that all members learn and are, therefore, better able to perform on a subsequent individual assessment measure as a result of their group experience. The second assumption is that assessment should focus on "unassisted" student learning, which means that students should not be exposed to sources of help and assistance such as classmates, parents, private tutors, educational programs on television or video, and so forth. This also is a misconception. All school learning is assisted and promoted by the instructional efforts of a wide variety of individuals within and outside of the school.

Assessment begins with a goal-setting conference. Once students' goals are set, students participate in the instructional program. The quality and quality of their academic learning, level of their reasoning, skills and competencies, attitudes, and work habits may be assessed by standardized and teacher-made tests, compositions and presentations, individual and group projects, portfolios, questionnaires, and learning logs and journals. The assessment data is used as part of a total quality learning procedure emphasizing continuous improvement. Teachers participate in colleagial teaching teams to ensure assessments are fair and complete. Finally, periodically teachers use the assessment data to give students grades.

My Assessment Plan

1. What are the purposes of the assessment?

   a. ______________________________

   b. ______________________________

   c. ______________________________

   d. ______________________________

2. What is the focus of the assessment?

   _____ Process Of Learning _____ Outcomes Of Learning

   _____ Process Of Instruction _____ Outcomes Of Instruction

3. In what setting will the assessment take place?

4. The assessment will be aimed at:

   _____ Academic Learning _____ Attitudes

   _____ Level Of Reasoning, Critical Thinking _____ Work Habits

   _____ Skills And Competencies

5. The assessment procedures used will be:

   _____ Standardized Tests _____ Portfolios

   _____ Teacher-Made Tests _____ Observation

   _____ Compositions _____ Interviews

   _____ Presentations _____ Questionnaires

   _____ Individual & Group Projects _____ Learning Logs & Journals

Meaningful And Manageable Assessment Through Cooperative Learning, Interaction Book Company, 7208 Cornelia Drive, Edina, MN 55435, (612) 831-9500, FAX (612) 831-9332

6. Who are the stakeholders and what is the level of their stakes in the assessment:

Stakeholder	Low Stake	Medium	High Stake
_____ Students & Parents			
_____ Teachers			
_____ Administrators			
_____ Policy-Makers			
_____ Colleges, Employers			

7. How will cooperative learning be used to make the assessment more meaningful?

8. How will cooperative learning be used to make the assessment more manageable?

Meaningful And Manageable Assessment Through Cooperative Learning, Interaction Book Company, 7208 Cornelia Drive, Edina, MN 55435, (612) 831-9500, FAX (612) 831-9332

The Teacher's Role in Cooperative Learning

Make Pre-Instructional Decisions

Specify Academic and Social Skills Objectives: Every lesson has both (a) academic and (b) interpersonal and small group skills objectives.

Decide on Group Size: Learning groups should be small (groups of two or three members, four at the most).

Decide on Group Composition (Assign Students to Groups): Assign students to groups randomly or select groups yourself. Usually you will wish to maximize the heterogeneity in each group.

Assign Roles: Structure student-student interaction by assigning roles such as Reader, Recorder, Encourager of Participation and Checker for Understanding.

Arrange the Room: Group members should be "knee to knee and eye to eye" but arranged so they all can see the instructor at the front of the room.

Plan Materials: Arrange materials to give a "sink or swim together" message. Give only one paper to the group or give each member part of the material to be learned.

Explain Task And Cooperative Structure

Explain the Academic Task: Explain the task, the objectives of the lesson, the concepts and principles students need to know to complete the assignment, and the procedures they are to follow.

Explain the Criteria for Success: Student work should be evaluated on a criteria-referenced basis. Make clear your criteria for evaluating students' work.

***Structure Positive Interdependence:** Students must believe they "sink or swim together." Always establish mutual goals (students are responsible for their own learning and the learning of all other group members). Supplement, goal interdependence with celebration/reward, resource, role, and identity interdependence.

Structure Intergroup Cooperation: Have groups check with and help other groups. Extend the benefits of cooperation to the whole class.

Meaningful And Manageable Assessment Through Cooperative Learning, Interaction Book Company, 7208 Cornelia Drive, Edina, MN 55435, (612) 831-9500, FAX (612) 831-9332

***Structure Individual Accountability:** Each student must feel responsible for doing his or her share of the work and helping the other group members. Ways to ensure accountability are frequent oral quizzes of group members picked at random, individual tests, and assigning a member the role of Checker for Understanding.

***Specify Expected Behaviors:** The more specific you are about the behaviors you want to see in the groups, the more likely students will do them. Social skills may be classified as **forming** (staying with the group, using quiet voices), **functioning** (contributing, encouraging others to participate), **formulating** (summarizing, elaborating), and **fermenting** (criticizing ideas, asking for justification). Regularly teach the interpersonal and small group skills you wish to see used in the learning groups.

Monitor and Intervene

***Arrange Face-to-Face Promotive Interaction:** Conduct the lesson in ways that ensure that students promote each other's success face-to-face.

Monitor Students' Behavior: This is the fun part! While students are working, you circulate to see whether they understand the assignment and the material, give immediate feedback and reinforcement, and praise good use of group skills. Collect observation data on each group and student.

Intervene to Improve Taskwork and Teamwork: Provide **taskwork assistance** (clarify, reteach) if students do not understand the assignment. Provide **teamwork assistance** if students are having difficulties in working together productively.

Evaluate and Process

Evaluate Student Learning: Assess and evaluate the quality and quantity of student learning. Involve students in the assessment process.

***Process Group Functioning**: Ensure each student receives feedback, analyzes the data on group functioning, sets an improvement goal, and participates in a team celebration. Have groups routinely list three things they did well in working together an done thing they will do better tomorrow. Summarize as a whole class. Have groups celebrate their success and hard work.

Meaningful And Manageable Assessment Through Cooperative Learning, Interaction Book Company, 7208 Cornelia Drive, Edina, MN 55435, (612) 831-9500, FAX (612) 831-9332

Cooperative Lesson Planning Form

Grade Level: ______________ Subject Area: ____________________ Date: ______________

Lesson: ____

Objectives:

1. Academic
2. Social

Decisions:

1. Group Size: ____
2. Method Of Assigning Students: ________________________________
3. Roles: ____
   ____
4. Room Arrangement: ____
5. Materials ____
   - ❑ a. One Copy Per Group
   - ❑ b. Jigsaw
   - ❑ c. Tournament
   - ❑ d. One Copy Per Person
   - ❑ e. Other

Explaining Task And Goal Structure

1. Task: ____
   ____
2. Criteria For Success: ______________________________________
   ____
3. Positive Interdependence: ___________________________________
   ____
4. Individual Accountability: ___________________________________
   ____
5. Intergroup Cooperation: _____________________________________
   ____
6. Expected Behaviors: ____
   ____

Assessment Made Easy With Cooperative Learning, Interaction Book Company, 7208 Cornelia Drive, Edina, MN 55435, (612) 831-9500, FAX (612) 831-9332

Monitoring And Intervening

1. Observation Procedure: ______ Formal ______ Informal
2. Observations By: _______ Teacher ________ Students ________ Visitors
3. Intervening For Task Assistance: ____________________
   ____
4. Intervening For Teamwork Assistance: ____________________
   ____
4. Other: ____________________
   ____

Evaluating and Processing

1. Assessment Of Members' Individual Learning: ____________________
   ____
2. Assessment Of Group Productivity: ____________________
   ____
3. Small Group Processing: ____________________
   ____
4. Whole Class Processing: ____________________
   ____
5. Charts And Graphs Used: ____________________
   ____
6. Positive Feedback To Each Student: ____________________
   ____
7. Goal Setting For Improvement: ____________________
   ____
8. Celebration: ____________________
   ____
9. Other: ____________________

Chapter Two: Goal Setting Conference

A Fable with a Sad Ending

Once upon a time, a young rabbit decided to go out into the world and seek his fortune. His parents gave him $300, wished him well, and he began his search. Before he had traveled very far, he met a pack rat. "*Hey, little rabbit, where are you going*?" asked the pack rat. "*I'm seeking my fortune*," replied the young rabbit. "*You're in luck*," said the pack rat. "*I have here a fashionable suit of clothes that I will sell to you for only $100. Then you can go seeking your fortune looking quite knowledgeable and successful because you're dressed in the latest up-to-date style*!" "*Say, that's fantastic*!" replied the young rabbit, who immediately bought the clothes, put them on, and continued his search for his fortune.

Soon he met a deer. "*Hey, little rabbit, where are your going*?" asked the deer. "*I'm seeking my fortune*," replied the young rabbit. "*You're in great luck*," said the deer. "*For only $100, I will sell you this motorcycle so you can go seeking your fortune at great and exciting speeds!*" "*Say, that's fantastic*!" replied the young rabbit, who immediately bought the motorcycle and went zooming across the countryside.

Soon he met a coyote. "*Hey, little rabbit, where are you going*?" asked the coyote. "*I'm seeking my fortune*," replied the young rabbit. "*You're in great luck*!" said the coyote. "*For only $100, I will let you take this shortcut*," said the coyote, pointing to his open mouth, "*and you'll save yourself years of time*!" "*Say, that's fantastic*!" replied the young rabbit. And paying his last $100 he put his head into the coyote's mouth, and was immediately devoured.

The moral of this story is: If you don't know where you're going, you are likely to end up somewhere you don't want to be! More specifically, the moral is that assessment practices can be the latest up-to-date fashion conducted with great energy and speed, but if the teacher and students do not know what they are trying to accomplish, their efforts at best may be futile and at worst destructive to the quality of ongoing learning and instruction.

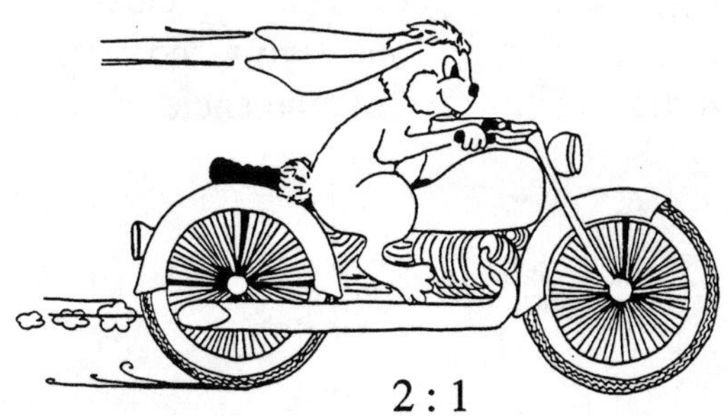

Meaningful And Manageable Assessment Through Cooperative Learning, Interaction Book Company, 7208 Cornelia Drive, Edina, MN 55435, (612) 831-9500, FAX (612) 831-9332

Why Goals Are Important

1. **Goals are guides for action**. They direct, channel, and determine what students and teachers do.

2. **Goals motivate behavior**. Goals are motivators and energizers. No goals, no motivation.

3. **Goals provide the basis for resolving conflicts**. Conflicts among students, among faculty and between students and faculty are resolved on the basis of what students and teachers want to accomplish.

4. **Goals are a prerequisite for assessment**. Without knowing what the purpose of the activity is, no assessment can be conducted.

START With Learning Goals

If a man does not know to which port he is sailing, no wind is favorable.

Seneca

All instruction is conducted for a purpose. Assessment begins with setting goals, progresses with progress checks, and ends with evaluating the extent to which the goals were accomplished. A **goal** is a desired state of future affairs. Learning to read or solve differential equations are learning goals. Goals are needed to assess the success of the student's efforts and the success of the instructional program. Even though school is not voluntary and students are in school to achieve goals that are by and large imposed on them, students and teachers are supposed to be bound together through a shared, emotional commitment to the vision of what they can accomplish if they all work together. Instruction begins with faculty inducing student commitment to what they are supposed to learn. Commitment is based on students understanding, accepting, and desiring to achieve instructional goals.

There are two aspects of ensuring student commitment to instructional goals. The **first** is to ensure that the instructional goals need to meet the START criteria (see Table 2.1). To be effective, goals need to be specific (so it is clear what needs to be done next), measurable (so progress can be tracked), challenging and offer a moderate risk of failure, relevant to students' interests, and aimed at competencies that will be transferred to real-life situations.

Table 2.1 "START" With Goals

Goal Characteristic	Definition Of Characteristic
S : Specific	Goals have to be specific enough so that they are clearly understood and a plan to achieve them can be developed. Specific goals indicate what needs to be done next. General and ambiguous goals do not guide action.
T : Measurable and Trackable	Students and the teacher must be able to determine the extent to which students have reached their learning goals. Goals must be operationalized so that the steps to achieving the goals are clear and understandable.
A : Challenging but Achievable	Students' goals must be just beyond their current competence level. Ideally, the goals will be challenging enough that the student has a 50/50 percent chance of achieving them. Students' must be able to achieve the learning goals if they work hard enough and utilize the support systems available to help them do so.
R : Relevant	Learning goals must be relevant to the student's interests, the parent's concerns, the instructional goals of the teacher, and the national, state, district, and school standards. Students must see the goals as meaningful and be personally committed to achieving them.
T : Transfer	Learning goals must be aimed at having students take what is learned and transfer it to "real-life" situations. Whatever students learn today, they should be able to use in other situations tomorrow.

The **second** way to ensure student commitment is to involve them in the process of forming the learning goals. Involvement leads to ownership which leads to commitment. **While indifferent to other's goals, individuals seek out opportunities to achieve their own goals and commit considerable energy to doing so**. The goal-setting conference is conducted in order to involve students in the goal setting process to ensure students take ownership of the learning goals and commit themselves to achieving the goals. In the goal-setting conference students translate the instructional objectives into specific performance goals they wish to achieve. It is within the goal-setting conference that external instructional objectives and expectations become reformed and internalized as personal ambitions. At the beginning of each day, week, instructional unit, course, semester, or year, students need to discuss thoroughly their learning goals, even when the goals are prescribed by faculty, parents, or their society. During the discussion the students should reword, reorganize, and review the goals until students feel a sense of "ownership" toward them. Such a discussion will clarify the students' understanding of the goals and help to clear away any misunderstandings concerning the tasks necessary to reach them. Many of the more effective assessment tools, furthermore, require students to participate in setting their learning goals and conducting assessments of how well they are achieving them.

Conferencing With Students

The process of assessment involves at least three types of conferences with each individual student (see Table 2.2). First, there is a **goal-setting conference** in which each student sets personal learning goals and publicly commits him- or herself to achieve them. In essence, each student makes a learning contract with him- or herself, the teacher, and a cooperative learning group that specifies what is to be learned and accomplished for either the class period, the day, the week, or the instructional unit. Second, there are periodic **progress-assessment conferences** in which the student's progress in achieving his or her goals is reviewed. What has been accomplished and what is yet to be done are detailed. The student's next steps in achieving his or her learning goals are discussed.

Table 2.2 Types Of Conferences

Conference	Individual Student	Cooperative Learning Group
Goal-Setting Conference	Each class period, day, week, or instructional unit each student sets personal learning goals and publicly commits him- or herself to achieve them in a learning contract.	Each class period, day, week, or instructional unit each cooperative group sets group learning goals and members publicly commit themselves to achieve them in a learning contract.
Progress-Assessment Conferences	The student's progress in achieving his or her learning goals is assessed, what the student has accomplished so far and what is yet to be done is reviewed, and the student's next steps are detailed.	The group's progress in achieving its learning goals is assessed, what the group has accomplished so far and what is yet to be done is reviewed, and the group's next steps are detailed.
Post-Evaluation Conference	The student explains his or her level of achievement (what the student learned and failed to learn during the instructional unit) to interested parties (student's cooperative learning group, teacher(s), and parents), which naturally leads to the next goal-setting conference.	The group explains its level of achievement (what the group has accomplished and failed to accomplish during the instructional unit) to interested parties (members, teacher(s), and parents), which naturally leads to the next goal-setting conference.

Meaningful And Manageable Assessment Through Cooperative Learning, Interaction Book Company, 7208 Cornelia Drive, Edina, MN 55435, (612) 831-9500, FAX (612) 831-9332

Third, there is a **post-evaluation conference** in which the level of student achievement is explained by the student to interested parties. The immediate interested parties may include the student and the student's cooperative learning group, teacher, and parents. Student-led conferences with parents are one example of a post-evaluation conference. Each student explains what he or she learned and failed to learn during the instructional unit or assessment period. This discussion may naturally lead into the next goal-setting conference.

This chapter focuses on the goal-setting conference. In a goal setting conference, each student must formulate both personal learning goals and goals for helping others in their group and class learn.

Cooperative Learning Groups And Goal Setting Conferences

Rank the following reasons why cooperative groups should be part of goal-setting conferences from most important (1) to least important (6). Share your ranking with your partner and listen to his or her ranking. Then come to consensus as to what the ranking should be.

_____ Makes groupmates part of the resources available to help students achieve their learning goals.

_____ Involves students in the diagnosis and goal setting process.

_____ Saves considerable teacher time and effort.

_____ Makes it possible for goal-setting conferences to be conducted at the beginning of each instructional unit.

_____ Provides the intellectual challenge necessary for higher-level reasoning to be used in setting learning goals.

_____ Creates a system for continuous monitoring and support for each student's efforts to achieve his or her learning goals.

Goal-Setting Conferences

Assessment begins with a goal setting conference. Each individual student has committed him- or herself to achieve two types of general learning goals. **First, the student has academic learning goals** determined by (a) what the student, parents, and teacher want the student to learn, (b) the national, state, district, and school standards and

Meaningful And Manageable Assessment Through Cooperative Learning, Interaction Book Company, 7208 Cornelia Drive, Edina, MN 55435, (612) 831-9500, FAX (612) 831-9332

guidelines, and (c) what post-secondary educational and career organizations require. **Second, the student has community learning goals for helping and encouraging other students to learn.** The classroom and school are learning communities in which each member has both a responsibility to maximize his or her own learning and a responsibility to help all other members of the community maximize their learning.

In addition to the individual learning goals of each student, **cooperative learning groups have academic learning goals**. For many assignments, such as completing science experiments, performing a play, making a video, giving a band concert, there are group goals as well as individual ones.

Individual students and cooperative learning groups develop their goals and commit themselves to achieving them in a goal-setting conference. A **goal-setting conference** is a meeting in which learning goals are formulated and a contract to achieve them is developed. Teachers have the choice of:

1. **Conducting Teacher - Student Conferences (T/S)**: Personally conducting a goal-setting conference with each individual student each day, week, semester, or year, or at the beginning of each instructional unit. This can easily lead to (a) role overload for the teacher due to the amount of time it takes to conduct a meaningful goal setting conference and (b) a classroom focus on individual learning only, which may isolate students and create the potential for egocentrism, selfishness, alienation, and learned helplessness.

2. **Conducting Teacher - Cooperative Learning Group Conferences (T/G)**: Personally conducting a goal-setting conference with each cooperative learning group. This cuts the time it takes to conduct the conferences considerably but may still lead to some teacher overload.

3. **Engineering And Supervising Cooperative Learning Group - Student Conferences (G/S)**: Having each cooperative learning group conduct a goal-setting conference with each one of its members while the teacher monitors and supervises.

4. **Engineering And Supervising Cooperative Learning Group - Cooperative Learning Group Conferences (G/G)**: Having each cooperative learning group conduct a goal-setting conference with another cooperative learning group and its members while the teacher monitors and supervises.

THE THREE PHASES OF GOAL SETTING

1. **Preparing for the goal-setting conference**. The preparation for the goal setting conference primarily involves gathering information, scheduling, planning the conference procedure, and planning how the follow-up will be conducted:

   a. The information gathered includes (1) the instructional objectives, what the student wants to learn, what the parents expect the student to learn, and the relevant school, district, state, and national guidelines and (2) the data on which to diagnose students' expertise in the area to be studied.

   b. Scheduling is complex if you are going to meet with each student individually, manageable if you are going to meet with each group, and relatively easy if you are going to have each group conference with its members or with the members of another group.

   c. Planning the conference involves making a time-line to be followed and using a set of forms to document that the procedure is followed. The overall goal is to involve each student in setting his or her learning goals in a way that results in a public contract specifying what is to be learned when and at what level.

   d. The planning of the follow-up includes scheduling the progress-assessment and post-evaluation conferences, planning the assessment program to measure the achievement of the goals and the degree to which the designated resources were effectively utilized.

2. **The goal-setting conference**. You either meet with each individual student or learning group or you teach the cooperative groups how to conduct the conference and monitor their effectiveness in conducting them.

3. **Follow-Up**. The follow-up includes facilitating the work of each student and group, conducting the progress-assessment conferences, assessing how effectively each student and group achieved their goals, and conducting the post-evaluation conferences. The information is then used in the next goal-setting conference.

Steps Of Teacher-Student Goal-Setting Conference

Step One: Diagnose: Your first step in conferencing with a student to set learning goals is to collect the available evidence of the student's expertise relevant to the subject matter to be studied. The evidence is derived from previous tests, performances, interviews, and so forth. You use this information to diagnose the student's (a) current level of knowledge and expertise relevant to the instructional unit, (b) pace of learning, and (c) ability to promote and encourage classmates' learning.

Step Two: START With The Student's Learning Goals: You and the student formulate the student's learning goals by (a) exploring all relevant expectations for the student's achievement and (b) making sure the goals match the "START" criteria. You discuss what the student wishes to learn, what you expect the student to learn, the relevant aspirations of parents, and the relevant school, district, state, and national guidelines. The requirements of post-secondary educational and career organizations may also be considered. Out of this discussion a set of learning goals are formulated. You always *start* with learning goals formulated by the student and the interested parties to guide the student's efforts to learn and help classmates learn.

Step Three: Organize Support Systems And Resources: You discuss with the student the support systems and resources the student needs to reach his or her learning goals successfully. The major support systems and resources include the student him- or herself, other members of the student's cooperative learning group and class, the teacher, technology, curriculum, and outside experts. You then work with the student and his or her classmates to organize these resources and structure them to promote the student's successful learning and achievement.

Step Four: Make Plan And Formalize Into A Learning Contract: The fourth step is for you and the student to make a plan, based on the learning goals formulated and the resources committed, detailing (a) the methods to be used to ensure the student achieves his or her goals and (b) a time-line specifying when and how the student's progress will be assessed. The plan is formalized into a learning contract by writing it down and both you and the student signing it.

Conferencing With Cooperative Learning Groups

Time is a major barrier to having a goal-setting conference with each student each week. In fact, very few teachers meet regularly with each student because most teachers simply do not have the time to do so. **Goal setting conferences can become more frequent when you (the teacher) meet with each cooperative learning group**. The steps of the conference are the same as they are for meeting with individual students.

Step One: Diagnose: Your first step in conferencing with a cooperative learning group to set learning goals is to collect the available evidence of the members' expertise relevant to the subject matter to be studied. The evidence is derived from previous tests, performances, interviews, and so forth. You use this information to diagnose members' (a) current level of knowledge and expertise relevant to the instructional unit, (b) pace of learning, and (c) ability to promote and encourage classmates' learning.

Step Two: START With The Group's Learning Goals: You and the group members formulate a set of learning goals by (a) exploring all relevant expectations for each member's achievement and (b) making sure the goals match the "START" criteria. The discussion focuses on what group members want to learn, what you expect each member to learn, the relevant aspirations of parents, and the relevant school, district, state, and national guidelines. The requirements of post-secondary educational and career organizations may also be considered. Out of this discussion a set of learning goals for the group and its members are formulated to guide each member's efforts to learn and help groupmates learn.

Step Three: Organize Support Systems And Resources: You discuss with the group the support systems and resources each member and the group as a whole need to reach the learning goals successfully. The major support systems and resources include the members themselves, other cooperative learning groups, the teacher, technology, curriculum, and outside experts. You then work with the group to organize these resources and structure them to promote the group's academic success.

Step Four: Make Plan And Formalize Into Learning Contract: The fourth step is for you and the group to make a plan, based on the learning goals formulated and the resources committed, detailing (a) the methods to be used to ensure the group achieves its goals and (b) a time-line specifying when and how the group's progress will be assessed. The plan is formalized into a learning contract by writing it down and both you and the group members signing it.

Goal:

Cooperative Learning Groups Conferencing With Their Members

You save considerable time in setting learning goals for each student by meeting with cooperative learning groups to do so rather than meeting with each student individually. You save even more time by having cooperative learning groups conduct the goal setting conferences for their members. **Goal setting conferences can become a regular part of classroom life when they are primarily managed by the cooperative learning group and monitored by the teacher**. While the groups are meeting, you circulate from group to group and monitor how well the groups are following the prescribed conferencing procedure. The conferencing steps are the same as they are for meeting with individual students.

Step One: Diagnose: The group collects the available evidence of the members' expertise relevant to the subject matter to be studied. The evidence is derived from previous tests, performances, interviews, and so forth. The group uses this information to diagnose members' (a) current level of knowledge and expertise relevant to the instructional unit, (b) pace of learning, and (c) ability to promote and encourage classmates' learning.

Meaningful And Manageable Assessment Through Cooperative Learning, Interaction Book Company, 7208 Cornelia Drive, Edina, MN 55435, (612) 831-9500, FAX (612) 831-9332

Step Two: START With The Group's Learning Goals: The group formulates a set of learning goals by (a) exploring all relevant expectations for each member's achievement and the achievement of the group as a whole and (b) making sure the goals match the "START" criteria. The discussion focuses on what group members want to learn, what you expect each member to learn, the relevant aspirations of parents, and the relevant school, district, state, and national guidelines. The requirements of post-secondary educational and career organizations may also be considered. Out of this discussion a set of learning goals for the group and its members are formulated to guide each member's efforts to learn and help groupmates learn.

Step Three: Organize Support Systems And Resources: The group discusses the support systems and resources each member and the group as a whole need to reach the learning goals successfully. The major support systems and resources include the members themselves, other cooperative learning groups, the teacher, technology, curriculum, and outside experts. The group organizes and structures these resources to promote the group's success.

Step Four: Make Plan And Formalize Into Learning Contract: The group makes a plan, based on the learning goals formulated and the resources committed, detailing (a) the methods to be used to ensure that each member achieves his or her learning goals and the group achieves its goals and (b) a time-line specifying when and how the progress of each member and the group as a whole will be assessed. The plan is formalized into a learning contract by writing it down. All group members and the teacher then sign it.

Goal:

Cooperative Learning Groups Conferencing With Another Group

Goal:

Two cooperative groups may be paired for the goal setting procedure. One group helps the other group (a) diagnosis each member's current level of expertise, pace of learning, and ability to assist groupmates' learning, (b) formulate learning goals that meet the START criteria and take into account the expectations of the various stake-holders, (c) organize the resources each member needs to achieve the goals, and (d) formalize the plan into a learning contract. Such a group-to-group goal setting conference increases the interdependence among groups and provides direct access to other groups as resources to help members achieve their goals.

FIGURE 2:3 GOAL-SETTING CONFERENCES

Teacher-Student (T/S)	Teacher-Group (T/G)	Group-Student (G/S)
Step One: Diagnose	**Step One: Diagnose**	**Step One: Diagnose**
Meet with student and use evidence of expertise (previous tests, performances, and so forth) to diagnose the student's (a) current level of knowledge and expertise relevant to the instructional unit, (b) pace of learning, and (c) ability to promote and encourage classmates' learning.	Meet with group and use evidence of members' expertise (previous tests, performances, and so forth) relevant to what is to be studied to diagnose members' (a) current level of knowledge and expertise, (b) pace of learning, and (c) ability to help each other learn.	The group collects available evidence of members' expertise (previous tests, performances, and so forth) relevant to what is to be studied to diagnose members' (a) current level of knowledge and expertise, (b) pace of learning, and (c) ability to promote other's learning.
Step Two: Set Goals	**Step Two: Set Goals**	**Step Two: Set Goals**
Discuss with student what the student should learn (with input from parents and other interested parties) and formulate goals that meet the START criteria.	Discuss with group what each member should learn (with input from parents and other interested parties) and formulate group goals that meet the START criteria.	The group formulates learning goals for each member and the group as a whole (with input from other interested parties) making sure the goals match the "START" criteria.
Step Three: Plan Support	**Step Three: Plan Support**	**Step Three: Plan Support**
Discuss with the student the support systems and resources the student needs (such as the student him- or herself, other members of the student's cooperative learning group and class, the teacher, technology, curriculum, and outside experts) and you organize and structure the resources to promote the student's achievement.	Discuss with the group the support systems and resources each member and the group need (such as the members themselves, other cooperative learning groups, the teacher, technology, curriculum, and outside experts) to reach the learning goals successfully. You organize and structure these resources to promote the group's success.	The group discusses the support systems and resources each member and the group need (such as the members themselves, other cooperative learning groups, the teacher, technology, curriculum, and outside experts) to reach the learning goals successfully. The resources are structured to promote the group's success.
Step Four: Make Plan	**Step Four: Make Plan**	**Step Four: Make Plan**
Formulate a plan, based on the learning goals and resources committed, detailing instructional methods and a time-line specifying when and how the student's progress will be assessed. The plan is formalized into a learning contract.	Formulate a plan, based on the learning goals and committed resources, detailing instructional methods and a time-line specifying when and how the group's progress will be assessed. The plan is formalized into a learning contract.	The group makes a plan, based on the learning goals and resources committed, detailing methods to be used and a time-line specifying when and how each member's and the group's progress will be assessed. The plan is formalized into a learning contract.

Meaningful And Manageable Assessment Through Cooperative Learning, Interaction Book Company, 7208 Cornelia Drive, Edina, MN 55435, (612) 831-9500, FAX (612) 831-9332

Summary And Conclusions

Assessment begins with setting goals. If there are no learning goals, there can be no assessment. Teachers may simply impose learning goals on students from their position of power and authority (*"In this unit you will learn the causes of the Civil War!"*) but there are many advantages to having students and other stake-holders involved in the goal setting process. **Students are far more motivated to achieve their personal goals than they are to achieve imposed instructional goals**. Many of the more effective assessment tools require student participation in setting learning goals and conducting the assessments.

Assessment involves three types of conferences with each student: A **goal-setting conference** to establish a contract containing the student's learning goals, **progress-assessment conferences** to determine the student's progress in achieving his or her goals, and a **post-evaluation conference** in which the student's accomplishments are explained to interested parties. Assessment begins with a goal-setting conference in which the student's learning goals and responsibilities for helping other students learn are established. The goal setting conference may be between the teacher and the student (T/S), the teacher and the cooperative learning group (T/G), the cooperative learning group and the student (G/S), and a cooperative learning group and another group (G/G). In all cases, the emphasis is on helping students set and take ownership for learning goals that meet the START criteria (specific, trackable, achievable, relevant, transferable). The goal-setting conference contains four steps: Diagnosis of current level of expertise, setting START goals, organizing support systems and resources to help each student achieve his or her goals successfully, and constructing a plan for utilizing the resources to achieve the goals and formalizing the plan into a learning contract.

The hard truth is that most teachers do not have the time to conference with each individual student, whether it is a goal-setting conference, a progress-assessment conference, or a post-evaluation conference. This does not mean that such conferences cannot happen. Teachers can engineer and supervise such conferences through appropriate use of cooperative learning groups.

Meaningful And Manageable Assessment Through Cooperative Learning, Interaction Book Company, 7208 Cornelia Drive, Edina, MN 55435, (612) 831-9500, FAX (612) 831-9332

Preparing For Goal-Setting Conference

Name: ______________________________ **Date:** _______ **Unit:** ________________

Class: ____________________ **Group:** _________________

Source	Preliminary Goals
Student	1. 2. 3. 4. 5.
Teacher	1. 2. 3. 4. 5.
Group	1. 2. 3. 4. 5.
Parents	1. 2. 3. 4. 5.

Goal:

Meaningful And Manageable Assessment Through Cooperative Learning, Interaction Book Company, 7208 Cornelia Drive, Edina, MN 55435, (612) 831-9500, FAX (612) 831-9332

Diagnosing Member's Expertise

Student's Name: ______________________ Date: ____________

Class: ______________ Group: ____________ Unit: ______________

Category	Low	Medium	High
Current Knowledge			
Pace Of Learning			
Ability To Help Others' Learn			
Implications For Setting Learning Goals	1. 2. 3.		

Directions:

1. For each category, write down a list of characteristics that would indicate a low, medium, or high level of aptitude and ability for this instructional unit.

2. On the basis of the member's past performances and interests, classify him or her into one of the levels for each category.

3. Discuss implications for setting learning goals for the group member.

Meaningful And Manageable Assessment Through Cooperative Learning, Interaction Book Company, 7208 Cornelia Drive, Edina, MN 55435, (612) 831-9500, FAX (612) 831-9332

Goals For Group Members

Group: ______________________ Date: __________ Unit: ______________

Goals	Member 1	Member 2	Member 3	Member 4
1.				
2.				
3.				
4.				
5.				
Signatures:				
Group Goals	1. 2. 3.			

Goal:

Directions:

1. Write out the learning goals for each member of your group for this instructional unit. Remember to include goals for helping and encouraging the learning of groupmates.

2. Make sure each goal meets the START criteria.

3. Have each group member sign for his or her goals. The signature indicates that the student understands the goals, agrees that they are challenging but realistic, and commits him- or herself to achieve them.

4. Set appropriate group goals for the instructional unit.

START With Learning Goals

1. Write the learning goal as specifically and precisely as you can.

2. On what date will the goal be achieved?

a. What will you finish the first class session?

b. What will you finish the second class session?

c. What will you finish the third class session?

d. And so forth?

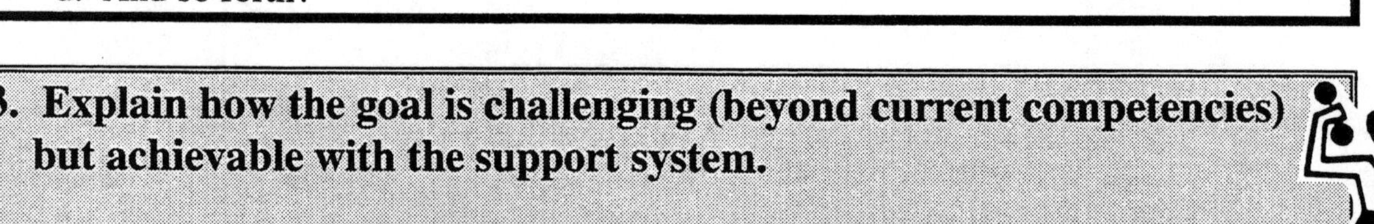

3. Explain how the goal is challenging (beyond current competencies) but achievable with the support system.

4. Explain how the goal is relevant to your interests, the instructional objectives, your group concerns, and your parent's concerns.

5. Explain how achieving the goal will allow you to use what is learned in other situations.

Meaningful And Manageable Assessment Through Cooperative Learning, Interaction Book Company, 7208 Cornelia Drive, Edina, MN 55435, (612) 831-9500, FAX (612) 831-9332

Organizing Support Systems And Resources

Name: ______________________________ Date: __________ Unit: ___________

To achieve each of the following goals, what resources do you need from each source? List your goals for this instructional unit across the top of the table. For each goal, list the resources you need from each of the sources listed. Add other sources relevant to the unit.

Sources	Goal 1	Goal 2	Goal 3
Self			
Groupmates			
Teacher			
Curriculum			
Technology			
Outside Experts			
Field Trips			
Other:			
Other:			

Meaningful And Manageable Assessment Through Cooperative Learning, Interaction Book Company, 7208 Cornelia Drive, Edina, MN 55435, (612) 831-9500, FAX (612) 831-9332

My Learning Contract

Learning Goals

My Academic Goals	My Responsibilities For Helping Others' Learn	My Group's Goals
1.		
2.		
3.		
4.		

THE PLAN FOR ACHIEVING MY LEARNING GOALS, MEETING MY RESPONSIBILITIES, AND HELPING MY GROUP IS:

THE TIME LINE FOR ACHIEVING MY GOALS IS:

Beginning Date:

First Road-Mark:

Second Road-Mark:

Third Road-Mark:

Final Date:

Signatures:

_______________________ _______________________

_______________________ _______________________

Meaningful And Manageable Assessment Through Cooperative Learning, Interaction Book Company, 7208 Cornelia Drive, Edina, MN 55435, (612) 831-9500, FAX (612) 831-9332

Chapter Three: Standardized Tests

What Are Standardized Tests

One of the most widespread assessment procedures used is standardized tests. While there are many critics of standardized tests, and considerable pressure to change them, in the foreseeable future they will be part of the assessment procedures in most school districts. Teachers should be able to use the results. **Standardized tests** are tests prepared for nationwide use (usually commercially) to provide accurate and meaningful information on students' levels of performance relative to others at their age or grade levels. In order to make test scores comparable, the tests are administered and scored under carefully controlled conditions that are uniform to all students so that students all over the country (and world) have equal chances to demonstrate what they know. Standard methods are used to develop items, administer the test, score it, and report the scores to interested audiences. Such tests are usually constructed by subject matter specialists and experts on testing.

Standardized tests are typically used to provide a yardstick (that teacher made tests cannot provide) against which to compare individuals or groups of students. The interpretation of scores on standardized tests are based on national and subnational norms. **Norms** are records of the performances of groups of individuals who have previously taken the test. The norms are used to determine how the score of any test taker compares with the scores of a sample of similar individuals. The test publishers provide one or more ways of comparing each student's raw score (number of correct answers) with the norming sample.

Standardized tests evolved and proliferated because of the unreliability of school transcripts. The Scholastic Aptitude Test (SAT), for example, was created in 1926 as an efficient and economical way for college admission officers to select the most promising students from the pool of applicants. The SAT test scores were found to be a better predictor of grades in college than were high school grades. Since that time standardized tests have been used to (a) select and place students into classes, programs, special schools, or colleges, and (b) decide whether a student should advance to the next level, (c) diagnose students' problems in learning, (d) determine honors, awards, and scholarships, (e) evaluate the effectiveness of instructional programs, (f) apply for federal funds, and (g) conduct research. Standardized test scores have become the yardstick for measuring the quality of schools, school districts, and even education within a state and the country as a whole.

There are two types of standardized tests: achievement and aptitude tests. **Achievement tests** focus on that knowledge and skills learned in school and may be

achievement batteries, diagnostic tests, and specific subject area tests. **Aptitude tests** focus on the potential maximum achievement of students and may measure general intellectual aptitude, aptitude to do well in college or certain vocational training programs, reading aptitude, mechanical aptitude, or perceptual aptitude. While aptitude tests and achievement tests are theoretically different, their results are so highly correlated that both may be considered achievement tests.

Criteria For Good Measurement Procedures

Criteria	Definitions
Reliability	**Reliability** exists when a student's performance remains the same on repeated measurements. On a norm-referenced measure, this means that when the measure is repeated and the raw scores of students are arranged in order from highest to lowest, all students will keep the same rank.
Validity	**Validity** means that the test actually measures what it was designed to measure, all of what it was designed to measure, and nothing but what it was designed to measure.
Objectivity	**Objectivity** is the agreement of (a) experts on the correct answer to a test item and (b) different scorers on what score should be assigned to a test paper or questionnaire.
Practicality	**Practicality** of a measure is determined by the cost per copy, the time it takes to administer it, and the ease of scoring, and other factors teachers have to take into account before deciding to use a particular measure.
Discrimination	When a norm-referenced measure is used, each item has to **discriminate** among students as high, medium, and low on the skill or knowledge being measured.
Norm-Referenced	Norm-referenced tests are designed to test a student's performance as it compares to the performances of other students.
Criteria-Referenced	Criteria-referenced tests are designed to compare a student's test performance to preset criteria defining excellence on learning tasks or skills.

Advantages Of Standardized Tests

1. Standardized tests are easily administered and they take little time away from instruction.

Meaningful And Manageable Assessment Through Cooperative Learning, Interaction Book Company, 7208 Cornelia Drive, Edina, MN 55435, (612) 831-9500, FAX (612) 831-9332.

2. Standardized tests provide a standard situation in which all students are required to answer the same questions. This ensures that all students may be evaluated on the same criteria--some students will not be evaluated on different criteria than others.

3. Standardized tests provide a permanent record of behavior when they are written (some tests can be oral). A permanent record of answers allows teachers to examine the same answers several times to ensure that the evaluation is fair and unbiased.

4. Standardized test scores allow simple comparisons between students, schools, districts, states, and nations. From the global comparisons provided an overall assessment can be made.

5. Standardized tests are used by psychometricians and major institutions and, therefore, they carry scientific credibility and tradition.

6. Standardized tests are unparalleled for certain purposes such as the large-scale, cost-effective assessment of large numbers of students on low-level cognitive objectives.

7. Standardized tests tend to have high predictive validity. Advanced placement tests, for example, accurately predict how students will perform in college courses.

Disadvantages Of Standardized Tests

1. **The content of standardized tests is problematic**. Standardized tests measure factual or declarative information and a narrow group of verbal skills (such as word recall, fluency, and recognition vocabulary). They tend not to measure depth of understanding, integration of knowledge, and production of discourse, let alone social progress, individual worth, or school effectiveness. Abstract verbal skills, for example, do not determine excellence in writing a poem, singing a lullaby, tutoring a child, or giving an order in a factory.

2. **The range of what can be assessed is limited**. Standardized tests are inadequate in assessing students' generative capabilities, such as (a) expressing themselves orally or in writing, (b) organizing and analyzing an abundance of data, (c) devising an experiment to answer an interesting question, and (d) working cooperatively with others.

3. **Standardized tests are of little help in identifying students** who need (a) support and help to succeed or (b) challenges beyond those offered by the curriculum because they are:

   a. **Not timely**. They are administered at most once per year and usually only once every several years.

Interpreting Standardized Test Scores

Statistic	Definition
Frequency Distribution	A listing of the number of people who obtain each score or fall into each range of scores on a test. This kind of information may be expresses as a simple graph, called a histogram or bar graph, where the horizontal or x axis indicates the number of possible scores and the vertical or y axis indicates the number of students who attained each score.
Measures Of Central Tendency	The **mean** is the sum of all scores in the class divided by the number of students. The **median** is the midpoint in the set of scores arranged in order, from highest to lowest. It is most useful when a few unusually high or low scores distort the mean.
Standard Deviation	The average of the differences of all students' scores from the mean score. A large standard deviation indicates that students obtained a wide range of scores on the test. A small standard deviation indicates that the range of scores is low and most students scored right around the mean.
Standard Score	An indication of how far each student is above or below the mean in a way that allows comparison of scores from different tests, regardless of the size of the class or the number of items on the test. To find the standard score you subtract the mean from the students' raw score and divide by the standard deviation.
Percentile Rank	The percent of the class with scores below that obtained by the student. Percentile rank can range from 0 to 100.
Grade-Equivalent Scores	The average of the scores of all students in the norming sample at that grade level. Grade-equivalent scores are generally listed in numbers, such as 11.4, 9.6, 7.2, or 3.5. The whole number gives the grade level and the decimals stand for tenths of a year. Grade-equivalent scores are easy to interpret and understand.
Standard Scores	How far they lie from the mean as measured by standard deviation units. Three common standard scores are the **z**-score, stanine score, and the normal curve equivalent. **Z-scores** have a mean of 0 and a standard deviation of 1. **Stanine** (a combination of the words, "standard nine") scores have a mean of 5 and a standard deviation of 2. The **normal curve equivalent** (NCE) scores range from 1 to 99 with a mean of 50 and a standard deviation of about 21.

Meaningful And Manageable Assessment Through Cooperative Learning, Interaction Book Company, 7208 Cornelia Drive, Edina, MN 55435, (612) 831-9500, FAX (612) 831-9332.

b. **Not aligned**. Any student in the school is potentially in need of special assistance at some point. And any student is potentially eligible for additional challenge. Unless teachers have the capability to assess frequently students on the curriculum they have no way of knowing which are which. To avoid letting students fall farther and farther behind or allow other students to endure repetition and slow pace (because they learn quickly or already knew what is being taught), assessment must be aligned with the curriculum and conducted regularly and frequently.

4. **Standardized tests are not helpful in assessing (a) student learning in specific courses or (b) achievement of district program goals**. A generic test for high school juniors, for example, will not yield information on the degree to which students have learned in a specific class on physics, auto mechanics, or family life. Prepared program goals (what students will have learned as a result of studying social studies or language arts) typically include such broad statements such as "*understand major historical trends*" or "*communicate effectively in speaking and writing*." Such goals involve higher-level outcomes not included in standardized tests.

5. **Standardized tests have limited use in assessing student exit outcomes**. Exit outcomes are statements of the knowledge and skills students will possess after completing schooling. Exit outcomes address the question, "*When students leave us what will they know and what can they do*?" Most schools use exit outcomes to guide curriculum planning and curriculum audits. Thus, if a district has an exit outcome relating to critical and creative thinking, faculty may examine the science program to ensure it does not rely solely on the memorization of acts and the performance of "cookbook" labs. In some schools, furthermore, a condition for graduation is that students demonstrate proficiency on the exit outcomes to a committee of teachers, community or business leaders, and other students. Such demonstrations may be an original garment design, a creative solution to a situation in auto mechanics, or a unique approach to a problem in trigonometry.

6. **Standardized tests are not useful in conducting external curriculum audits**. In order to determine the quality of a school or district curriculum, student performance must be compared with students from all over the state or nation, using the same procedures and techniques and the results shared. While this is precisely the purpose of a standardized test, the tests are not capable of assessing the full range of the curriculum, all the types of knowledge and skills that educators and the community consider important. A curriculum audit should reflect the entire range of the curriculum deemed important by educators and the community.

7. **When standardized test results are used for high-stake purposes, there is a temptation to cheat in some manner**. There are many stories about schools that exclude low-achieving students from a standardized test because including them would depress their average score and cause them to lose face (or worse) in

comparison with other schools. There are also stories about teachers who unfairly coach their students on the test items or provide unauthorized assistance during the actual assessment.

8. **The impact standardized tests have on instruction is problematic**. Test construction emphasizes basic skills and neglects many of the most important outcomes of schooling. When teachers "teach to the test" they will emphasize basic skills at the expense of higher-order reasoning skills.

9. **The limited use for standardized test results is a problem**. Standardized tests predict how many years of conventional education a student will attain. They do not, however, predict occupational success in such fields as medicine, engineering, teaching, scientific research, and business.

Cautions

In and of themselves, tests are incapable of harming students. It is the way tests results are used that is potentially harmful to students. Even the best tests can create problems if their results are misused. The issue is not whether standardized tests should exist, but rather how their results should be used. Some helpful hints are as follows.

1. **Make sure you are using the right tests**. Schools often devise new goals and curriculum only to assess their success by tests that are not relevant to either the goals or the new materials. Whatever the purposes of assessment, they cannot be reached unless the correct tests are used.

2. **Do not use the results of standardized tests to judge the success of local programs and goals**. Standardized tests cover large segments of subject matter or general abilities related to learning. They focus on general goals common to schools across the country and are not suitable for evaluating instruction in a limited unit or judging how well a strictly local instructional goal is accomplished.

3. **Assume that test results are fallible and not always accurate.** Low scores can be the result of (a) poor health, negative moods, and distractions, (b) lack of test taking skills, and (c) inability to take tests well due to such factors as anxiety. Every test score contains possible error. Many students who score poorly on standardized tests excel in school, college, or occupations.

4. **Use more than a single test score to make important decisions**. Given the possibility of error that exists for every test score, a single test score is too suspect to serve as the sole criterion for any crucial decision. Supporting evidence is needed.

Meaningful And Manageable Assessment Through Cooperative Learning, Interaction Book Company, 7208 Cornelia Drive, Edina, MN 55435, (612) 831-9500, FAX (612) 831-9332.

5. **Do not set arbitrary minimums for performance on tests.** Using arbitrary minimums to make critical decisions is inherently unfair. If the standard is arbitrarily set at 85, for example, there may be no valid reason to predict that a person who scores 86 will perform better in the future than a person who scores 84. Tests do not have sufficient validity and reliability to make such fine distinctions.

6. **Remember that a test does not measure <u>all</u> the content, skills, or behaviors of interest.** Tests are limited to what they cover, which is usually a sample of what a student knows or can do. Another test that samples differently could get quite different results. Scores are approximations of students' knowledge and competencies.

7. **Remember, in some cases there is no alternative to standardized tests.** The SAT and GRE provide important information, as do advanced placement tests. Standardized tests have their place and if used appropriately, provide information that cannot be currently obtained any other way.

How To Help Your Students Do Better On Standardized Tests

There are three steps to helping students do better on standardized tests: (a) making students comfortable in the test-taking situation, (b) showing students how to complete tests efficiently, and (c) helping students see their scores on standardized tests as a cause for neither pride or shame.

The first step is the warm-up. It involves familiarizing students with the mechanics of the testing situation. Pass out facsimiles of the answer sheet and have students practice filling in their names and other information. Rehearse the preliminary instructions, using the exact language the manual advises. Practice arranging the seats according to the seating plan suggested by the test makers. Give the students the proper pencils and have them practice filling in answer sheets rapidly, since speed is essential on a standardized test and neatness does not help one's score. Have them practice, watching for students who tend to lose their place or have trouble marking the proper boxes. It is especially helpful to have them practice reading the questions on one sheet and marking the answers on another sheet. The purpose of such warm-up procedures is to make the mechanics of test-taking so familiar that students will be relaxed and competent when faced with the real thing.

The second step is the dry run. Use old copies of the test that contain questions no longer used to familiarize students with question format, the vocabulary of instructions, and the general appearance of the test. Have students devise their own best strategies for test taking and then share their ideas with one another. Look through the test to determine if any special skills such as reading graphs and charts are needed. If so, drill

students on those skills. Tell students whether they should guess or avoid guessing. Since skimming is a vital skill, have students practice reading passages both aloud and silently, stressing only key words, and reading passages with the question and answers in mind. At the end of each practice session, discuss with students the following rules for test taking:

1. As quickly as possible, complete the entire test or section. Answer at first only questions you are sure of and those with obvious answers. Lightly mark the questions that make you pause and return to them later.

2. Leave a minute at the end of the test to fill in any blank boxes. Guess on every question you don't know if there is no penalty for doing so.

3. Do not get interested in the reading passages or any information contained in the test. Standardized tests are not for learning or thinking. They are for gauging how well students take tests.

4. Never argue with answers. Simply try for the answers the testing agency is going to score as being correct.

Step three is the follow-through. This involves letting students know that what was tested was their ability to take tests and their scores are cause for neither pride nor shame. The real work completed during the school year measures achievement and ability.

Summary

Standardized tests are tests prepared for nationwide use (usually commercially) to provide accurate and meaningful information on students' levels of performance relative to others at their age or grade levels. National and subnational normative data are provided for most standardized instruments so that student performance can be compared to other than local norms. Standardized tests scores may be used to evaluate the effectiveness of instructional programs, select and place students, diagnose students' problems in learning, and conduct research. There are two types of standardized tests--achievement and aptitude. Standardized achievement tests may be achievement batteries, diagnostic tests, and specific subject are tests. Aptitude tests may be general intelligence tests or multifactor aptitude batteries. Standardized tests ensure that all students are evaluated by the same criteria. They yield more accurate and fairer evaluations than unsystematic observations. On the other hand, standardized achievement and aptitude tests measure a narrow group of verbal skills and primarily contain multiple-choice items that do not allow students to demonstrate complex cognitive and problem solving skills.

Meaningful And Manageable Assessment Through Cooperative Learning, Interaction Book Company, 7208 Cornelia Drive, Edina, MN 55435, (612) 831-9500, FAX (612) 831-9332.

To interpret standardized test scores, you need to understand frequency distributions, measures of central tendency and standard deviation, percentiles, grade equivalents, and normal curve equivalents. The criteria that standardized tests (and all other measurement procedures) have to meet are reliability, validity, objectivity, practicality, and discrimination. A measure is **reliable** if it is a consistent and accurate measure. A measure is **valid** if it measures what it is supposed to measure. A measure has **objectivity** if there is agreement among (a) experts on the correct answer to a test item and (b) different scorers on what score should be assigned to a test paper or questionnaire. **Practicality** is determined by the cost of and ease with which a measure can be used. A measure **discriminates** if it differentiates among high, medium, and low achieving students.

Teachers can help their students score higher on standardized tests by making students comfortable in the test-taking situation, showing students how to complete tests efficiently, and helping students see their scores on standardized tests as neither a cause for pride or shame. In holding teachers accountable for student scores on standardized tests, it should be remembered that teachers can only provide an opportunity for students to learn, they cannot make students learn.

Standardized Tests: Planning Form

1. Ways I will drill students on the mechanics of taking standardized tests:

a.

b.

c.

d.

2. Ways I will drill students on test-taking skills:

a.

b.

c.

d.

3. Ways I will teach students how to interpret standardized test scores:

a.

b.

c.

d.

Meaningful And Manageable Assessment Through Cooperative Learning, Interaction Book Company, 7208 Cornelia Drive, Edina, MN 55435, (612) 831-9500, FAX (612) 831-9332.

Analyzing Standardized Tests

1. Select a standardized test that either you or your students have taken. Note the type of questions used in the test. Write sample questions of the types used in the tests that are appropriate for your students. Have your students practice with the questions until you are sure they are familiar with how to answer each type of question.

2. Choose several of the test questions in the standardized test. Analyze and label them according to the following categories:

   a. Prior knowledge needed.

   b. Higher-level reasoning needed.

   c. More than one answer seems correct.

   d. Ambiguous question.

   e. Recall is required.

   f. Culturally biased.

   g. Other:

Comment On Your Findings:

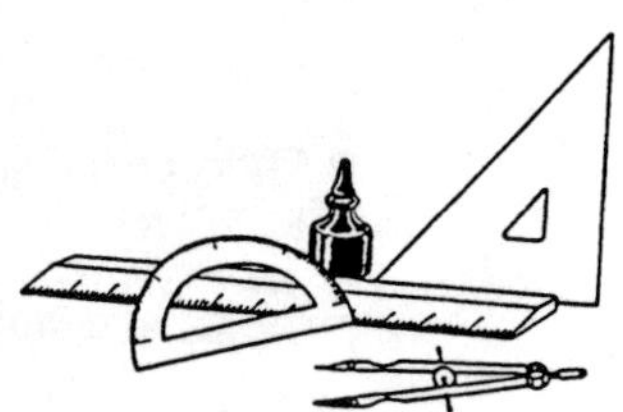

Cooperative Learning: Classroom Observation

Teacher:_________________________ Date:____________ Observer: ______________

Teacher Actions	Implementation	Comments
Objectives	❑ Academics ❑ Social Skills	
Positive Interdependence	❑ Group Goal ❑ Group Celebration/Reward ❑ Resources Shared/Jigsawed ❑ Roles Assigned ❑ Shared Identity	
Group Composition	❑ Random ❑ Teacher Selected	
Seating Arrangement	❑ Clear View/Access to Groupmates, Teacher ❑ Clear View/Access to Materials	
Individual Accountability	❑ Each Student Tested Individually ❑ Students Check Each Other ❑ Random Student Evaluated ❑ Role: Checker for Understanding	
Define Social Skills	❑ Define (T-Chart) ❑ Demonstrate/Model ❑ Guided Practice ❑ Assign As Role	
Observation Of Taskwork And Teamwork	❑ Teacher Monitors And Intervenes ❑ Students Monitor ❑ Formal Observation Form ❑ Informal (Anecdotal) Observation	
Teacher Feedback: Teamwork Skills	❑ Class ❑ Group ❑ Individual ❑ Frequency And Quality Of Use ❑ Charts and Graphs Used ❑ Positive Feedback To Each Student	
Group Processing	❑ Analysis/Reflection: Teamwork & Taskwork ❑ Goal Setting For Improvement ❑ Celebration	
General Climate	❑ Group Products Displayed ❑ Group Progress Displayed ❑ Aids To Group Work Displayed	

Meaningful And Manageable Assessment Through Cooperative Learning, Interaction Book Company, 7208 Cornelia Drive, Edina, MN 55435, (612) 831-9500, FAX (612) 831-9332.

Chapter Four: Teacher-Made Tests

Testing Students

Tests are given to assess student learning, increase student learning, and guide instruction. From five to fifteen percent of all class time is used in administering written teacher-made tests. **Teacher-made tests** are written or oral assessments of student achievement that are (a) not commercially produced or standardized and (b) designed specifically for the teacher's students. They tend to be used more frequently, to cover more of the curriculum, and count more for final grades than other forms of assessment and evaluation. Ideally, teacher-made tests will be used to increase learning, guide instruction, and provide insight into what students need to be taught next. Actually, they are used primarily to measure final achievement and give grades at the end of an instructional unit. Teacher-made tests are almost always of the paper-and-pencil variety and may be classified as either objective or essay tests.

Objective Tests

Advantages	Disadvantages
Allow Broad Sampling Of Knowledge	Very Time Consuming To Construct
Assess Knowledge Quickly & Efficiently	Highly Subjective In Choosing Questions
Can Be Easily Scored And Analyzed	Difficult To Write Unambiguous Questions
Can Be Administered To Large Groups	Rely On Recognition And Recall
Prevent Bias In Scoring	Require A Specific, Predetermined Answer
Measure Student Knowledge Without Bias Of Writing, Grammatical, Neatness Skills	Penalize Poor Readers

Objective tests are frequently used because they can be easily scored and analyzed (once a key is constructed), given to large numbers of students, take very little time to administer and score, and are free of bias in scoring and in requiring unrelated skills such as writing. Since objective tests allow teachers to sample the content of an instructional unit more fully (because more questions can be asked and students can answer them more quickly), efficiency and reliability tend to be high. Their **pitfalls** are that they are highly subjective in determining what questions to ask and how to ask them, it takes considerable time and skill to write good objective questions, rely on recognition and

Meaningful And Manageable Assessment Through Cooperative Learning, Interaction Book Company, 7208 Cornelia Drive, Edina, MN 55435, (612) 831-9500, FAX (612) 831-9332

recall to assess knowledge and skills, and penalize poor readers. There are several types of objective test items: multiple-choice, true-false, matching, short-answer, and interpretive.

Guidelines For Writing Multiple-Choice Items

1. Write the stem first. The stem should present a problem, stand on its own without qualification, include most of the item, be as short as possible, and be clearly worded. Phrases or words that would begin every choice should be part of the stem.
2. Use the negative ("not") infrequently in the stem, but underline it to make it noticeable when you do.
3. Include only one correct or clearly best response.
4. Make all alternatives grammatically consistent with the stem. Each choice should have the same grammatical form (such as a verb) at its beginning.
5. Make all alternative responses equal in length. Avoid making the correct response either the longest or the shortest. Often the longest alternative is correct, because absolutely correct answers often require qualification and precision.
6. Make all the incorrect responses equally plausible. Do not include responses that are absurd or unbelievable.
7. Place the correct response in each possible position equally often.
8. Avoid the use of "none of these" as an alternative because too often it reduces the possible correct choice to one or two items.
9. Never make the answer to one question depend on knowing the answer to another.
10. Avoid using (a) no-exception words such as "never," "all," "none," and "always" (they signal an incorrect response) and (b) qualifying words such as "often," "seldom," "sometimes," "typically," "generally," and "ordinarily" (they signal correct responses).

Multiple-Choice Items

Multiple-choice items consists of a direct question or incomplete statement (called the stem) followed by two or more possible answers (called responses), only one of

which is to be selected. Students can be instructed to choose either the correct answer or the best answer. An example of a multiple-choice item is:

Drilling a hole with a drill that has one lip ground longer than the other will result in a hole that is:

a. oversized *c. bell-mouthed*

b. out-of-round *d. undersized*

The **advantages** of multiple-choice items is that many levels of cognitive understanding can be assessed, they are easy to grade, and guessing is difficult. The **disadvantages** are that writing good items is difficult and time-consuming, especially if higher-level reasoning is to be tested, the items test only recognition of the correct answer, and it is difficult to provide feedback on each item. Teachers should ensure that they write questions that require translation, interpretation, application, analysis, and evaluation. Too often, multiple-choice test items assess only at the knowledge level.

True-False Items

In **true-false items** students identify the correctness of facts, statements, definitions, and principles. An example of a true-false item is:

T F A virus is the smallest known organism.

Guidelines For Writing "True-False Items

1. Use statements that are clearly true or false without qualification.
2. Avoid absolute words such as "all," "always," and "never."
3. Restrict each statement to a single idea.
4. Use an approximately equal number of true and false items.
5. Do not use the exact wording of the textbook in the questions.
6. Make all items approximately the same length.
7. Avoid trivial and general statements.
8. Have students make false statements true to encourage higher-level thinking.

Meaningful And Manageable Assessment Through Cooperative Learning, Interaction Book Company, 7208 Cornelia Drive, Edina, MN 55435, (612) 831-9500, FAX (612) 831-9332

True-false items have the **advantages** of being easy to construct and quick to be answered and scored. Thus, a large amount of knowledge can be sampled in a short amount of time. Their **disadvantages** are that students' scores can be influenced considerably by guessing and only lower-level learning can be measured.

Matching Items

A **matching question** consists of a list of concepts and a list of responses. Students match one of the responses to each concept, which requires them to categorize and associate. An example of a matching question is:

Match the names of psychologists with the concept they popularized.

_____*Carl Rogers*	a. *mastery learning*
_____*Abraham Maslow*	b. *fully functioning person*
_____*Benjamin Bloom*	c. *self-actualization*
	d. *competency motivation*

The **advantages** include the ability to cover considerable material in a small amount of space, ease of scoring, and ability to assess discrimination between similar events or issues. The **disadvantages** include being restricted to measuring factual information and the ease with which students can cheat.

Guidelines For Writing Matching Items

1. Keep the lists as short as possible (six items or less).
2. Keep the lists as homogeneous as possible (do not mix names with dates).
2. List more responses than concepts to reduce guessing.
3. Arrange the lists in alphabetical or chronological order.
4. State in the directions the basis on which the matching is to be done.

Short Answers And Completion Items

In **short-answer and completion items** students are required to supply a brief answer consisting of a name, word, phrase, or symbol. An example of a short-answer question is:

A figure that has three sides is called a _______________.

Their **advantages** are that they are easy to write, require recall of information, and guessing is not likely to be successful. Their **disadvantage** is that they measure only lower level learning.

Guidelines For Writing Short-Answer Questions

1. Ensure only one answer is correct.	2. Ask a direct question.
3. Put the blank toward end of the sentence.	4. Use blanks of equal length.
5. Ensure the answer is brief and definitive.	6. Have one blank per sentence.
7. In computation problems state the degree of precision expected.	8. For completion items, put blanks in a column on the right side of the paper.

Interpretive Items

Interpretive items are objective questions based on a graph, diagram, map, or descriptive paragraph. They require students to interpret written or pictorial material and, therefore, they can measure complex learning in a more structured form than can essay items. The **disadvantages** are that they test at the recognition level, are difficult and time consuming to construct, favor good readers, and measure only the ability to solve problems presented in a structure form. When writing interpretative items teachers should ensure that the questions are at an appropriate reading level and require analysis and interpretation.

Essay Tests

Essay tests consist of a few questions requiring students to write paragraphs or themes as answers. Essay items require students to recall, select, organize, and apply what they have learned and express it in their own words. The **advantages** of essay tests are that they can be used to assess students' recall of what was learned, understanding of concepts and principles, ability to organize material and develop arguments, and the ability to apply what a student knows. Essay questions are especially useful in measuring higher-level reasoning processes (analysis, synthesis, and evaluation) and the ability to express oneself in writing.

There are several **disadvantages** to essay tests. The first is that only a few questions can be asked, so that often a representative sample of the content to be tested cannot be requested. Secondly, nonverbal students and students who do not write well may be penalized by the exclusive use of essay tests. The third and fourth disadvantages are that essay tests take a great deal more time to score than do objective tests and are difficult to score in an objective and reliable way. The scoring of essay questions is notoriously unreliable. Different teachers may give different grades to the same answers and teachers may give different scores to the same answer at different times. A relatively poor answer has been found to receive a higher grade when it is read after an even poorer one than when it is read after a much better one. Teachers have been found to be give lower grades to students whose handwriting is illegible, whose paper is untidy, or whose grammar or spelling is faulty. Although there are procedures for increasing the reliability of essay test grading, they require a great deal of discipline and commitment on the part of the teacher.

Guidelines For Writing Essay Questions

1. Gear questions directly toward desired outcomes of the instructional program not easily assessed by objective items (e.g., analysis, synthesis, argumentation).

2. Define assessment criteria and point values. Be sure the criteria clearly communicate how questions should be answered. Inform students which items will be weighted heavier than others and how much time they should spend on each question.

3. Make questions specific. Avoid broad and ambiguous questions (e.g., discuss..., tell all you know about...).

4. Allow students sufficient time to complete the questions.

5. Adopt procedures to make scoring as objective as possible, such as (a) outlining model answers before scoring tests, (b) prepare assessment criteria in advance, (c) assess all answers for one question before going on to the next, (d) begin assessing by scanning a random sample of the papers, (e) apply the same criteria to all papers (if one student is penalized for spelling and grammar, all students should be), and (f) have colleagues score a number of papers with your criteria and compare their assessments with yours.

Short-Essay Items

Short-essay items require students to recall, explain, and apply specific information they have learned in their own words. Students are required to write short, succinct answers in which they reveal how much they know. Students may give an answer from two or three sentences to a page. Short essay items have the same advantages and disadvantages as essay items. **Advantages** include that they can be used to elicit a wide variety of student responses from defining terms to comparing and contrasting important concepts or events. They can be used to assess higher level reasoning in the form of analysis, synthesis, and evaluation. And guessing is minimized. **Disadvantages** include scoring responses reliably and the time required to assess student responses.

Test Blueprints

Whether a test consists of essay or objective questions, it needs to measure accurately and fairly the parts of the subject area covered in instruction. A blueprint of a test can be constructed to ensure that the test covers a representative, accurate sample of what is covered in the learning unit. In most cases you will not have the time to test students' knowledge and performance on everything covered in the class. Your tests, therefore, will only partially sample what students know and can do. The more precisely and completely learning goals are described at the beginning of a unit, the easier it will be to (a) include an adequate sample of the most significant topics on a test and (b) use the types of test items that are most appropriate for measuring the desired learning outcomes. A test blueprint can also serve as a guide to students preparing for an exam. Imagine, for example, that you have been teaching a unit on mathematics that includes fractions, multiplication, division, measuring, and decimals. During the time spent on the unit, the major emphasis was placed on fractions. Thus, the test blueprint would be as follows:

Test Blueprint

Subject Area	Routine Computation	Taught Procedures	Total
Fractions	10	5	15
Multiplication	5	3	8
Division	5	3	8
Measuring	5	3	8
Decimals	5	3	8
Total	30	17	47

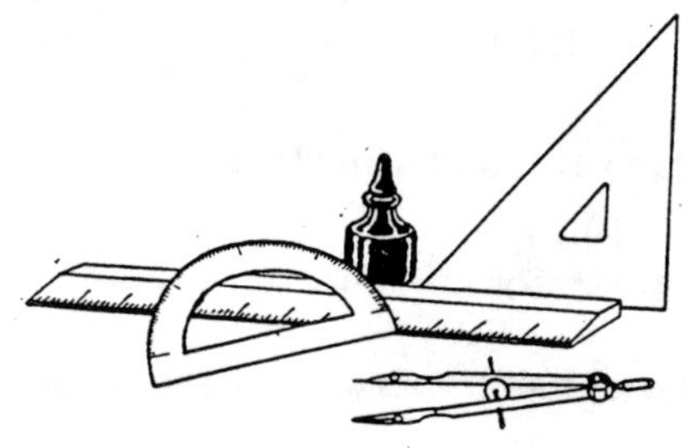

Meaningful And Manageable Assessment Through Cooperative Learning, Interaction Book Company, 7208 Cornelia Drive, Edina, MN 55435, (612) 831-9500, FAX (612) 831-9332

Guidelines For Teacher-Made Tests

1. Construct test items to reflect instructional objectives and desired outcomes.

2. Each student should have a neatly and accurately typed copy of the test. Teachers should avoid whenever possible writing items on the board or reading them aloud to the class. All items of the same format should be grouped together.

3. Vary the question types (true-false, multiple-choice, fill-in-the-blank, matching, short-response, essay).

3. Divide question types into separate sections.

4. Precede each set of items with clear completion instructions and the total amount of credit (points) possible for each question (e.g., multiple-choice [3 points each]).

5. Vary levels of questions from recognition, recall, processing, analysis, integrative, application.

6. Within each type of item, arrange the questions from simple to complex (easiest to hardest).

7. For broad, integrative, complex questions (e.g., essay and graphic organizer questions), give students a choice in the questions they select to answer.

8. Administer the test so that cheating is eliminated or detected.

9. Provide a criterion-referenced grading scale so students know what score represents a certain grade (e.g., A = 93-100, B = 85-92, C = 75-84, D = 65-74; F = Below 65).

10. Make sure reading level is appropriate to your students.

11. Give sufficient time for all students to finish. Informed students of time remaining.

12. Type or print the test clearly and leave space between questions and sections to facilitate easy reading and responding.

13. Include a variety of visual, oral, and kinesthetic tasks.

14. Vary the way the test is given for students with special needs.

Your Checklist For Your Tests

1. _____ All items relate to the instructional objectives and desired learning outcomes.
2. _____ There are _____ different question types in the test.
3. _____ Each question types is in a separate section.
4. _____ The directions for the overall test and each section are clear.
5. _____ Questions of _____ different levels have been included.
6. _____ Questions are arranged from simple to complex.
7. _____ Students have a choice of essay and graphic organizer questions.
8. _____ Point values are given for each section .
9. _____ Students have been informed of the criterion-referenced grading scale.
10. _____ The reading level is appropriate to your students.
11. _____ Each question is easy to read and respond to.
12. _____ The test has been adapted for students with special needs.

Cooperative Learning And Teacher-Made Tests

There are at least three ways cooperative learning can be used as part of a testing procedure: Group-individual-group procedure, weekly group tests with an individual final exam, and group discussion tests.

Group Preparation, Individual Test, Group Test Procedure

Tests may be given both to assess and increase student learning. There are two advantages of cooperative learning groups in administrating traditional tests (Johnson, Johnson, & Holubec, 1993; Johnson, Johnson, & Smith, 1991). **First**, allowing students to work together before an assessment can level the playing field by enabling students to compare understandings and ensure that they all have the same background knowledge to prepare for the assessment. **Second**, following the assessment allowing students to work in groups immediately (a) allows each group member to discover what he or she did and did not understand, (b) allows each group member to discover where the information required to answer the questions is in the course materials, and (c) allows the group to provide remediation to members who did not understand the course content covered in the test.

The sequence of using cooperative learning groups in testing is (a) students work together in cooperative learning groups to review the material to be covered in the test, (b) each student takes the test individually, and (c) students retake the test in the cooperative learning group (**Group Preparation, Individual Test, Group Test**). Students are assigned to cooperative learning groups that are heterogeneous in terms of reading and math ability. The groups study together all week. On Thursday, the groups meet to ensure that all group members know and understand the material on which they will be tested. On Friday, an examination is given. The students take the test individually, making two copies of their answers. One answer sheet they hand in to the teacher (who then scores the answers). If all members of the group score above a present criterion (such as 90 percent correct) on the individual tests, then each member receives a designated number (such as five) of bonus points. The bonus points are added to their individual score to determine their individual grade for the test. The students keep the second answer sheet. After all members have finished the test, the group meets to take the test again. Their **task** is to answer each question correctly. The **cooperative goal** is for all group members to understand the material covered by the test. For any answer that they disagree about or are unsure of, they are required to find the page and paragraph in the text that contains the answer. The teacher randomly observes the groups to check that they are following the procedure.

The GIG Procedure For Giving Tests

You should frequently give tests and quizzes to assess (a) how much each student knows and (b) what students still need to learn. Whenever you give a test, cooperative learning groups can serve as bookends by preparing members to take the test and providing a setting in which students review the test. Using the following procedure will result in (a) optimizing each student's preparation for the test, (b) making each student accountable to peers for his or her performance on the test, (c) assessing how much each student knows, (d) assessing what students still need to learn, (e) providing students with immediate clarification of what they did not understand or learn, (f) providing students with immediate remediation of what they did not learn, (g) preventing arguments between you and your students over which answer are correct and why. The procedure is.

1. Students prepare for, and review for, a test in cooperative learning groups.

Meaningful And Manageable Assessment Through Cooperative Learning, Interaction Book Company, 7208 Cornelia Drive, Edina, MN 55435, (612) 831-9500, FAX (612) 831-9332

2. Each student takes the test individually, making two copies of his or her answers. Students submit one set of answer to you to grade and keep one set for the group discussion.

3. Students retake the test in their cooperative learning groups.

Preparing For A Test In Cooperative Groups

Students meet in their cooperative learning groups and are given (a) study questions and (b) class time to prepare for the examination. The task is for students to discuss each study question and come to consensus about its answer. The cooperative goal is to ensure that all group members understand how to answer the study questions correctly. If students disagree on the answer to any study questions, they must find the page number and paragraph in the resource material explaining the relevant information or procedures. When the study/review time is up, the students give each other encouragement for doing well on the upcoming test.

Taking The Test Individually

Each student takes the test individually, making two copies of his or her answers. The task (and individual goal) is to answer each test question correctly. Students submit one copy of the answers to you (the teacher). You score the answers and evaluate student performance against a preset criterion of excellence. Students keep one copy for the group discussion. After all group members have finished the test, the group meets to take the test again.

Retaking The Test In Cooperative Groups

Students meet in their cooperative learning groups and retake the test. The **task** is to answer each question correctly. The **cooperative goal** is to ensure that all group members understand the material and procedures covered by the test. Members do so by (a) reaching consensus on the answer for each question and the rationale or procedure underlying the answer and (b) ensuring that all members can explain the answer and the rationale or procedure. The procedure is for members to:

1. Compare their answers on the first question.

2. If there is agreement, one member explains the rationale or procedure underlying the question and the group moves on to question two.

3. If there is disagreement, members find the page number and paragraph in the resource materials explaining the relevant information or procedures. The group is responsible for ensuring that all members understand the material they missed on the test. If necessary, group members assign review homework to each other. When all members

agree on the answer and believe other members comprehend the material, the group moves on to question two.

4. The learning groups repeat this procedure until they have covered all test questions.

5. The group members celebrate how hard members have worked in learning the material and how successful they were on the test.

Weekly Group Tests and Individual Final Exam

To maximize students' higher-level reasoning and long-term retention of knowledge, the following procedure may be followed. Assign students to cooperative learning groups of four members and have them complete their assignments together all week. The groups should be heterogeneous in terms of math and reading ability. On Friday, an examination is given.

Each cooperative group is divided into two pairs. Each pair takes the test, conferring on the answer to each question. The **task** is to correctly answer each question. The **cooperative goal** is to have one answer for each question that both agree upon and both can explain. They cannot proceed until they agree on the answer. Once the two pairs are finished, the cooperative group of four meets and retakes the test. Their **task** is to answer each question correctly. The **cooperative goal** is for all group members to understand the material covered by the test. Group members confer on each question. On any question to which the two pairs have different answers or members are unsure of the answer, they find the page number and paragraph in the textbook where the answer is explained. Each group is responsible for ensuring that all members understand the material they missed on the test. If necessary, group members assign review homework to each other. The teacher randomly observes each group to ensure that they are answering the questions correctly. Each cooperative group then hands in one answer sheet with a list of all members. Each member signs the answer sheet to verify that (a) he or she understands the content and (b) all other group members understand the content covered by the test. All group members are given equal credit for successfully passing the test.

At the end of the grading period, each student takes an individual final examination. If any student scores below a preset criterion (such as 90 percent), then the cooperative group meets and reviews the content with the student until the student can successfully pass the test. This rarely happens, as the group members have verified each week that they all are learning the assigned content.

Group Discussion Test

For the **group discussion test** students meet with their cooperative base group and discuss the content of the assigned reading. The **purpose** of the group discussion test is for students to have a thorough, intellectually stimulating, creative, fun, and practically useful discussion of the assigned texts. More specifically, the **task** is to demonstrate mastery and deeper-level understanding of the assigned readings. This task is to be accomplished **cooperatively**. Members are to generate one set of answers for the group and all members must agree with and be able to explain the answers. During the group test group members should focus on:

1. Integrating relevant theory, research, and practical experiences.
2. Analyzing in depth possible answers to the question in order to achieve insights into the issue.
3. Thinking divergently.
4. Critically examining each other's reasoning and engaging in constructive controversy.
5. Making the examination a fun and enjoyable experience for everyone.

A number of discussion questions are attached. These questions are aimed at being **integrative** in the sense that material from many different chapters and books are relevant to answering them. The **responsibilities of each group member** are to:

1. Choose two of the suggested discussion questions. For each question think carefully about the answer. Make sure that your answer combines material from many different chapters of the assigned texts as well as your own relevant personal experiences and background. Learn the answer to the questions thoroughly as you will be the **group expert** on what the text books have to say about the issue highlighted in the question.
2. Plan how to lead a group discussion on the question that will require higher-level reasoning, critical thinking, conceptual integration of material from many different chapters of the assigned texts, and a working knowledge of the specific relevant theories and research findings. In order to do so you will need to prepare for each group member (a) a typed outline of the answer to the question with the relevant page numbers in the assigned text books and (b) copies of relevant written information to facilitate discussion. As members of your group may be visual rather than auditory learners, **prepare visuals** such as diagrams, charts, and cartoons to help them learn, think critically about, and conceptually integrate the relevant theories, research, and practical experiences.

Meaningful And Manageable Assessment Through Cooperative Learning, Interaction Book Company, 7208 Cornelia Drive, Edina, MN 55435, (612) 831-9500, FAX (612) 831-9332

3. Come to the examination prepared to contribute to the discussion of each question and to learn, think critically about, and conceptually integrate the theory, research, and practical experiences relevant to each question discussed.

The group discussion test should cover at least one question from each member. Since each member will come prepared to lead a discussion on two questions, flip a coin to select which question will be part of the examination. **Guidelines** to follow are:

1. Stick to the questions. It is easy to go off on tangents.

2. Cite specific theories, research, and concepts discussed in the texts. Refer to specific pages. It is easy to make overly broad generalizations and to state personal opinions that are not supported by current knowledge.

3. Refer to personal experiences. Comparing the theories and research findings against your personal and practical experiences is valuable and often allows for integration of several concepts. Do not chat about "what happened to me."

4. Set time limits for each question and stick to these limits rigidly.

5. Encourage disagreement and controversy. All viewpoints and positions should be encouraged as long as they can be supported by theory and research. Follow the rules for constructive controversy.

6. Take responsibility for both task and maintenance actions. Your group has a definite task to accomplish (i.e., demonstrate understanding of the field of social psychology), but the discussion should be enjoyable as well as a productive learning experience.

7. All members must participate actively to (a) contribute to the learning of others and (b) demonstrate overtly to the other members of the group that he or she has read the texts and mastered the content of the course.

To document that the group test did take place and that the criteria for passing were met by all group members, each member will be required to sign the certification form. Make sure that there are no "free-loaders." Do not sign off for a group member unless he or she arrived at the examination fully prepared and participated actively in the discussion of each question. If any group member was absent, the group is to determine what the member has to do to make up the test.

The group will be expected to hand in a **report** consisting of the certification form, a listing of the questions discussed with a summary of the answers and conclusions generated by the discussion, a description of the procedures followed, and a subjective evaluation of the learning resulting from the experience.

Meaningful And Manageable Assessment Through Cooperative Learning, Interaction Book Company, 7208 Cornelia Drive, Edina, MN 55435, (612) 831-9500, FAX (612) 831-9332

Group Exam Certification Form

We, the undersigned, certify that we have participated in the group discussion examination and have met the following criteria:

1. We understand the basic concepts, theories, and bodies of research presented in the texts and lectures.
2. We know the major theorists and researchers discussed in the texts and lectures.
3. We can apply the theories and research findings to practical situations.
4. We can conceptualize a research question and design a research study to test our hypotheses.
5. We have submitted our choice of questions and a brief summary of each answer we have formulated as a group.

Name	Signature	Date

Academic Tournament

An alternative to the individual test is an academic tournament. An **academic tournament** is an objective test (usually recognition or total recall level) conducted in a game format. The **purpose** of the tournament is to determine which cooperative learning group best learned the assigned material. The procedure (adapted from the Teams-Games-Tournament procedure created by David DeVries and Keith Edwards [1974]) is as follows:

1. **Assign students to heterogeneous cooperative learning groups whose members are of different achievement levels**. One high, two medium, and one low achieving student, for example, may be placed in one group. Group members study the assigned material and complete the assignments together and prepare each other for the tournament.

Meaningful And Manageable Assessment Through Cooperative Learning, Interaction Book Company, 7208 Cornelia Drive, Edina, MN 55435, (612) 831-9500, FAX (612) 831-9332

2. **Assign students to competitive triads.** A class tournament is structured around a game in which each student competes as a representative of his or her team with students of equal achievement levels from other teams. When students compete, they should be placed in homogeneous groups based on previous achievement. Groups of three maximize the number of winners in the class (pairs tend to make the competition too personal). Rank the students in each cooperative learning group from highest to lowest on the basis of their previous achievement. Given that only one student from a group can be in a competitive triad, assign the three highest achieving students in the class to Table 1, the next three to Table 2, and so on until the three lowest achieving students in the class are in the bottom table. This creates equal competition within each triad and makes it possible for students of all achievement levels to contribute maximally to their team scores if they do their best. Figure 1 illustrates the relationship between the cooperative learning groups and the competitive triads.

3. **Arrange the classroom.** The room should be arranged so that the triads are separated from each other and students within each triad sit close to each other.

4. **Prepare instructional materials.** During the tournament the students play an instructional game for 10 to 30 minutes. Make a game sheet consisting of about 30 items, a game answer sheet, and a copy of the rules. Make a set of cards numbered from 1 to 30. On each card write (a) one question from the game sheet and (b) the number of the question on the answer sheet. The questions can be either recognition or recall questions.

5. **Conduct the tournament.** The tournament is conducted to determine which cooperative learning group best learned the assigned material. Students receive points according to how well they mastered the material (compared with the other two members of their tournament triad). The procedure for playing the game is in the **Rules Of Play Instruction Sheet** given below.

6. **Determine winning cooperative learning group.** A team score is derived by adding the scores of all the individual members. Team scores are then ranked and announced. The winning group is congratulated.

Meaningful And Manageable Assessment Through Cooperative Learning, Interaction Book Company, 7208 Cornelia Drive, Edina, MN 55435, (612) 831-9500, FAX (612) 831-9332

Rules Of Play

This tournament is being conducted to determine which cooperative learning group has best learned the assigned material. You will receive points according to how well you have mastered the assigned material (compared to the other two members of your tournament triad). The points of the members of your cooperative learning group will be added together to determine a group score. The cooperative learning group with the most points wins.

1. You have been given a deck of specially constructed cards and an answer sheet. To start the game, shuffle the cards and place them face down on the table. Play is in a clockwise rotation. Three rotating roles are assigned to players (roles are rotated in a clockwise direction after each question):

    a. **Question Reader**: Player draws a card, reads it aloud.

    b. **Answer Giver**: Player decides whether or not to give an answer.

    c. **Answer Checker**: If an answer is given, the player reads the answer to the question from the answer sheet (regardless of whether the answer is challenged).

2. To play, the question-reader takes the top card from the deck, reads it aloud. The question-giver has a choice of two responses:

    a. Says he does not know or is not sure of the answer. The two other students may then volunteer to answer the question (the question-reader has the first chance to answer the question). If no one wants to answer, the card is placed on the bottom of the deck.

    b. Answers the question and asks if anyone wants to challenge his or her answer. The player on the answer giver's right has the first right of challenge.

3. If there is no challenge, the answer-checker reads the answer on the answer sheet out loud.

    a. If correct, the answer-giver keeps the card.

    b. If incorrect, the card is placed on the bottom of the deck.

4. If there is a challenge, the challenger gives an answer.

    a. If answer-giver is correct, he or she keeps the card and the challenger must give up one of his or her cards (which is placed on the bottom of the deck).

b. If the answer-giver is incorrect and the challenge is correct, the challenger keeps the card.

c. If both the answer-giver and the challenger are incorrect, then the card is placed on the bottom of the deck.

5. The roles are rotated after each question.

6. The game ends when there are no more cards in the deck. Players count their cards and determine who has the most, second most, and least cards. The ranking is converted into points.

Ranking	Points
First Place	6 Points
Second Place	4 Points
Third Place	2 Points
Two Tie For First Place	5 Points Each
Three Tie For First Place	4 Points Each
Two Tie For Second Place	3 Points Each

TOURNAMENT SCORING SHEET

Tournament Triad: ______________________ **Date:** ________ **Unit:** ________

Write the names of the triad members in the top row of the table. For each question answered, place a plus (+) for each question the student gets right and a minus (-) for each question the student gets wrong. Total the number right for each member and rank the three members from who got the most questions right to who got the least questions right.

Question			
1.			
2.			
3.			
4.			
5.			
6.			
7.			
8.			
9.			
10.			
Total			

Meaningful And Manageable Assessment Through Cooperative Learning, Interaction Book Company, 7208 Cornelia Drive, Edina, MN 55435, (612) 831-9500, FAX (612) 831-9332

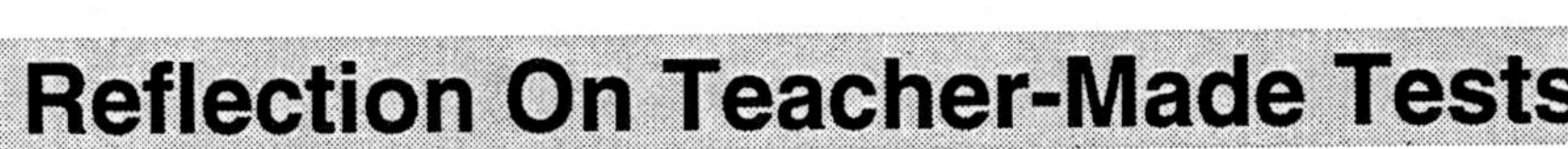

Reflection On Teacher-Made Tests

1. Choose a unit you are going to teach soon.

2. Decide whether to emphasize essay or objective test items. Explain why one is more useful than the other for assessing the outcomes of this unit. Indicate what percentage of the questions will be:

   _____ Essay Questions

   _____ Objective Questions

   _____ 100 Percent

3. Summarize the strengths and weaknesses of each type of question and explain why you have decided on the percentages you have.

4. Of the objective questions you are going to include in the test, indicate the percentage that will be each of the following types:

   _____ Multiple Choice Questions

   _____ True-False Questions

   _____ Matching Questions

   _____ Short Answer And Completion Questions

   _____ Interpretative Questions

   _____ 100 Percent

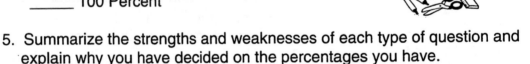

5. Summarize the strengths and weaknesses of each type of question and explain why you have decided on the percentages you have.

6. **List five pieces of advice for teachers on constructing tests:**

   a.

   b.

   c.

   d.

   e.

Meaningful And Manageable Assessment Through Cooperative Learning, Interaction Book Company, 7208 Cornelia Drive, Edina, MN 55435, (612) 831-9500, FAX (612) 831-9332

Chapter Five: Compositions And Presentations

Student Performances And Cooperative Learning

Aesop tells of a man who visited foreign lands and, when he returned to his home, could talk of little except his wonderful adventures during his travels and the great deeds he had done. One of his feats was an amazing leap he had made in a city called Rhodes. "*My leap was so great*," he said, "*no other person could leap anywhere near that distance! Many people witnessed my leap and if you go to Rhodes they will tell you that what I say is true.*" "*No need for witnesses*," one of his listeners said, "*Imagine this city is Rhodes. Now, show us how far you can jump*!" The moral of this tale is: **Actual performances count, not descriptions of what a person believes he or she can do.**

It is not enough to ask students to describe their skills, students have to demonstrate what they can do in actual performances that others can view and assess. **Student performance** refers to a set of actions students engage in to demonstrate their level of skill in enacting a procedure or creating a product. These performances can include performing a music recital, presenting a play, participating in a discussion, creating a newspaper, conducting a science experiment, presenting a mock trial, engaging in a debate, giving a speech, and writing a composition.

To assess performances frequently and effectively, you may wish to enlist the help of cooperative learning groups. With the use of cooperative learning, you can amazingly kill five birds with one stone. **First**, students must engage in the performances frequently to gain expertise. The more frequently students write, for example, the better writers they potentially can become. Ideally, students should write every day. Cooperative learning groups provide an arena in which performances can be developed, practiced, and perfected.

Second, in learning how to engage in a performance, students need to receive immediate and detailed feedback on the quality of their performance. Peer editing of compositions in cooperative teams, for example, enables students to receive continuous feedback on their writing.

Third, to engage in a performance skillfully, students must observe and analyze the performances of others. In order to learn how to play baseball, for example, one must watch others play baseball and analyze how they field and bat. In order to learn how to write well, students must study other people's writing and analyze what is good about it and what could be improved. In order to learn how to present well, students must observe others present and analyze what is effective and ineffective. Cooperative learning groups

Meaningful And Manageable Assessment Through Cooperative Learning, Interaction Book Company, 7208 Cornelia Drive, Edina, MN 55435, (612) 831-9500, FAX (612) 831-9332

provide a setting in which students can observe and analyze how peers write, present, and engage in other performances.

Fourth, assessing the quality of performances is time-consuming. If students write every day, someone has to read their compositions and give critical but helpful feedback. The clear fact is, you do not have the time to assess numerous performances daily. The labor intensive nature of performance assessment means that you have to engineer assessment systems that involve others beside yourself. You do not have to assess every performance of each student. You do have to create a system that ensures that each performance of every student gets assessed. Cooperative learning groups provide a source of labor that enables you to require students to write and present frequently if not daily.

Fifth, assessing others' performances teaches students how to improve their own performances. From assessing their groupmates' performances, students increase their understanding of (a) what constitutes a high quality performance, (b) what actions are required to engage in a high quality performance, and (c) the criteria to be used in assessing their own performances.

In other words, involving cooperative learning groups in assessing members' performances allows students to engage in the performance frequently, receive immediate and detailed feedback on their efforts, observe closely the performances of others and see what is good or lacking in others' performances, provide the labor needed to allow students to engage in performances frequently and receive feedback on their efforts, and increase their understanding of what constitutes a high-quality performance.

This chapter covers the use of cooperative learning groups in assessing two common types of student performances: compositions and presentations.

Cooperative Writing and Editing Pairs

When your lesson includes students writing an essay, report, poem, story, or review of what they have read, you should use cooperative writing and editing pairs.

Tasks: Write a composition and edit other students' compositions.

Criteria For Success: A well-written composition by each student. Depending on the instructional objectives, the compositions may be evaluated for grammar, punctuation, organization, content, or other criteria set by the teacher.

Cooperative Goal: All group members must verify that each member's composition is perfect according to the criteria set by the teacher. Students receive an individual score on the quality of their compositions. You can also give a group score based on the total

Meaningful And Manageable Assessment Through Cooperative Learning, Interaction Book Company, 7208 Cornelia Drive, Edina, MN 55435, (612) 831-9500, FAX (612) 831-9332.

number of errors made by the pair (the number of errors in their composition plus the number of errors in their partner's composition).

Individual Accountability: Each student writes his or her own composition.

Procedure:

1. The teacher assigns students to pairs with at least one good reader in each pair.

2. Student A describes to Student B what he or she is planning to write. Student B listens carefully, probes with a set of questions, and outlines Student A's composition. The written outline is given to Student A.

3. This procedure is reversed with Student B describing what he or she is going to write and Student A listening and completing an outline of Student B's composition, which is then given to Student B.

4. The students research individualistically the material they need to write their compositions, keeping an eye out for material useful to their partner.

5. The two students work together to write the first paragraph of each composition to ensure that they both have a clear start on their compositions.

6. The students write their compositions individualistically.

7. When completed, the students proofread each other's compositions, making corrections in capitalization, punctuation, spelling, language usage, topic sentence usage, and other aspects of writing specified by the teacher. Students also give each other suggestions for revision.

8. The students revise their compositions, making all of the suggested revisions.

9. The two students then reread each other's compositions and sign their names (indicating that they guarantee that no errors exist in the composition).

While the students work, the teacher monitors the pairs, intervening where appropriate to help students master the needed writing and cooperative skills. When students complete their compositions, students discuss how effectively they worked together (listing the specific actions they engaged in to help each other), plan what behaviors they are going to emphasize in the next writing pair, and thank each other for the help and assistance received.

Meaningful And Manageable Assessment Through Cooperative Learning, Interaction Book Company, 7208 Cornelia Drive, Edina, MN 55435, (612) 831-9500, FAX (612) 831-9332

WRITING TOGETHER:

How My Partner And I Are Going To Write Two Of The World's Greatest Compositions

Step One: Creating A Partnership. Identify your partner, say hello, and make sure you have all the materials (pen, paper, topic) you need to complete the assignment of writing a composition. You are to work cooperatively with your partner to ensure that both write a high quality composition. You will receive two scores for the composition. The first is based on the quality of your composition. The second is based on the total number of errors made by you and your partner (the number of errors in your composition plus the number of errors in your partner's composition).

Step Two: Outlining The Compositions. Flip a coin to see who is Student A and who is Student B. Student A describes to Student B what he or she is planning to write. Student B listens carefully, probes with a set of questions, and outlines Student A's composition. The written outline is given to Student A. This procedure is then reversed with Student B describing what he or she is going to write and Student A listening and completing an outline of Student B's composition, which is then given to Student B. If your partner does not understand how to construct an outline, teach him or her how to do so.

Step Three: Researching Your Topic And Collecting Helpful Materials. This can be done cooperatively or individually. In either case, search for information on your topic and keep an eye out for material useful to your partner. Teach your partner what you know about using reference materials and the library, and learn what he or she knows.

Step Four: Writing The First Paragraph (Or Sentence). Work cooperatively with your partner to write the first paragraph of each composition. First write the starting paragraph of Partner A's composition and then of Partner B's composition. Make sure there is a clear and coherent beginning to both compositions.

Step Five: Writing Your Composition By Yourself. Working by yourself, write the best draft of the assignment that you can. Try to meet the criteria for the assignment set by the teacher. Any draft, however, is better than no draft. Write something.

Step Six: Editing Your Partner's Composition. Trade compositions with your partner. Carefully read what your partner has written. Make suggestions as to how your partner may improve his or her composition and better meet the criteria set by the teacher. Suggest corrections in capitalization, punctuation, spelling, language usage, topic sentence usage, and other aspects of writing specified by the teacher. When both you and your partner have finished, explain your suggestions to your partner and listen carefully to his or her explanations of the suggested revisions for your composition.

Meaningful And Manageable Assessment Through Cooperative Learning, Interaction Book Company, 7208 Cornelia Drive, Edina, MN 55435, (612) 831-9500, FAX (612) 831-9332.

Step Seven: Rewriting Your Composition (The Second Draft!). Things get better the second time around. Working individualistically, carefully consider the suggestions made by your partner to improve your composition. Decide which ones you want to use. Revise your composition to make it better and to better meet the criteria set up by the teacher.

Step Eight: Re-Editing Your Partner's Composition. Trade compositions with your partner again. Carefully read what your partner has written. Consider how your partner may improve his or her composition. Make constructive suggestions as to how your partner may do so. Keep in mind the criteria set by the teacher. When both you and your partner have finished editing, explain your suggestions to your partner and listen carefully to his or her explanations of how you may improve your composition. Keep revising your composition until both you and your partner agree that it meets all the criteria set by the teacher and is ready to be turned in.

Step Nine: Signing Off. When you and your partner agree that your composition is the best it can be under the circumstances, you sign your name as the author of the composition and your partner signs as the editor who personally guarantees that no errors exist in the composition and the composition is ready to be read by the teacher.

Step Ten: Discussing The Quality Of Your Partnership (How Well Did We Work Together?). With your partner, discuss the effectiveness of your partnership. List specific actions each did that helped the other to write a good composition. Think of how each could work together even better next time. Thank each other for the help and assistance received, and celebrate the success of your partnership.

Partnership Processing Form

1. My actions that helped my partner learn:
   a.
   b.
   c.
2. Actions I could add or improve on to be an even better partner next time:
   a.
   b.
   c.

Writing A Persuasive Argument

Thesis Statement (A statement that you want others to agree with and accept, but expect others to challenge)

Rationale (The facts, information, and theories gathered that validate the thesis statement, arranged in a logical structure to lead to a conclusion)

Conclusion (A statement that is logically derived from rationale and is the same as the thesis statement)

Author: ______________________________ **Editor:** ______________________________

Persuasive Argument Composition Rubric

Name: ______________________________ Date: __________ Grade: ____

Title Of Composition: ____

Scoring Scale: Low 1--2--3--4--5 High

Criteria	Score	Weight	Total
Organization: Thesis Statement And Introduction Rationale Presented To Support Thesis Conclusion Logically Drawn From Rationale Effective Transitions		6	(30)
Content: Topic Addressed Reasoning Clear With Valid Logic Evidence Presented To Support Key Points Creativity Evident		8	(40)
Usage: Topic Sentence Beginning Every Paragraph Correct Subject-Verb Agreement Correct Verb Tense Complete Sentences (No Run-Ons, Fragments) Mix Of Simple And Complex Sentences.		4	(20)
Mechanics: Correct Use Of Punctuation Correct Use Of Capitalization Few Or No Misspellings		2	(10)
Scale: 93-100=A, 87 - 85-92=B, 77-84=C		20	(100)

Comments:

Meaningful And Manageable Assessment Through Cooperative Learning, Interaction Book Company, 7208 Cornelia Drive, Edina, MN 55435, (612) 831-9500, FAX (612) 831-9332

Reflection On Peer Editing And Assessment

Benefits To Editee	Benefits To Editor
1.	1.
2.	2.
3.	3.
4.	4.
5.	5.
6.	6.
7.	7.
8.	8.
9.	9.
10.	10.

Presenting Together:

How My Partner And I Are Going To Give Two Of The World's Greatest Presentations

Step One: Creating A Partnership. Identify your partner, say hello, and make sure you have all the materials (pen, paper, topic) you need to complete the assignment. The learning **tasks** are for students to (a) prepare a presentation, (b) make a presentation, and (c) assess its effectiveness. The presentation has to include visuals and/or active participation by the audience. The **cooperative goal** is to ensure that all group members learn the material they study and develop and deliver a high-quality presentation on it.

Step Two: Selecting A Topic. Each person, working individualistically, selects a topic to present (or considers the one assigned by the teacher) and collects their initial thoughts about what they may say.

Step Three: Outlining The Presentations. Flip a coin to see who is Student A and who is Student B. Student A describes to Student B what he or she is planning to present. Student B listens carefully, probes with a set of questions, and outlines Student A's presentation. The written outline is given to Student A. This procedure is then reversed with Student B describing what he or she is going to present and Student A listening, completing an outline of Student B's presentation, and giving it to Student B. Teach your partner what you know about how to construct an outline and learn what your partner knows.

Step Four: Researching Your Topic And Collecting Helpful Materials. This can be done cooperatively or individually. In either case, search for information on your topic and keep an eye out for material useful to your partner. If your partner does not know how to use reference materials and the library effectively, teach him or her how to do so.

Step Five: Writing The Introduction. Work cooperatively with your partner to write the introduction for your presentation. First write the introduction for Partner A's presentation and then of Partner B's presentation. Make sure there is a clear and coherent beginning to both presentations.

Step Six: Planning Your Presentation By Yourself. Working by yourself, plan the first version of your presentation. Try to meet the criteria for the assignment set by the teacher. Any version, however, is better than no version. Plan something.

Step Seven: Presenting Your Initial Version. Combine your pair with another pair into a group of four. Each person gives his or her presentation. The other three members carefully analyze the presentation (using the assessment rubric) and make suggestions

Meaningful And Manageable Assessment Through Cooperative Learning, Interaction Book Company, 7208 Cornelia Drive, Edina, MN 55435, (612) 831-9500, FAX (612) 831-9332

as to how it may be improved. The teacher rotates throughout the class and samples as many presentations as he or she can. When all four members have finished, discuss how each may revise his or her presentation and make it better.

Step Eight: Re-Planning Your Presentation (The Second Version!). Things get better the second time around. Working individualistically, carefully consider the suggestions made by your groupmates to improve your presentation. Decide which ones you want to use. Revise your presentation to make it better and to better meet the criteria set up by the teacher.

Step Nine: Giving Your Presentation. Combine your pair with a different pair to form a new group of four. Each member gives his or her presentation. The other three members critically analyze the presentation (using the assessment rubric) and consider how the presentation may be improved. The teacher will rotate throughout the class and sample the presentations of as many students as he or she can. Listen carefully to the feedback you receive from the other three members on how you may improve your presentation. The teacher may wish to collect the assessment forms completed by the group members to help him or her assess the quality of each student's presentations.

Step Ten: Discussing The Quality Of Your Partnership (How Well Did We Work Together?). With your partner, discuss the effectiveness of your partnership. List specific actions each did that helped the other to make a high quality presentation. Think of how each could work together even better next time. Thank each other for the help and assistance received, and celebrate the success of your partnership.

Partnership Processing Form

1. My actions that helped my partner learn:

   a.

   b.

   c.

2. Actions I could add or improve on to be an even better partner next time:

   a.

   b.

   c.

Meaningful And Manageable Assessment Through Cooperative Learning, Interaction Book Company, 7208 Cornelia Drive, Edina, MN 55435, (612) 831-9500, FAX (612) 831-9332.

Oral Presentations Rubric

Name: ______________________________ ***Date:*** ____________

Title Of Presentation: ______________________________

Criterion	Rating	Comments
Addresses Subject, Scholarly, Informative		
Organized (introduction, body, conclusion)		
Creative Reasoning And Persuasiveness		
Intriguing (audience wants to find out more)		
Interesting, Transitions, Easy To Follow, Concise		
Volume, Enunciation, Eye Contact, Gestures		
Involving (audience active, not passive)		
Visual Aids, Props, Music		
Other:		
Total		

For each criterion, rate the presentation between 1 (very poor) to 5 (very good).

Meaningful And Manageable Assessment Through Cooperative Learning, Interaction Book Company, 7208 Cornelia Drive, Edina, MN 55435, (612) 831-9500, FAX (612) 831-9332

Preparation Papers

To prepare for each lesson, you ask students to complete a short writing assignment. Even if you do not grade the papers, it compels students to organize their thoughts and take some responsibility for the lesson's success.

1. Students' **task** is to write a short paper (one to two pages) on an aspect of the assigned readings to prepare for class. Before each lesson (class session) students:

   a. Choose a major theory, concept, idea, or person discussed in the assigned reading.

   b. Write a one to two page analysis of it (1) summarizing the relevant assigned readings and (2) adding relevant material from another source (book, journal, magazine, newspaper) to enrich the analysis.

2. Students meet in their base groups of four members. The base groups stay the same for the entire semester or year. Create the **cooperative structure** by having students bring multiple copies of their paper to class (one for each member of their group and one for you). Each member presents a two to three minute summary of his or her paper. Before the next class session the members of the cooperative group read, edit, and criticize the paper. They complete an assessment form for each member's paper. Members then sign each member's paper. The signature means that they have read the paper and have provided feedback to improve their groupmates' writing skills.

3. The cooperative groups summarize what they have learned from members' papers and how it applies to the topic of the lesson.

Preparation Paper Assessment Form

Points Possible	Criteria	Points Earned
10	Has A Clear, Accurate, Descriptive Title	
10	Begins With A Position Statement	
10	Each Paragraph Is Indented	
10	Each Paragraph Begins With A Topic Sentence	
10	Capitalization, Appearance, Punctuation, Spelling	
10	Includes Information From Two Or More Sources	
10	Includes Persuasive Supporting Sentences	
10	Includes Analysis And Critical Thinking	
10	Ends With Conclusions	
10	Other:	
100	**Total**	

Write specific suggestions on how to improve the paper on the back of this page.

Meaningful And Manageable Assessment Through Cooperative Learning, Interaction Book Company, 7208 Cornelia Drive, Edina, MN 55435, (612) 831-9500, FAX (612) 831-9332.

Reflection: My Strengths and Growth Goals

1. The best aspects of my skills in writing are...

2. An interesting part of my rationale is...

3. Things I learned from editing my partner's writing are...

4. My next step(s) in improving my writing are...

5. Aspects of writing on which I could be more skilled are...

TEACHER APPRAISAL SYSTEM

1. Provides Opportunities For Students To Participate Actively And Successfully:

_____ Varies Activities Appropriately

_____ Structures Cooperative Groups Appropriately

_____ Monitors And Interacts With Cooperative Groups Appropriately

_____ Intersperses Pair Discussions During Lectures

_____ Extends Students' Responses And Participation

_____ Provides Time For Thoughtful Responses

2. Assesses And Provides Feedback On Student Progress During Instruction:

_____ Defines Instructional Task Clearly

_____ Defines Criteria For Success Clearly

_____ Systematically Observes Students At Work In Cooperative Groups

_____ Solicits Responses, Explanations, And Demonstrations For Assessment

_____ Structures Peer Assessment And Corrective Feedback

_____ Structures Peer Support For High Quality Work

_____ Reinforces Correct Responses And Performances

_____ Provides Corrective Feedback And Clarifies

_____ Reteaches When Needed

3. Organizes Students And Materials:

_____ Secures Student Attention

_____ Gives Clear Directions

_____ Maintains Appropriate Grouping And Seating Arrangements

_____ Moves Students Into Groups And From Group To Group Smoothly

_____ Has Materials, Aides, Facilities Ready

_____ Provides Clear Cooperative Structure For Learning Groups

Meaningful And Manageable Assessment Through Cooperative Learning, Interaction Book Company, 7208 Cornelia Drive, Edina, MN 55435, (612) 831-9500, FAX (612) 831-9332.

Chapter Six: Projects

Nature Of Projects

A **project** is an assignment aimed at having students produce something themselves on a topic related to the curriculum rather than just "reproduce" knowledge on tests. Projects are a traditional part of the curriculum. Projects are assigned at all grade levels in such subjects as music, media, art, science, language arts, and social studies. Projects may involve models, maps, pictures, tables, graphs, collages, photographs, plays, films, or videotapes. The assignments are aimed at enhancing students communication, reasoning, technical, interpersonal, organizational, decision-making, and problem-solving skills. Projects may be done by individual students, cooperative learning groups, whole classes, schools, and communities. Projects may involve both in-class and out-of-class research and development. Projects allow students to be creative, use multiple modes of learning, and explore their own multiple intelligences. The disadvantages of projects are that they are difficult to assess and to store.

Why Use Projects

Despite the assessment challenges posed by projects, they are very useful assignments that achieve objectives that may not be achieved in any other way. Projects:

1. Allow students to be creative and inventive in integrating diverse knowledge and skills.

2. Allow students to demonstrate and clarify their multiple intelligences through the use of diverse medias (see page 6:2).

3. Require students to use, integrate, apply, and transfer a wide variety of diverse information and skills into a final product.

4. Require students to engage in procedures (such as scientific investigation and inquiry) that promote higher-level outcomes.

5. Give students the opportunity to formulate their own questions and then try to answer them.

6. Accommodate different achievement levels by allowing students to complete projects at varying levels of difficulty.

Meaningful And Manageable Assessment Through Cooperative Learning, Interaction Book Company, 7208 Cornelia Drive, Edina, MN 55435, (612) 831-9500, FAX (612) 831-9332.

Multiple Intelligences

Intelligence	Definition
Linguistic	Ease in producing language (writers, poets, storytellers). Related to written and spoken words and language
Logical-Mathematical	The ability to reason and to recognize abstract patterns (scientists, mathematicians). Often called "scientific thinking" because it deals with deductive reasoning, numbers, and the recognition of abstract patterns.
Musical/Rhythmic	Sensitivity to pitch and rhythm (composers, instrumentalists). Recognition of tonal patterns, including various environmental sounds, and on a sensitivity to rhythm and beats.
Visual/Spatial	The ability to create visual-spatial representations of the world and to transfer these representations either mentally or concretely (architects, sculptors, engineers). Relies on the sense of sight and being able to visualize an object, and the ability to create internal mental images.
Bodily / Kinesthetic	Using the body to solve problems, to create products, and to convey ideas and emotions (athletes, surgeons, dancers). Related to physical movement and the knowing of the body, including the brain's motor cortex which controls body motion.
Interpersonal	The ability to understand other people and to work effectively with them (salespeople, teachers, politicians). Operates primarily through person-to-person relationships and communication. Relies on all other intelligences.
Intrapersonal	Personal knowledge about one's own emotions or self. Relates to inner states of being, self-reflection, metacognition, and awareness of spiritual realities.

(Adapted from White, Blythe, & Gardner, 1992)

7. Give students with reading and writing problems an alternative method of demonstrating learning and competencies, which may result in increased academic self-esteem.

8. Provide opportunities for positive interaction and cooperation among classmates.

9. Provide a forum for students to share their learning and accomplishments with other students, classes, parents, and the community.

How To Assign Projects

The wide variety of meaningful outcomes achieved by projects make them a valuable and flexible teacher tool. Their richness and complexity make them ideally suited for cooperative learning groups. Given below are the steps for assigning a project (a) in general and (b) specifically for cooperative learning groups.

General Steps

1. Assign a variety of projects throughout the year. Structure the projects so that students (a) have some choice in the focus or topic of their projects, (b) can use a variety of intelligences in completing them, and (c) have to use higher level reasoning skills such as induction and problem solving, and (d) can be creative and divergent in their approach to the assignment.

2. For each project list the dates for when the project starts, when each part of the project should be completed, when the initial draft is submitted for peer editing and initial teacher reaction, and when the final product is due.

3. Show students samples or models of completed projects. A variety of projects ranging from excellent to poor will help students develop a frame of reference on what is and is not an acceptable finished product.

4. Have students develop specific criteria to assess the quality of the completed projects. The criteria may include timeliness, appearance, originality, quality, evidence, reflection, richness of ideas, and presentation. Students develop indicators of excellent, medium, and inadequate products. If students want to make a video, for example, they can view several videos and then develop a rating scale that differentiates high quality from medium and low quality videos. The best video they view can be a benchmark to which they aspire. Students need to understand the components of a good project and then use indicators to guide them in their work.

5. Teach students a rubric supplied by you (the teacher) that is standardized for the school, district, or state. Learning a standardized rubric to use in assessing the quality of projects gives students a more sophisticated frame of reference to use in reflecting on their own work.

6. Have students complete the project with help and assistance from faculty.

7. Have students present their completed projects to some or all of their classmates. In viewing classmates' projects, students use the rating scale developed and the standardized rubric to assess projects' quality. A peer-editing cycle is very useful at this point (see Chapter 5).

8. Students turn in their projects to be assessed by the faculty.

Group Projects

The usual rule for cooperative learning groups is that students learn in a group and are subsequently assessed as individuals (Johnson, Johnson, & Holubec, 1993). While in school individual assessment is more common than group assessment, in real life it may be just the opposite. In most organizations, the success of the organization as a whole, divisions in the organization, and teams in the division are focused on more frequently than is the success of each individual employee. **Authentic assessment, therefore, most often means group assessment.** Thus, there are times when a classroom assignment may be given requiring a group report, exhibit, performance, video, or presentation.

Students and assessment procedures need to be clearly briefed when the purpose of assessment is to measure group productivity. Students are given the **task** of completing the assigned project. The **cooperative goal** is for group members to complete one project in which everyone has contributed a share of the work, everyone can explain its content and how it was conducted, and everyone can present it to the class. In addition to the general steps discussed above, the **procedure** is:

1. Students are assigned an initial project and are placed in cooperative learning groups to complete it. The required materials are provided.

2. The group completes the project, ensuring that all members contributed, agreed on, and can explain the results. The teacher systematically observes each group and provides feedback and coaching.

3. The group hands in their report to the teacher, each member presents the results to a section of the class, and a test may be given on the content of the project.

4. The assignment can be extended by the teacher presenting the relevant algorithm, procedure, concept, or theory required to complete the project. Students are then asked to apply what they have just learned in a more complex project.

Meaningful And Manageable Assessment Through Cooperative Learning, Interaction Book Company, 7208 Cornelia Drive, Edina, MN 55435, (612) 831-9500, FAX (612) 831-9332.

Group Project Rubric

Class:________________________________ Type Of Project:_____________

Students:______________________________________ Date: ____________

Write the indicators for each of the three levels (inadequate, medium, superior)

Low	Middle	High
Criterion One:		
•	•	•
•	•	•
•	•	•
Criterion Two:		
•	•	•
•	•	•
•	•	•
Criterion Three:		
•	•	•
•	•	•
•	•	•
Criterion Four:		
•	•	•
•	•	•
•	•	•

Comments: ____

____

____.

Our Group!

Meaningful And Manageable Assessment Through Cooperative Learning, Interaction Book Company, 7208 Cornelia Drive, Edina, MN 55435, (612) 831-9500, FAX (612) 831-9332.

Example: Brochure On A Vocational Program

Assignment: Each group selects and researches a vocational program and prepares an instructional brochure to present to the class.

SCORING RUBRIC

1. Criterion: **Quality Of Research**

1---------2---------3---------4---------5

One Source — Three Sources — Five Sources

2. Criterion: **Question And Answer Section**

1---------2---------3---------4---------5

Many Factual Errors — Some Factual Errors — No Factual Errors

3. Criterion: **Graphics**

1---------2---------3---------4---------5

No Graphics — Good Graphics — Dazzling Graphics

4. Criterion: **Organization**

1---------2---------3---------4---------5

Random — Clear — Overwhelming

5. Criterion: **Oral Presentation**

1---------2---------3---------4---------5

Incomprehensible — Clear — Inspiring

Comments:

Group Grade

Grading Score: ______

22 - 25 Points = A

18 - 21 Points = B

13 - 17 Points = C

8 - 12 Points = D

Meaningful And Manageable Assessment Through Cooperative Learning, Interaction Book Company, 7208 Cornelia Drive, Edina, MN 55435, (612) 831-9500, FAX (612) 831-9332.

Create A Project

1. List the projects you will assign students during the course.

   a.

   b.

   c.

   d.

2. Select one of the projects you listed write out the steps you will follow in assigning the project.

Examples Of Projects

Mythological Rap Song: Write and present a rap song about the gods and goddesses in Greek mythology	**Pamphlet: Select and research a disease and prepare an instructional pamphlet to present to the class.**
Select a famous writer, artist, politician, or philosopher from the Renaissance period and become that person on a panel of experts.	Research an international conflict in the world today (for each country a student researchers a different aspect of the country related to the war--history, resolutions, maps, and so forth)
Teaching cycles through gardening (different students are in charge of seeds, fertilizing, and so forth)	**Paint a mural of the history of the earth and humankind (each group takes a section--Greek, Roman, middle ages art)**
Videotape of a community project	Time-line (personal, history, literature, art, geology)
Writing plays, skits, role plays	**School or class newspaper**
Running a school post-office	Mock court
International festival with multi-cultural activity	**Mural based on reading**
Groups write alternative endings with dramatizations	Create a new invention using the computer
Turn a short story or event in history into a movie	**Design an ideal school and have class enact it**
Newscast	Science fair projects

Meaningful And Manageable Assessment Through Cooperative Learning, Interaction Book Company, 7208 Cornelia Drive, Edina, MN 55435, (612) 831-9500, FAX (612) 831-9332.

College Admissions Rating Form

Please describe what you think is important about the applicant that will help us differentiate this student from other applicants. Describe the applicant's academic and personal qualities, especially his or her intellectual purpose, motivation, relative maturity, integrity, ability to work with others, interpersonal skills, leadership potential, independence, originality, capacity for growth, special talents, and enthusiasm.

No Basis	Academic Skills And Potential	Below Average	Average	Above Average	Top 5%
	Creative, Original Thought				
	Motivation				
	Independence, Initiative				
	Intellectual Ability				
	Academic Achievement				
	Written Expression Of Ideas				
	Oral Expression Of Ideas				
	Disciplined Work Habits				
	Potential For Growth				
	Ability To Work With Others				
	Summary Evaluation				

Meaningful And Manageable Assessment Through Cooperative Learning, Interaction Book Company, 7208 Cornelia Drive, Edina, MN 55435, (612) 831-9500, FAX (612) 831-9332.

Chapter Seven: Student Portfolios

What Is A Portfolio

Architects, artists, writers, and performers have used portfolios for some time to represent the quality of their work. Portfolios can also be used in collecting, assessing, and evaluating student work. A **portfolio** is an organized collection of evidence accumulated over time on a student's or group's academic progress, achievements, skills, and attitudes. It consists of work samples and a written rationale connecting the separate items into a more complete and holistic view of the student's (or group's) achievements or progress toward learning goals.

Portfolios can cover one semester, one year, or several years. They may represent student work in one, several, or all subject areas. They can include the work of one student or a group of students. They may be presented in file folders, notebooks, boxes, or video disks. They may be the property of the student or they may be passed from teacher to teacher. There are no hard and fast rules as to the contents of a portfolio. Portfolios may contain any relevant item, such as:

Completed homework, in-class assignments	Self-reflection and analysis checklists
Tests (teacher made, curriculum supplied)	Group products
Compositions (essays, reports, stories)	Evidence of social skills
Presentations (recordings, observations)	Evidence of work habits and attitudes
Investigations, inventions, projects	Anecdotal records, narrative reports
Logs or journals	Standardized test results
Observation checklists (teacher, classmates)	Photo, autobiographic sketch
Creative products (drawings, paintings, sculptors, pottery, dances, thespian activities)	

In elementary classes, portfolios can include all subject areas. In middle schools, students may keep a portfolio that reflects an integrated curriculum. In high schools, students may build employment portfolios to be used when students graduate. Some portfolios are graded while others help students reflect on their progress and set future learning goals. The contents of a portfolio may be determined by:

1. **The student**: Students can decide what to include in their portfolio.

Meaningful And Manageable Assessment Through Cooperative Learning, Interaction Book Company, 7208 Cornelia Drive, Edina, MN 55435, (612) 831-9500, FAX (612) 831-9332.

2. **The cooperative learning group**: The student's cooperative learning group can recommend what the student include in his or her portfolio.

3. **The teacher, school, and district**: Faculty can specify work samples or components to be included in the portfolio. Manhattan Communication College faculty, for example, added an essay requirement to what was originally just a collection of a student's work. A mathematics teacher might require a demonstration of the student's ability to make connections between two or more branches of mathematics (for example, an algebraic proof of a geometry theorem or a graphic solution of an algebra problem). In some school districts teachers are provided with a work sample menu, work sample descriptions, and supporting documentation. Teachers then decide on which work samples they want their students to include in their portfolios and distribute the descriptions assessment rubrics to students.

Work Sample
1. The skills and knowledge that are the focus of the description.
2. A summary statement of the materials expected from the student.
3. Several sample classroom assignments to help make the descriptions more concrete.
4. The scoring criteria for assessing the quality of the work sample.

Why Use Portfolios

1. **Portfolios give students the opportunity to direct their own learning** by (a) documenting their efforts, achievements, development, and growth in knowledge, skills, expressions, and attitudes, (b) using a variety of learning styles, modalities, and intelligences, (c) assessing their own learning and deciding which items best represent their achievements and growth, and (d) setting their future learning goals.

2. **Portfolios can be used to determine students' level of achievement.** Portfolios allow students to present a holistic view of their highest academic achievements, skills, and competencies.

3. **Portfolios can be used to determine students' growth over time.** Portfolios allow students to present their work over a period of time to show how they are progressing in achieving their learning goals (initial ideas, early drafts, first critiques, interim and

final drafts, feedback from peers and teachers, and some suggestions of how one will build on the current project in future endeavors).

The Best Works Portfolio

Subject Area	Individual Student	Cooperative Group
Science	The best solution to a scientific problem posed by the instructor, review of a scientific article, laboratory work conducted, original hypothesis formulated, position paper on a scientific issue, log or journal entry from a long-term experiment.	The best scientific experiment conducted, project completed
Mathematics	The best solution to a problem posed by the instructor, description of how to solve a mathematical problem, review of a mathematics article, biography of mathematician, original mathematics theory developed, photo/diagram/concept map of a mathematical idea investigated.	The best project completed, small business planned and initiated
Language Arts	The best compositions in a variety of styles--expository, humor/satire, creative (poetry, drama, short story), journalistic (reporting, editorial columnist, reviewer), and advertising copy.	The best dramatic production, video project, TV broadcast, newspaper, advertising display
Social Studies	The best historical research paper, opinion essay on historical issue, commentary on current event, original historical theory, review of a historical biography, account of academic controversy participated in.	The best community survey, paper resulting from academic controversy, oral history compilation, multi-dimensional analysis of historical event, press corps interview with historical figure.
Fine Arts	The best creative products such as drawings, paintings, sculptors, pottery, poems, thespian performance.	The best creative products such as murals, plays written and performed, and inventions made and built.

4. **Portfolios can be used to understand how students think, reason, organize, investigate, and communicate**. Portfolios can provide insight into students'

reasoning and intellectual competencies by documenting students' progression of thought and work in achieving their learning goals.

The Process Portfolio

Subject Area	Individual Student	Cooperative Group
Science	Documentation (running records or logs) of using the scientific method to solve a series of laboratory problems.	Documentation (observation checklists) of using the scientific method to solve a series of laboratory problems.
Mathematics	Documentation of mathematical reasoning through double-column mathematical problem-solving (computations on the left side and running commentary explaining thought processes on the right side).	Documentation of complex problem-solving and use of higher-level strategies.
Language Arts	Evolution of compositions from early notes through outlines, research notes, response to others' editing, and final draft.	Rubrics and procedures developed to ensure high quality peer editing.
Social Studies	Evolution of speech from early notes through outlines, research notes, final draft, and response to critiques.	Step-by-step documentation of historical research project.
Fine Arts	"History" of any piece of student's creative work, from its original conception through first, second, third attempts and final product.	Biography of school of artists who worked together to create a new form of artistic expression.

5. **Portfolios provide an effective way of collecting and demonstrating achievement on a broad range of outcomes that cannot be assessed as effectively by paper and pencil methods**. Examples of these outcomes include, persistence, growth, pride and ownership of work, problem-solving, higher-level thinking, the ability to work with others and self-evaluation.

6. **Portfolios can be used to communicate student efforts, progress toward accomplishing learning goals, and accomplishments** to peers, teachers, parents, college admission officers, and so forth. Portfolios allow students to present their work as a whole in relation to standards and criteria. In addition, portfolios allow teachers and other interested audiences to consider multiple sources of data when they examine what students know and can do.

7. **Portfolios can be used to evaluate and improve curriculum and instruction.** Portfolios provide a broad view on the effectiveness of the curriculum and instruction thereby allowing teachers to improve and enhance their instructional methods and curriculum materials. Portfolios have been found to change instruction as a result of changing the criteria against which student work is evaluated. The use of portfolios has also been found to change the way students' evaluate their own work. Students are taught the criteria against which their work will be judged. This improves their ability to think more deeply and creatively and analyze the strengths and weaknesses of their work.

Contents Of Portfolios

1. **Cover sheet** that creatively reflects the nature of the student's (or group's) work.
2. **Table of contents** that includes the title of each work sample and its page number.
3. The **rationale** explaining what work samples are included, why each one is significant, and how they all fit together in a holistic view of the student's (or group's) work.
4. The **work samples.**
5. A **self-assessment** written by the student or the group members.
6. **Future goals** based on the student's (or group's) current achievements, interests, and progress.
7. **Other's comments and assessments** from the teacher, cooperative learning groups, and other interested parties such as the parents.

How To Use Student Portfolios

The student's portfolio represents the quality of student learning throughout the grading period. While the teacher may give quizzes, tests, homework assignments, and projects during the course, the portfolio represents an overall, more holistic view of what the student has learned and accomplished. There are important aspects of the teacher's role in using portfolios that occur (a) before the instructional unit or grading period begins, (b) during the instructional unit or grading period, and (c) following the instructional unit or grading period.

The first step is to prepare for the use of portfolios. Guidelines for developing a portfolio program include the following. Before the term, semester, year, or course begins faculty must decide on:

1. **What type of portfolio to use.** Portfolios may be constructed by having:

   a. Individual students keep personal portfolios with the input and help of teachers.

   b. Individual students keep personal portfolios with the input and help of their cooperative learning groups (the teacher monitors the process and provides help and assistance to the groups when it is needed).

   c. Cooperative base groups keep group portfolios with the input and help of teachers. Group portfolios include documentation of:

      1. The work of the group as a whole.

      2. The work of each individual member.

2. **The purposes and objectives of the portfolio.** Because there are so many varieties of portfolios, faculty should think through what they want portfolios to accomplish before requiring them. Will students hand in the portfolio to the faculty, will it serve as the focus of a discussion with faculty, will it be used in student-parent conferences, or will students keep their portfolios?

3. **What categories of work samples should go into the portfolio.** What are the skills, competencies, and knowledge students should demonstrate and what assignments will show evidence of these skills, competencies, and knowledge? How much of a student's work should go into his or her portfolio? Will the portfolio include an assignment (such as an essay or a competency matrix) that helps students reflect on their learning?

4. **How will the pieces in the portfolio be selected**? While the teacher may specify the categories of work samples and the criteria by which they will be assessed and evaluated, students may select which pieces best represent their work and meet the criteria in each category.

5. **How will the portfolio be assessed and evaluated**? Who will develop the rubrics? Who will do the assessing and evaluating? Will students be involved?

In planning how to use portfolios as part of your assessment process, do not try to do too much with a portfolio program. Start out slowly. Do not try to use portfolios to assess everything.

The second step is to manage the portfolios during the semester or course. During the course or semester, portfolios are managed in the following way.

1. **Faculty explain to students the portfolio process** and the categories of work samples to be included in the portfolio.

2. **Faculty develop rubrics to assess and evaluate the student's work samples.** Students may participate in developing some or all the rubrics.

3. **Students complete assignments** knowing that some or all of them will be included in the final portfolio. All assignments may be kept in a "working portfolio" during the grading period.

4. **Students reflect on and self-assess the quality and quantity of their work and progress toward their learning goals.**

The third step is to manage the portfolio process at the end of the grading period. Once all the work samples have been completed, the selections for the portfolio must be made and organized into a coherent representation of the student's or group's work.

1. **Faculty specify a certain number and type of products to be included in the final portfolio.** One product, for example, might be included from each instructional unit conducted during the grading period.

2. **Students decide which items to include in their final portfolio.** The advice of the teacher and the student's cooperative learning group may be taken into account in selecting the final items. The student has the opportunity to revise his or her work and make the products better. The students understand what the criteria are for each assignment so they know the standards by which the teacher will grade them.

3. **Students describe the progress made in achieving their learning goals during the grading period.**

4. **The cooperative learning group describes the progress the student has made in achieving his or her learning goals during the grading period.**

5. **Faculty conduct a summative evaluation** and gives a grade or score indicating their judgment as to the quality and quantity of the student's work. The scoring

of student portfolios, however, often suffers from problems in reliability. Different teachers give different scores to the same portfolio and the same teacher may give the same portfolio different scores at different times. **There are a number of options for grading**:

a. The portfolio is not graded because each entry has been previously graded during the grading period.

b. Each individual entry is given a grade and the portfolio is not graded.

c. One grade is given to the entire portfolio on the overall quality and quantity of the work products included.

6. **Post-Conferences are held**. The options for post-conferences include:

   a. The student and the teacher.

   b. The student and the cooperative learning group.

   c. The student (and the cooperative learning group) and his or her parents (with the teacher).

   d. The student and visitors at a portfolio exhibition.

7. **A decision is made on whether, how, or what parts of the portfolio are to be passed on to the next teacher**. The portfolios of seniors may be used in the interview process for a job or college.

Individual Portfolios With Help From Cooperative Learning Group

The cooperative procedure for using portfolios is similar to that used for peer-editing of compositions. The **task** is for each student to create a portfolio. The **criteria for success** is a well constructed portfolio by each student. The **cooperative goal** is for all group members to verify that each member's portfolio is perfect according to the criteria set by the teacher. Students receive an individual score or grade on the quality of their portfolio. The teacher can also give bonus points based on the quality of all members' portfolios. Each student is **individually accountable** to create his or her own portfolio. The procedure is as follows (Johnson, Johnson, & Holubec, 1993):

1. The teacher assigns students to cooperative base groups with at least one good reader and writer to each group.

Cooperative Group Portfolio

What is a cooperative base group?	A **cooperative base group** is a long-term, heterogeneous cooperative learning group with stable membership. It may last for one course, one year, or for several years. Its purposes are to give the support, help, encouragement, and assistance each member needs to make good academic progress and develop cognitively and socially in healthy ways.
What is a group portfolio?	A **group portfolio** is an organized collection of group work samples accumulated over time and individual work samples of each member.
What are its contents?	Cover that creativity reflects group's personality Table of contents Description of the group and its members Introduction to portfolio and rationale for the work samples included. Group work samples (products by the group that any one member could not have produced alone) Observation data of group members interacting as they worked on group projects. Self-assessment of the group by its members. Individual members' work samples that were revised on the basis of group feedback (compositions, presentations, and so forth). Self-assessment of members including their strengths and weaknesses in facilitating group effectiveness and other members' learning. List of future learning and social skills goals for the group and each of its members. Comments and feedback from faculty and other groups

2. The teacher explains individual portfolios. The teacher describes the categories of work samples that students will have to place in their portfolios and the criteria that will be used to assess and evaluate each sample.

3. Group members complete a series of individual assignments related to their learning goals with each other's help and assistance. Compositions, for example, go through a peer editing process to ensure that they meet the criteria set by the teacher.

5. Faculty and group members monitor the groups as they work and collect data on interaction among members.

6. Students select work samples from each specified category to include in their portfolio. Each member explains his or her proposed portfolio to the group. Group members give the student feedback concerning the quality of his or her presentation and help him or her choose the specific pieces that best represent the

Meaningful And Manageable Assessment Through Cooperative Learning, Interaction Book Company, 7208 Cornelia Drive, Edina, MN 55435, (612) 831-9500, FAX (612) 831-9332.

quality of his or her work (taking into account the assessment criteria) and, therefore, should be included in the student's portfolio. If possible, a chart or graph is drawn showing the student's progress.

7. Faculty conduct a summative evaluation of the student's portfolio.

8. Post-conferences are held between (a) the student and the faculty and (b) the student and his or her parents (possibly with the help of cooperative learning group but always with the assistance of the teacher).

The **task** is for each cooperative base group to create a group portfolio. The **criteria for success** is that the portfolio meets the criteria specified by the faculty and/or students. The **cooperative goal** is for all group members to verify that the group's portfolio meets the criteria. Each student is **individually accountable** to contribute his or her part of the portfolio and help complete the overall group portions of the portfolio. The procedure is:

1. **The teacher assigns students to cooperative base groups** with at least one good reader and writer to each group. The teacher structures identity interdependence by having groups choose names, create a group symbol, and so forth.

2. **The teacher explains group portfolios**. The teacher describes the categories of work samples that each group will have to place in their portfolio and the criteria that will be used to assess and evaluate each sample.

3. **The group completes a series of group projects** (that any one member could not complete alone) related to the learning goals of its members. Examples include creating a new invention using the computer, turning a short story or historical event into a movie/video, or research a vocational program and create an informational brochure about it.

4. **Group members complete a series of individual assignments related to their learning goals with each other's help and assistance**. Presentations, for example, go through a peer editing process to ensure that they meet the criteria set by the teacher.

5. **Faculty and group members monitor the groups as they work** and collect data on interaction among members.

6. **Faculty specify the categories of group and individual work samples that go into the group portfolio.**

7. **Group members select the group projects to include in the group's portfolio** that best represent the quality of learning or progress toward learning groups of the group as a whole (taking into account the assessment criteria).

Meaningful And Manageable Assessment Through Cooperative Learning, Interaction Book Company, 7208 Cornelia Drive, Edina, MN 55435, (612) 831-9500, FAX (612) 831-9332.

8. **The group includes in its portfolio evidence of teamwork** such as charts and grafts documenting constructive patterns of interaction among members. The data result from members' and faculty's observations of the patterns of members' interactions and members' processing and self-assessments of how well the group is functioning. Descriptions of group celebrations are also included.

9. **Members select individual work samples from each specified category to include in the group portfolio.** Each member explains his or her proposed work samples to groupmates. Group members give each member feedback concerning the quality of his or her presentation and help the member choose the specific pieces that best represent the quality of his or her work (taking into account the assessment criteria) and, therefore, should be included in the group's portfolio. If possible, a chart or graph is drawn showing the student's progress.

10. **Faculty conduct a summative evaluation of the group's portfolio.**

11. Post-conferences are held between (a) the group and the faculty and (b) the cooperative group and members' parents.

Involving Students In Developing Rubrics

1. Develop a list of potential criteria to use in evaluating portfolios. The potential criteria may be derived from having students interview each other about potential criteria and from the teacher supplying what he or she thinks are important criteria.

2. Have cooperative groups of students rank order the criteria from most important to least important. Then have the groups share their rankings and discuss until there is consensus on the criteria by the entire class.

3. Construct a rubric for each criteria starting with the one ranked most important by listing indicators of low, middle, and high proficiency.

4. Have students apply the rubrics to sample performances.

5. Have students apply the rubrics to their own and each other's work samples and portfolios.

(Based On Procedure Developed By Laurie Stevahn)

Preparing To Use Portfolios

1. Who will construct the portfolios:

    ____ Individual students with teacher input and help.

    ____ Individual students with the input and help of cooperative learning groups.

    ____ Cooperative base groups (whole group work and individual members' work) with teach input and help.

2. What type of portfolio do you want to use?

    _____ Best Works Portfolio _____ Process/Growth Portfolio

3. What are the purposes and objectives of the portfolio?

    a.

    b.

    c.

4. What categories of work samples should go into the portfolio?

    a.

    b.

    c.

    d.

5. What criteria will students or groups use to select their entries?

    a.

    b.

    c.

6. Who will develop the rubrics to assess and evaluate the portfolios?

    _____ Faculty _____ Students

Meaningful And Manageable Assessment Through Cooperative Learning, Interaction Book Company, 7208 Cornelia Drive, Edina, MN 55435, (612) 831-9500, FAX (612) 831-9332.

Final Portfolio

Student/Group: ______________________ **Time Frame & Dates:** ___________

Grade Level: ___________ **Subject(s):** _________________________________

Purpose: ____ **Best Work** _____ **Process/Growth**

Selection	Points	Comments
1.		
2.		
3.		
4.		
5.		
6.		
7.		
Total Grade		

Comments:____

____

____

Suggested/Future/Goals:____

____

____

Final Portfolio Grade:_________ **Faculty:**________________________________

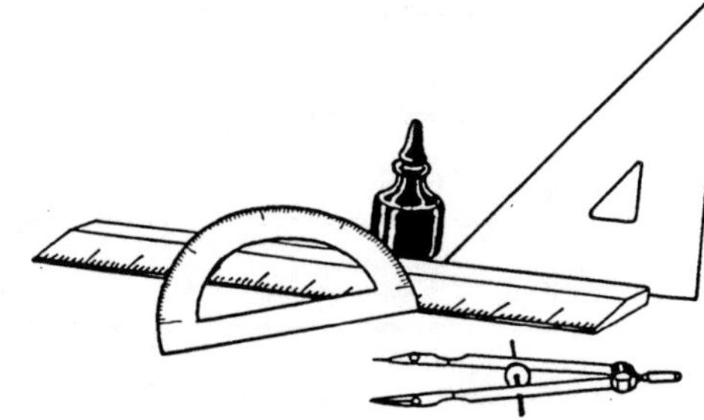

Meaningful And Manageable Assessment Through Cooperative Learning, Interaction Book Company, 7208 Cornelia Drive, Edina, MN 55435, (612) 831-9500, FAX (612) 831-9332.

GROUP PORTFOLIO

Group: ______________________________ **Time Frame & Dates:** ____________

Grade Level: ___________ **Subject(s):** ____________________________________

Purpose: ____ **Best Work** _____ **Process/Growth**

Group Projects	Assessment Criteria
Chosen To Be Included	**Rationale**
Teamwork Data / Student	**Teamwork Data / Teacher**

Meaningful And Manageable Assessment Through Cooperative Learning, Interaction Book Company, 7208 Cornelia Drive, Edina, MN 55435, (612) 831-9500, FAX (612) 831-9332.

Reflecting On Portfolios

Reflect on your potential use of portfolios. Write down the pluses and minuses of doing so along with any interesting ideas that come to mind.

Plus	Minus	Interesting
1.	1.	1.
2.	2.	2.
3.	3.	3.
4.	4.	4.
5.	5.	5.
6.	6.	6.

Math Portfolio: Points Of Focus

Computations	Knowing Basic Computation Procedures
Problem-Solving	Developing And Executing Strategies
Mathematical Communication	Reading And Writing In Mathematics
Mathematical Disposition	Having Healthy Attitudes Toward Mathematics
Technology	Using Computers And Graphing Calculators
Connections	Relating Mathematics To Other Subjects
Teamwork	Working Cooperatively With Others To Learn Math

Meaningful And Manageable Assessment Through Cooperative Learning, Interaction Book Company, 7208 Cornelia Drive, Edina, MN 55435, (612) 831-9500, FAX (612) 831-9332.

Student-Led Conferences

The purpose of the post-evaluation conference is to review the student's progress in achieving his or her learning goals. In the post-evaluation conference the student explains his or her level of achievement (what the student learned and failed to learn) to interested parties (cooperative learning group, teacher, parents), which naturally leads to the next goal-setting conference. Student-led conferences with parents are one example of a post-evaluation conference.

Student-led conferences involve three groups of individuals: Parents, students, and teachers. They are a modification of the traditional teacher-parent conference. Instead of the teacher explaining to the parent what the student has been studying and how well the student is learning, the teacher (a) helps the student prepare a portfolio and a presentation, (b) helps the student explain to his or her parent what has been learned, and (c) assess how well the conference went. There are three phases to student-led conferences:

1. **Preparation For The Conference**: In the Charlevoix-Emmet Intermediate School District, there are five procedures for students to do before a conference:

    a. Make an invitation to parents to attend the conference with the date, time, and place specified.

    b. Create a portfolio.

    c. Practice the introduction to the conference.

    d. Role-play the conference to practice their presentations.

    e. Set up the room for the conference.

    The cooperative learning group prepares each member for the conference by helping him or her compile a portfolio. The portfolio includes the student's (a) best work in the various subject areas, (b) progress reaching his or her learning goals, and (c) ways he or she has helped groupmates reach their goals. Once the portfolio is constructed, the group helps the student prepare effective presentation aids and practice and refine their conference presentation. In preparing and practicing their presentation, students become well rehearsed in presenting their work and the rubrics used to evaluate it. They master the language needed to communicate about their learning goals and academic efforts, and learn how to describe their progress.

2. **Conducting The Conference**: Each student, with the teacher serving as a co-leader and coach, presents his or her work to his or her parents and discusses the next steps they will take in improving their academic accomplishments. Placing students in

Meaningful And Manageable Assessment Through Cooperative Learning, Interaction Book Company, 7208 Cornelia Drive, Edina, MN 55435, (612) 831-9500, FAX (612) 831-9332.

charge of the conference makes each student individually accountable, encourages students to take pride in their work, and encourages student-parent communication about school performance. A procedure for conducting the conference is:

a. The student picks up the portfolio and goes to the table designated for the conference and sits down with his or her parents.

b. The student introduces the portfolio to his or her parents, explaining what the portfolio is and giving an overview of what it contains. A portfolio organizer and table of contents helps this part of the presentation.

c. The student explains each section of the portfolio explaining the rationale for why each work sample was included and why it represents a significant indicator of learning. A student, for example, might show writing samples from September, October, and November to show how his or her skills have been improving.

d. The teacher moves from conference to conference monitoring the presentations and giving help and assistance when it is needed. When the teacher arrives, the student introduces the teacher to his or her parents.

e. The student concludes the presentation with a summary of what has been accomplished and what is yet to be done.

f. The student asks his or her parents to write any comments or suggestions they have for the student and to complete a reaction form to the conference. If the parents wish to have a conference only with the teacher they may sign up to do so.

g. The student returns the portfolio to its place and reflects on how well the conference went.

3. **Assessment Of The Quality Of The Conference**: An assessment of the student's progress is made by (a) the student, (b) the cooperative learning group, (c) the teacher, and (d) the parents.

Portfolio Organizer

Name: ______________________ Date: ________ Class: __________

Reading	Writing
Science	**Math**
Social Studies	**Physical Education**

I Believe I Do The Following Well:

1. ____

2. ____

3. ____

Your Comments And Suggestions Are:

____

____

____

____

____

Meaningful And Manageable Assessment Through Cooperative Learning, Interaction Book Company, 7208 Cornelia Drive, Edina, MN 55435, (612) 831-9500, FAX (612) 831-9332.

Chapter Eight: Observing Students

Assessment Through Observing Students Learn

The only thing that endures over time is the law of the farm: I must prepare the ground, put in the seed, cultivate it, water it, then gradually nurture growth and development to full maturity...there is no quick fix.

Stephen Covey

Teachers are always observing and noticing what is going on around them. They look to see who is and who is not on task, which students are out of their seat, which students look puzzled, and which students are finished and waiting for their next assignment. Observation is a primary, yet often underutilized, tool of assessing learning and instruction. By and large, little attention has been devoted to training teachers how to engage in unbiased observation of student performances and students' efforts to learn. **Observation** is aimed at recording and describing behavior as it occurs. Its **purpose** is to provide objective data about:

1. **The quality of student performances**. Many student performances may only be assessed through direct observation procedures. Many performances, such as giving a speech, playing tennis, helping a classmate, reciting a poem, or drawing a picture can only be assessed through observational methods.

2. **The processes and procedures students use in completing assignments**. To improve continuously the process of learning, students must receive feedback concerning their actions in completing an assignment. The process of learning is primarily assessed through observation.

3. **The processes and procedures teachers use in conducting lessons**. If teachers are to improve continuously they need feedback on their actions in conducting class sessions and teaching a course. The process of instruction is primarily assessed through observation.

A major problem with observation is the potential for lack of objectivity by the observers. An example of biased observing may be seen in a study conducted by Hastorf and Cantril (1954). They asked Dartmouth and Princeton college students to watch a film of the football game between the two schools. The game was an unusually rough one in which many penalties had been called. The Princeton quarterback, an all-American, left the game in the second quarter with a broken nose and a mild concussion. The Dartmouth quarterback left the game in the third quarter with a broken leg. The

Meaningful And Manageable Assessment Through Cooperative Learning, Interaction Book Company, 7208 Cornelia Drive, Edina, MN 55435, (612) 831-9500, FAX (612) 831-9332.

Dartmouth and Princeton college students were asked to watch the film and record the number and severity of the infractions committed by the two teams. Dartmouth won the game and its students saw the two teams committing an equal number of violations. The Princeton students saw the Darmouth players as committing more than twice as many fouls as the Princeton team. A solution to the problem of bias is the use of **structured coding systems**, which require observers to categorize each group behavior into an objectively definable category.

In using observation as an assessment tool, you need to:

1. Understand the basics of observing.
2. Prepare for observing by:
    a. Deciding which student behaviors, actions, and skills are to be observed.
    b. Deciding who will be the observers.
    c. Making a sampling plan.
    d. Constructing an observation sheet to record the frequencies of targeted actions that are appropriate for the age of the students.
    e. Training the observers.
3. Observe and record how often each student performs the specified behaviors. Observation procedures may be formal or informal.
4. Summarize the observations in a clear and useful manner to give feedback to each student and group and help students analyze the observation data and reflect on how:
    a. Effectively they are learning and helping each other learn.
    b. They may behave more effectively next time.

Five Minute Walk

1. Select actions to observe.
2. Construct observation sheet.
3. Plan route through the classroom.
4. Gather data on every group.
5. Feedback the data to the groups and/or to the class as a whole.
6. Chart / graph the results.

The Basics Of Observing

In order to use observation for assessment purposes, it is necessary to understand the basic nature of observation. Working with a partner, complete the following activities that will define and explain the nature of observing.

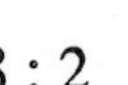

Meaningful And Manageable Assessment Through Cooperative Learning, Interaction Book Company, 7208 Cornelia Drive, Edina, MN 55435, (612) 831-9500, FAX (612) 831-9332.

1. Observing The Characteristics Of Your Setting

1. You have five minutes to write down as many characteristics of your setting as possible.

1.	6.
2.	7.
3.	8.
4.	9.
5.	10.

2. Form a triad and compare your observations:

   a. What did each of you observe?

   b. In what sequence were your observations made?

   c. How did you decide what to write down and what not to?

   d. Did the format of the task influence what you observed?

2. Differentiating Between Objective And Subjective

1. Ensure all triad members understand the difference between:

   a. **Objective** (factors or details all members could readily agree upon).

   b. **Subjective** (unique perceptions, biases, or individual points of view that all members might not agree upon).

2. Label each observation recorded in the above exercise as either an "O" or "S."

3. Differentiating Between Descriptions And Inferences

1. Identify the descriptive (D) and the interpretative (I) statements given below:

   _____ a. Sam held his hand up 90 seconds before the teacher called on him.

   _____ b. Helen made sarcastic remarks about the teacher.

   _____ c. Roger laughed four times during the meeting.

_____ d. David was embarrassed when they sang "Happy Birthday."

_____ e. Roger is holding the golf club in his left hand.

_____ f. Keith does not like the lesson.

_____ g. Dale is confused by the teacher's explanation.

_____ h. Edythe is not talking enough.

_____ i. John has his back to his group.

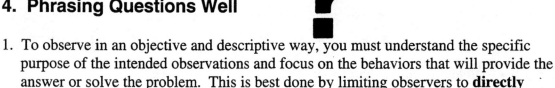

4. Phrasing Questions Well

1. To observe in an objective and descriptive way, you must understand the specific purpose of the intended observations and focus on the behaviors that will provide the answer or solve the problem. This is best done by limiting observers to **directly observable behaviors.**

2. Determine which of the questions given below are well phrased in that they allow the observer to focus on **directly observable behavior.**

Questions	Well Phrased	Poorly Phrased	Reason(s)
1. Are males more restless than females during the lesson?			
2. How many questions did students ask during the lesson?			
3. Is the teacher encouraging students to disagree and challenge each other?			
4. How many students are studying during free-time?			

5. Differentiating Between Category And Sign Systems

1. **Category system** requires the observer to list a set of categories so that every observed behavior can be recorded into one, and only one, of a series of mutually exclusive categories. The categories must be exhaustive for a particular dimension so that every observed behavior can be categorized.

Meaningful And Manageable Assessment Through Cooperative Learning, Interaction Book Company, 7208 Cornelia Drive, Edina, MN 55435, (612) 831-9500, FAX (612) 831-9332.

2. A **sign system** involves listing beforehand a limited number of specific kinds of behavior of interest to the observer. An observer using a sign system approach records only those behaviors that fall into one of the preconceived categories listed. Many behaviors would not be recorded if they did not fit into the specified categories.

Category System Of Observing

Category	Member 1	Member 2	Member 3
Gives Information			
Asks For Other's Information			
Gives Direction To Group's Work			
Summarizes Members' Ideas			

Sign System Of Observing

Group Member	Explains Concept	Draws Representation	Withdraws
1.			
2.			
3.			
4.			

6. Understanding Types Of Categories

1. **Mutually exclusive** categories are precisely distinguishable and independent from other categories. Non-mutually-exclusive categories are **over-lapping** (a behavior can be coded in more than one category).

2. **Exhaustive** categories exist when every instance of observed behavior can be classified in one of the available categories.

3. Examine the categories below. Decide if they are (a) mutually exclusive or over-lapping and (b) exhaustive or nonexhaustive. Put a "yes" or "no" in each box.

Meaningful And Manageable Assessment Through Cooperative Learning, Interaction Book Company, 7208 Cornelia Drive, Edina, MN 55435, (612) 831-9500, FAX (612) 831-9332.

Categories	Mutually Exclusive	Exhaustive
Asking A Question Stating An Opinion Explaining A Concept Telling A Joke		
Being Silent Talking		
Looking Out The Window Looking At The Book Looking At The Teacher		
Standing Sitting Lying Prone		

Time Sampling Observation Form

Group Member	10:00	10:15	10:30	11:00	Total

Event Sampling Observation Form

Group Member	Sits Down	Reads	Writes	Draws	Total

Meaningful And Manageable Assessment Through Cooperative Learning, Interaction Book Company, 7208 Cornelia Drive, Edina, MN 55435, (612) 831-9500, FAX (612) 831-9332.

7. Understanding Types Of Sampling

1. **Time sampling** occurs when the observer records the occurrence or nonoccurrence of selected behavior(s) within specified, uniform time limits.

2. **Event sampling** occurs when the observer records a given event or category of events each time it naturally occurs.

3. Construct an observation form of each type.

Summary

The basics of observing include being aware of the characteristics of the setting, differentiating between objective and subjective observations, differentiating between descriptions and inferences, the phrasing of questions, differentiating between category and sign systems, differentiating between mutually exclusive and over-lapping and between exhaustive and nonexhaustive categories, and understanding the difference between time sampling and event sampling. Given your understanding of these basics, you are now ready to prepare for observing.

Preparing For Observing

In preparing for observing, you state your instructional objectives in the appropriate behavioral form. The objectives should describe student behavior that is observable and countable. Then you decide which actions to observe, who will observe, what the sampling plan will be, and how the observers will be trained. You then construct your observation form.

Which Actions Will We Observe?

1. **On or off task**. You can observe students' work to determine if they are on task completing their work or are off task engaging in some other activity than the prescribed academic learning.

2. **Academic efforts, procedures, and strategies**. You can assess many learning outcomes (such as depth of understanding, level of reasoning, mastery of problem solving procedures, meta-cognitive thinking) only by opening a "*window into students' minds*" and observing students "*thinking outloud.*" Cooperative learning groups provide such a window.

3. **Social skills**. One of the many advantages of cooperative learning is that it allows teachers, students, and other interested parties to assess students' mastery of the interpersonal and small group skills needed to work with others.

Who Will Observe?

1. **Teachers:** You, the teacher, are always an observer. In every lesson, you systematically roam from group to group. You gather specific information on the interaction of members in each group. When necessary, you intervene to improve students' efforts to learn and to help classmates learn.

2. **Students:** When students become experienced in working in cooperative learning groups, you should train them to be observers. Students may be roving observers who circulate throughout the classroom and monitor all learning groups. Similar to the teacher, student roving observers need a sampling plan to ensure that they observe all groups an approximately equal amount of time. Students may also observe their own groups (one observer per group). In this case, student observers remove themselves slightly from the group so they are close enough to see and hear the interaction among group members but are not tempted to participate in the academic task. Observers do not comment or intervene while the group is working. You set aside a time near the end of the class period for the learning groups to review the content of the lesson with the observer. The role of observer rotates so that each group member is an observer an equal amount of time.

3. **Visitors:** Visitors should not be allowed to sit and watch a lesson passively. When someone visits your classroom, hand them an observation form, explain the role of the observer, and put them to work. Visitors may be roving observers or they may observe one single group, depending on the purpose of their visit.

Making Sampling Plan For Roving Observers

Before the lesson begins you plan how much time you will spend observing each learning group (this is a **sampling plan**). You may observe one learning group for the entire class period, collecting information on every member. Or, if the class period lasts for 50 minutes and there are ten groups in the class, you may decide to observe each group for five minutes. Or, you may observe each group for two minutes and rotate through all the groups twice during one class period. If you decide you should intervene in a group or with a student, you temporarily suspend the sampling plan and then resume it after the intervention is over.

Constructing An Observation Form

Observation forms or check-sheets are used to answer the question, "*How often are certain actions or events happening?*" **Observation forms** are used to tally and count the number of times a behavior, action, or event is observed in a specified time period. An example is given below. The form has to be designed so that all potential observers can use it (that is, age appropriate). **A structured observation form is created by:**

1. Defining exactly what behaviors, actions, skills, or events are being observed (all observers have to be looking for the same thing).

2. Determining the time period during which the data will be collected (minutes to weeks).

3. Entering the actions to be observed in the first column (each action or skill is placed in a separate row, the final row is reserved for the total of the columns).

4. Making an additional column for each member of the group, and making a final column to record the total for each row on the form.

5. Making sure all columns are clearly labeled and wide enough to enter data.

Observation Form

Observer: ______________________________ **Date:** __________ **Grade:** __________

Actions	Edythe	Keith	Dale	Total
Contributes Ideas				
Encourages Participation				
Checks For Understanding				
Gives Group Direction				
Other:				
Total				

After the observers are appointed and the observation form is constructed, the form is explained to the observers and the class as a whole. Teachers should make sure that all students understand what the observation form is and how it will be used.

Meaningful And Manageable Assessment Through Cooperative Learning, Interaction Book Company, 7208 Cornelia Drive, Edina, MN 55435, (612) 831-9500, FAX (612) 831-9332.

Being An Observer

1. Use one observation form for each group. Place a tally mark in the appropriate row and column when a student engages in one of the targeted actions. Look for patterns of behavior in the group. Do not worry about recording everything, but observe as accurately and rapidly as possible.

2. Make notes on the back of the observation form if something takes place that should be shared with the group but does not fit into the actions being observed.

3. Write down specific positive and important contributions by each group member (to ensure that every member will receive positive feedback).

4. After the learning session is over, total the columns and rows. Transfer the totals to long-term record sheets and the appropriate charts or graphs. The observation forms should be dated and kept to assess the growth of the students and groups. When a group is observed more than once during a class session, different colored ink may be used. This allows group members to assess their skill development at a glance.

5. Give the information gathered to the group and assist group members in deriving conclusions. Show the observation form to the group, holding it so all members can see it. Ask the group, ***"What do you conclude about (a) your participation in the group and (b) the group functioning in general?"*** Ensure all group members receive positive feedback about their efforts to learn and help their groupmates learn. After small group processing, there is whole class processing.

6. Help group members set goals for improving their competence in engaging in the social skills during the next group meeting by asking, ***"What could you add to be even a better group tomorrow than you were today?"*** Have members discuss the goals and publicly commit to achieving them. Emphasize the continuous improvement of students' competencies and group effectiveness.

Training Observers

If students or visitors are to be used as observers, they must be trained to follow observation procedures, use the observation forms, and follow the sampling plan. Minimal training can make students quite proficient observers. Take a few minutes after an observation period to chat with students about what they learned in doing the observing. Occasionally, sit side-by-side with a student observer and check your counts against his or hers. Discuss any discrepancy. Videotaping a group working and then having everyone in the class observe it and compare their observations with classmates is an excellent way of training students. An advantage of a videotape is that it may be replayed and analyzed several times.

Observing

Observing Students "On-Task" Behavior

The simplest use of observation procedures is to observe each student and determine whether the student is engaged in academic learning or is off-task. This type of observation can be used when students work individually by themselves or when students are working in cooperative learning groups. The observation form consists of a list of students in the class, two columns to indicate either on-task or off-task behavior, and a column for comments.

Observing On-Task Behavior

Class:___________________ Group:_____________ Date:__________

Students	On-Task	Off-Task	Comments
Frank			
Helen			
Roger			
David			
Edythe			
Keith			
Dale			
Tai			
Roberta			
Phillip			
Juan			

Meaningful And Manageable Assessment Through Cooperative Learning, Interaction Book Company, 7208 Cornelia Drive, Edina, MN 55435, (612) 831-9500, FAX (612) 831-9332.

Window Into Students' Minds: Observing Academic Efforts

Many students may be unaware of their reasoning processes while they are engaged in academic work. When asked, "*How do you solve this problem*?" many students may respond, "*I don't know; I just do it.*" Such an answer is usually not acceptable. If students can not accurately describe the reasoning procedures and sequences they use before, during, and after problem solving, they have not really learned the material.

The assessment issue is, "*How do you make covert cognitive reasoning overt and therefore open to correction and improvement*?" While paper-and-pencil tests and homework assignments indicate whether students can determine the "correct" answer, they usually do not reveal students' cognitive reasoning and depth of understanding. The only way to determine whether students really understand a procedure or concept is to listen to them explain it to someone else. Such oral explanations can be obtained either by (a) listening to students' explanations as they work in cooperative learning groups or (b) interviewing a student and requesting a detailed explanation of reasoning processes.

Systematic observation of cooperative learning groups allows teachers to attain a "*window*" into students' minds and thereby:

1. **Determine the extent to which students do or do not understand what they are studying.** This helps teachers to pinpoint areas of learning that need to be focused on or retaught.

2. **Make internal covert reasoning processes and procedures overt so they can be examined, corrected, and improved**. Many students, while able to derive the "correct answer," may misunderstand the basic principles and concepts involved. They may, for example, list correctly the phases of the moon without any understanding of what causes the moon to pass through different phases. Learning outcomes such as level of reasoning, mastery of problem solving procedures, and meta-cognitive thinking cannot be measured by pencil-and-paper homework assignments and tests. They can only be assessed by observing students "*thinking out loud*" as they explain to each other how to solve a problem or complete the assignment.

3. **Assess aspects of learning and intelligent behavior** such as persistence, using a variety of strategies, flexibility in thinking, metacognition, commitment to high quality work, and commitment to continuous improvement.

4. **Assess performances** such as singing, dancing, dramatic enactments, or athletic skills. Any performance (playing music, dancing, singing, giving a speech) may be better assessed with observation than with any other assessment procedure.

5. **Assess transfer and application of what is being learned.**

The procedure for obtaining a window into students' minds is to:

1. Assign students to small cooperative groups and give them an academic assignment that requires them to use problem-solving and reasoning procedures.

2. Assign one member of each group the role of "*checker for understanding*." The checker-for-understanding is given the responsibility for asking other group members to explain the procedures and processes they are using to solve a problem or complete a task.

Checklist For 'Persistence'

Indicators	Observed Frequently	Observed Sometimes	Not Yet Observed
Accesses Information			
Does Not Give Up			
Tries Several Strategies			
Seeks Several Solutions			
Other:			
Other:			

3. Construct an observation checklist. An **observation checklist** is a record keeping device for teachers to use to keep track of the degree to which each student has demonstrated a targeted behavior, action, skill, or procedure. Checklists include students' names, space for four to five targeted behaviors, a code or rating scale to signify the level of mastery (+ = frequently; @ = sometimes; - = not yet), a space for comments or anecdotal notes, and a space to record the date so that developmental growth can be examined. Checklists may be used to observe students during lessons, on the playground, on field trips, in hallways. They can be used to observe students individually, in groups, with younger students, with older students, or with adults. An example of a checklist is observing for student persistence.

4. Move from group to group gathering observation data about the quality of the explanations and intellectual interchange occurring among group members.

5. Summarize and analyze the data to assess the effectiveness of students' efforts to learn and the instructional program, give students appropriate feedback, and help them reflect on how to improve their learning efforts.

Cooperative learning groups offer a unique opportunity for immediate (a) diagnosis of level of understanding, (b) feedback from peers, and (c) remediation to correct misunderstandings and fill in gaps in students' understanding. Training students to observe each other's cognitive reasoning and strategies for solving problems and completing assignments will facilitate the cycle of immediate diagnosis-feedback-remediation.

Observing For Social Skills

The third use of observation procedures is to assess students' social skills. In addition to evaluating efforts to achieve academically, teachers need to assess and evaluate students' efforts to work together cooperatively. This is covered in Chapter 9.

Unstructured Observations

The use of structured observation schedules is not the only way to observe pupil behavior. As long as you are hearing or seeing the class, you are observing. Informal, off-the-cuff observation is always taking place; the challenge is to become aware of it and make it as accurate and helpful as possible. Becoming more precise in your natural observing of pupils is called informal or unstructured observation. **Unstructured observations** is the recording of significant, specific events involving pupils. The emphasis is on the significant; it is not necessary to record an observation for each pupil each day. Teachers eavesdrop by making observations that are:

1. Specific (they don't degenerate into generalities).
2. Brief enough to write down quickly.
3. Capture an important aspect of the behavior of one or more pupils.
4. Provide help in answering questions about (a) students' efforts to maximize their own and each other's learning and (b) the successful implementation of instructional strategies and procedures.

Eavesdropping differs from the use of structured observation schedules in that it is concerned primarily with qualitative incidents which may occur somewhat infrequently. You will want to develop a procedure for unstructured observation that allows you to make a permanent record of incidents as they are taking place. A stenographer's notebook, a few 3x5 inch index cards in a pocket, or scratch paper can facilitate the

Meaningful And Manageable Assessment Through Cooperative Learning, Interaction Book Company, 7208 Cornelia Drive, Edina, MN 55435, (612) 831-9500, FAX (612) 831-9332.

immediate recording of observations. Such notes need to be placed in a log so that they are organized in a permanent way. You may wish to write down positive incidents on cards and file them under the student's name (after they have been used to give the student feedback). You can then access the cards in parent conferences as examples of the student's competencies and positive qualities.

Anecdotal Observations

Observer:______________________________ Date:__________

Note 1: Group:________ Student(s):______________________

Note 2: Group:________ Student(s):______________________

Note 3: Group:________ Student(s):______________________

Note 4: Group:________ Student(s):______________________

Guidelines For Observing

Guideline One: Use a formal observation sheet to count the number of times students engage in the targeted behaviors. The more concrete the data, the more useful it is to you and your students. A variety of observation instruments and procedures that you can use for these purposes are in Johnson, Johnson, and Holubec (1993, 1995).

Guideline Two: Try not to count too many different behaviors at one time. You may wish to choose two to four behaviors from our observation sheet to record the first

Meaningful And Manageable Assessment Through Cooperative Learning, Interaction Book Company, 7208 Cornelia Drive, Edina, MN 55435, (612) 831-9500, FAX (612) 831-9332.

few times you observe. Once you have used the observation sheet several dozen times, you will be able to keep track of all the behaviors included.

Guideline Three: Sometimes you may use a simple checklist in addition to a systematic observation form. An example of the checklist is given below.

Guideline Four: Focus on positive behaviors that are celebrated when they are present and a cause for discussion when they are missing.

Guideline Five: Supplement and extend the frequency data with notes on specific student actions. Especially useful are skillful interchanges that you observe and can share with students later as objective praise. You can also share them with parents in conferences or telephone conversations.

Observation Checklist

Behavior	Yes	No	Comments
1. Do students understand the task?			
2. Are students thinking out loud by explaining step-by-step how to complete the assignment?			
3. Are students challenging each other's reasoning and searching for new information and understandings?			
4. Are students engaging in the social and cognitive skills they are expected to practice in this lesson?			

Guideline Six: Train students to be observers. Student observers can obtain more complete data on each group's functioning. For very young students you must keep the system very simple, perhaps only "*Who talks?*" Many teachers have had good success with student observers, even in kindergarten. One of the more important things for you to do is to give the class adequate instructions (and perhaps practice) on gathering the observation data and sharing it with the group. The observer is in the best position to learn about the skills of working in a group. We can remember one first grade teacher who had a student who talked all the time (even to himself while working alone). He tended to dominate any group he was in. When she introduced student observers to the class, she made him an observer. One important rule for observers was not to interfere in the task but to gather data without talking. He was gathering data on who talks and he did a good job, noticing that one student had done quite a bit of talking in the group whereas another had talked very little. The next day when he was a group member, and there was another observer, he was seen starting to talk, clamping his hand over his mouth and glancing at the observer. He knew what was being observed and he didn't want to be the only one with marks. The observer often benefits in learning about how to behave more competently.

Guideline Seven: When you use student observers, allocate several minutes at the end of each group session for the group to teach the observer what members of the group have just learned. Often important changes are made during this review.

Guideline Eight: You may wish to use cooperative learning enough so that students understand what it is and how they should behave in helping each other learn before introducing student observers. Whether or not you use student observers, however, you should always monitor cooperative learning groups while they work.

Guideline Nine: Be open to discovering unexpected and unplanned outcomes. Unexpected outcomes can be the most interesting, and the next time you teach the same lesson you may wish to include them in the list of expected outcomes.

Summarizing Observations, Giving Feedback, Facilitating Analysis

Aesop tells of the consequences of not processing the effectiveness with which group members work together. A lion had been watching three bulls feeding in an open field. He had tried to attack them several times, but they had kept together, and helped each other to drive him away. The lion had little hope of eating them, for he was no match for three strong bulls with their sharp horns and hoofs. He could not keep away from that field, however, for he could not resist watching a good meal, even when there was little chance of his getting it. One day, however, the bulls had a quarrel. When the hungry lion came to look at them and lick his chops (as he was accustomed to doing), he found them in separate corners of the field. They were as far away from one another as they could get. It was then easy for the lion to attack them one at a time. He did so with the greatest satisfaction and relish. In failing to process their problems in working together and continually increase the effectiveness of their cooperation, the bulls forgot that their success came from their unity.

At the end of the lesson, (a) the observations are summarized and organized to give to students and other stake-holders (such as parents), (b) each student receives (and gives) feedback on the effectiveness of his or her efforts to learn and help classmates learn, (c) students are helped to analyze and reflect on what actions were helpful and unhelpful in contributing to the achievement of their goals, (c) students make decisions about what actions to continue or change and sets goals for improving the quality of their work, and (d) students celebrate their success.

Meaningful And Manageable Assessment Through Cooperative Learning, Interaction Book Company, 7208 Cornelia Drive, Edina, MN 55435, (612) 831-9500, FAX (612) 831-9332.

Charts And Graphs

To display the results of observations so that students, parents, and other interested parties may interpret them two charts are helpful: the bar chart and the run chart.

Constructing A Bar Chart

1. List the actions, conditions or causes you wish to monitor.

2. Collect the data on the number of times the actions conditions, or causes occurred in a predetermined period of time.

3. On the left-hand axis, list the measurement scale by recording the total number of actions, conditions, or causes on the left vertical axis.

4. Under the horizontal axis, write the actions, conditions, or causes observed. They may be placed in descending order (the most frequently occurring action to the left and the least occurring to the right):

    a. Identify the action, condition, or cause with the largest total. Working from left to right, (1) label the first bar on the horizontal axis of the chart with the action, condition, or cause, (2) record the total in the blank space, and (3) draw a vertical bar stretching from 0 to the total frequency of occurrence using the measurement scale on the left-hand axis as a guide.

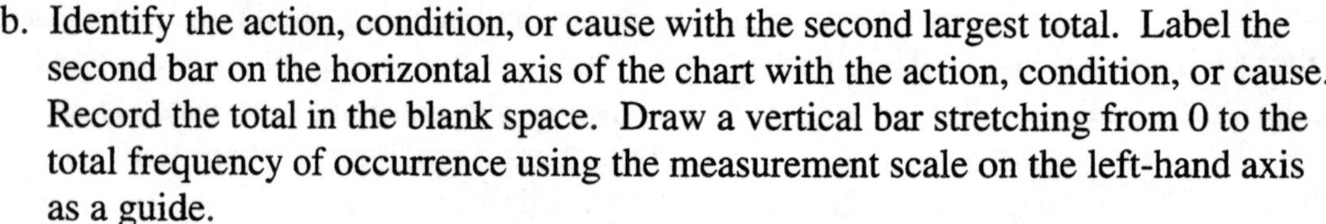

    b. Identify the action, condition, or cause with the second largest total. Label the second bar on the horizontal axis of the chart with the action, condition, or cause. Record the total in the blank space. Draw a vertical bar stretching from 0 to the total frequency of occurrence using the measurement scale on the left-hand axis as a guide.

    c. Continue this procedure until every action, condition, or cause has been recorded on the chart in sequence from most to least frequently occurring.

5. Students and/or other audiences make an action plan by noting which actions are engaged in at an appropriate level and which should be increased or decreased.

Meaningful And Manageable Assessment Through Cooperative Learning, Interaction Book Company, 7208 Cornelia Drive, Edina, MN 55435, (612) 831-9500, FAX (612) 831-9332.

Long-Term Progress: Weekly Bar Chart

Group Members: ____

____

Class: __________________ Subject Area: ______________________

50
45
40
35
30
25
20
15
10
5

Contributes Ideas | Encourages Others | Integrates Summarizes | Helps Groupmates

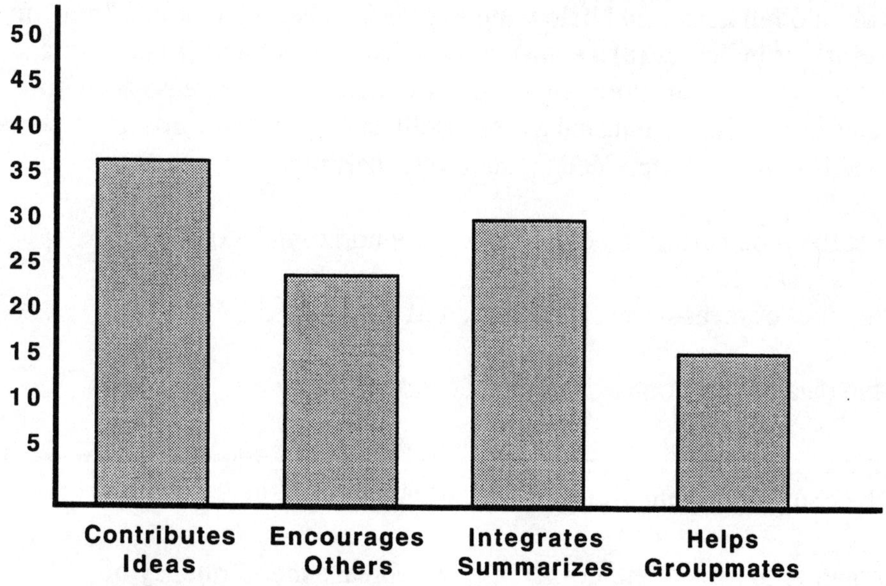

Long-Term Progress: Run Chart

Group Members: ____

____

Class: __________________ Subject Area: ____________ Skill: SUMMARIZES ____

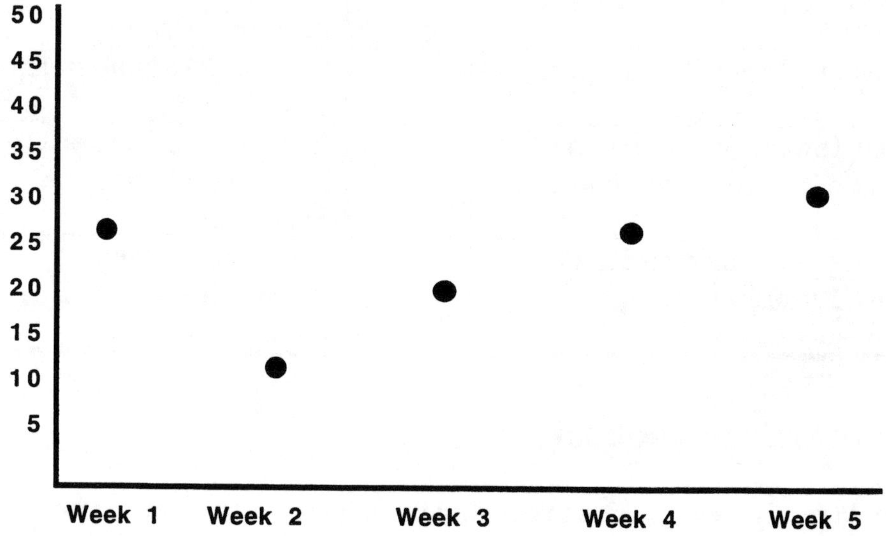

50
45
40
35
30
25
20
15
10
5

Week 1 | Week 2 | Week 3 | Week 4 | Week 5

Meaningful And Manageable Assessment Through Cooperative Learning, Interaction Book Company, 7208 Cornelia Drive, Edina, MN 55435, (612) 831-9500, FAX (612) 831-9332.

Run Chart

A **Run Chart** is used to monitor the process over time to see whether or not the long-range average is changing (see Figure 2.6). In a Run Chart data points are plotted on an x-y axis in chronological order. There are two guidelines for identifying meaningful trends or shifts in the average. First, when monitoring any process, an equal number of points should fall above and below the average. When nine points "run" on one side of the average, it indicates (a) a statistically unusual event and (b) the average has changed. Second, when six or more points steadily increase or decrease with no reversals, it indicates a statistically unusual event. Both cases point towards an important change the team needs to investigate. You create a run chart by:

1. Marking off the time period to be used along the horizontal axis.

2. Entering the unit of measurement along the left vertical axis.

3. Entering the data as it becomes available.

4. Analyzing the (historical) trend revealed by the position of the data points (each point can be compared to the overall average).

5. Making a plan as to how to either increase or decrease the frequency of occurrence of the targeted action, condition, or cause.

Feedback Checklist

Feedback	Yes	No, Start Over
Is Feedback Given?		Was Not Given Or Received, Start Over
Is Feedback Generating Energy In Students?		Students Are Indifferent, Start Over
Is Energy Directed Towards Identifying And Solving Problems So Performance Is Improved?		Energy Used To Resist, Deny, Avoid Feedback, Start Over
Do Students Have Opportunities To Take Action To Improve Performance?		No, Students Are Frustrated And Feel Like Failures, Start Over

Giving And Receiving Feedback

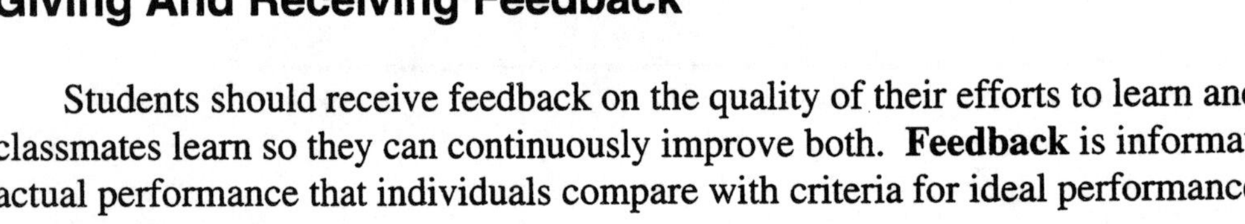

Students should receive feedback on the quality of their efforts to learn and help classmates learn so they can continuously improve both. **Feedback** is information on actual performance that individuals compare with criteria for ideal performance. When

Meaningful And Manageable Assessment Through Cooperative Learning, Interaction Book Company, 7208 Cornelia Drive, Edina, MN 55435, (612) 831-9500, FAX (612) 831-9332.

feedback is given skillfully, it generates energy, directs the energy toward constructive action, and transforms the energy into action towards improving the performance of the teamwork skills. The results may include a decrease in the discrepancy between actual and real performance, increased self-efficacy, and empowerment to be even more effective next time. The following **checklist** may help in assessing the effectiveness of feedback.

Reflecting On And Analyzing Feedback

A common teaching error is to fail to provide a time and structure for students to reflect on and analyze the quality of their efforts to learn and help classmates learn and make decisions about what actions to continue or change. Ways to facilitate and assess this process are:

1. Each student summarizes (a) the feedback received, (b) what actions were helpful and unhelpful in increasing his or her own and others' academic learning, and (c) what actions he or she has decided to continue or change. The student then places the reflections in a folder with his or her completed academic work and hands it in to the teacher.

2. The student does a mind-map representing the secrets to his or her success.

3. The student rates him- or herself on a series of dimensions on a bar chart.

Varying the procedures for reflection and analysis keeps the processing vital and interesting. At the end of the processing, students should set goals for improving the effectiveness of their efforts to learn and helping others do likewise.

Giving Personal Feedback In A Helpful, Non Threatening Way

_____ 1. Focus feedback on behavior (not on personality traits).

_____ 2. Be descriptive (not judgmental).

_____ 3. Be specific and concrete (not general or abstract).

_____ 4. Make feedback immediate (not delayed).

_____ 5. Focus on positive actions (not negative ones).

_____ 6. Present feedback in a visual (such as a graph or chart) as well as auditory fashion (not just spoken words alone).

Meaningful And Manageable Assessment Through Cooperative Learning, Interaction Book Company, 7208 Cornelia Drive, Edina, MN 55435, (612) 831-9500, FAX (612) 831-9332.

Summarizing Observation Data: An Example

Imagine you have finished observing a cooperative learning group with four members. You can either provide direct feedback to each student or you can show them the data and ask them to reach their own conclusions about their participation. If you decide to give direct feedback, you might say:

Helen contributed ten times, Roger seven times, Edythe five times, and Frank twice. Frank encouraged others to participate ten times, Edythe five times, and Roger and Helen twice. Roger summarized five times, Frank twice, and Helen and Edythe once.

If you decided to let the students reach their own conclusions, you might say:

Look at the totals in the rows and columns. What conclusions could you make about:
a. Your participation in the lesson.
b. The effectiveness of the group in completing the assignment.

In summarizing, you might say:

Each of you will wish to set a personal goal for how you can be even more effective tomorrow than you were today. What actions did you engage in most and least? What actions were more and least appropriate and helpful under the circumstances (summarizing right after someone else summarized may be inappropriate and not very helpful)? What other actions would have helped the group work more effectively? Decide on a personal goal to increase your effectiveness and share it with the other group members.

Observation Form

Students	Contributes Ideas	Encourages Others To Contribute	Integrates, Summarizes	Totals
Frank				
Helen				
Roger				
Edythe				
Totals				

Meaningful And Manageable Assessment Through Cooperative Learning, Interaction Book Company, 7208 Cornelia Drive, Edina, MN 55435, (612) 831-9500, FAX (612) 831-9332.

Set Improvement Goals

After reflecting on the feedback received, students set improvement goals specifying how they will act more skillfully in the next course session. Students should publicly announce the behavior they plan to increase. The goal should be written down and reviewed at the beginning of the next class session. Goal setting is the link between how students did today and how well they will do tomorrow. Goal setting can have powerful impact on students' behavior as there is a sense of ownership of and commitment to actions that a student has decided to engage in (as opposed to assigned behaviors).

Celebrating

Lessons end with students celebrating their hard work and success. Celebrations are key to encouraging students to persist in their efforts to learn (Johnson & Johnson, 1993). Individual, small-group, and whole-class celebrations should take place. Feeling successful, appreciated, and respected builds commitment to and enthusiasm for learning as well as self-efficacy about mastering subject-matter and cooperating with classmates.

Summary

Observation is aimed at recording and describing behavior as it occurs. Its purpose is to provide objective data about the quality of student performances, the processes and procedures students use in completing assignments, and the processes and procedures teachers use in conducting lessons. Using observation as an assessment tool requires that teachers understand the basis of observing, know how to prepare for observing, know how to observe, and know how to summarize and organize the data for use by students, parents, and other stake-holders.

The basics of observing include being aware of the characteristics of the setting, differentiating between objective and subjective observations, differentiating between descriptions and inferences, the phrasing of questions, differentiating between category and sign systems, differentiating between mutually exclusive and over-lapping and between exhaustive and nonexhaustive categories, and understanding the difference between time sampling and event sampling.

Preparing for observing involves deciding what actions to observe, who will observe, what the sampling plan will be, constructing an observation form, and training observers to use the form. Conducting observations may focus on students' "on-task" behavior, academic efforts, or social skills. Observations may be formal and informal, structured and unstructured. In summarizing observations, the data may be displayed in bar or run charts, feedback is then given to the students or other interested parties, the recipients reflect on the feedback and set improvement goals.

Weekly Report Form

Name: ______________________________ **Date:** __________ **Class:** __________

Date	On-Task Work	Contributes Ideas	Integrates, Summarizes	Helps Classmates	Completes Assignments
Totals:					

Comments:

Meaningful And Manageable Assessment Through Cooperative Learning, Interaction Book Company, 7208 Cornelia Drive, Edina, MN 55435, (612) 831-9500, FAX (612) 831-9332.

PLANNING FOR OBSERVING

1. The student actions I wish to observe are:

2. The observers will be:

3. The sampling plan will be:

4. The observation form will be:

5. The observers will be trained in the following way:

6. The observations will focus on:

7. The results will be portrayed by:

8. The results will be presented to:

9. The ways reflection and goal setting will be facilitated are:

Cooperative Learning: Classroom Observation

Teacher:__________________________ Date:_____________ Observer: _______________

Teacher Actions	Implementation	Comments
Objectives	❑ Academics ❑ Social Skills	
Positive Interdependence	❑ Group Goal ❑ Group Celebration/Reward ❑ Resources Shared/Jigsawed ❑ Roles Assigned ❑ Shared Identity	
Group Composition	❑ Random ❑ Teacher Selected	
Seating Arrangement	❑ Clear View/Access to Groupmates, Teacher ❑ Clear View/Access to Materials	
Individual Accountability	❑ Each Student Tested Individually ❑ Students Check Each Other ❑ Random Student Evaluated ❑ Role: Checker for Understanding	
Define Social Skills	❑ Define (T-Chart) ❑ Demonstrate/Model ❑ Guided Practice ❑ Assign As Role	
Observation Of Taskwork And Teamwork	❑ Teacher Monitors And Intervenes ❑ Students Monitor ❑ Formal Observation Form ❑ Informal (Anecdotal) Observation	
Teacher Feedback: Teamwork Skills	❑ Class ❑ Group ❑ Individual ❑ Frequency And Quality Of Use ❑ Charts and Graphs Used ❑ Positive Feedback To Each Student	
Group Processing	❑ Analysis/Reflection: Teamwork & Taskwork ❑ Goal Setting For Improvement ❑ Celebration	
General Climate	❑ Group Products Displayed ❑ Group Progress Displayed ❑ Aids To Group Work Displayed	

Meaningful And Manageable Assessment Through Cooperative Learning, Interaction Book Company, 7208 Cornelia Drive, Edina, MN 55435, (612) 831-9500, FAX (612) 831-9332.

My Checklist For Cooperative Groups

Name: ______________________ **Date:** _________ **Class:** ______

1. When I knew an answer or had an idea, I shared it with the group.

   Never 1---2---3---4---5 All The Time

2. When my answer did not agree with someone else's, I tried to find out why.

   Never 1---2---3---4---5 All The Time

3. When I did not understand something, I asked others to explain.

   Never 1---2---3---4---5 All The Time

4. When someone else did not understand, I explained it until he or she did.

   Never 1---2---3---4---5 All The Time

5. I tried to make the people in the group feel appreciated and respected.

   Never 1---2---3---4---5 All The Time

6. Before I signed my name to our paper, I made sure that I understood everything, agreed with the answers, and was confident that all other members understood the answers.

   Never 1---2---3---4---5 All The Time

Observation Form

Observer: ______________________________ **Date:** __________ **Grade:** _______

Assignment: ____

Action					Total
Contributes Ideas					
Describes Feelings					
Encourages Participation					
Summarizes, Integrates					
Checks For Understanding					
Relates New To Old Learning					
Gives Direction To Work					
Total					

Directions For Use: (a) Put the names of the group members above each column. (b) Put a tally mark in the appropriate box each time a group member contributes. (c) Make notes on the back when interesting things happen that are not captured by the categories. (d) Write down one (or more) positive contribution made by each group member.

Meaningful And Manageable Assessment Through Cooperative Learning, Interaction Book Company, 7208 Cornelia Drive, Edina, MN 55435, (612) 831-9500, FAX (612) 831-9332.

Observing For Indicators Of Criteria

Name: ____________________ **Date:** __________ **Grade:** __________

Assignment: ______________________________________

Directions: List the criteria you wish to observe and specify indicators that describe the criteria. Then observe the student and record the frequency with which he or she engages in each indicator action.

Criteria				Total
1:				
a:				
b:				
c:				
2:				
a:				
b:				
c:				
3:				
a:				
b:				
c:				
4:				
a:				
b:				
c:				

Comments:

Meaningful And Manageable Assessment Through Cooperative Learning, Interaction Book Company, 7208 Cornelia Drive, Edina, MN 55435, (612) 831-9500, FAX (612) 831-9332.

Weekly Observation Form

Teacher: ______________________________ **Date:** __________ **Class:** _______

Assignment: ____

Directions: List the students to be observed in column one, list the social skill each student is supposed to engage in column two, and note the frequency of the use of the skill for each day of the week. Then total the daily frequencies.

Student	Social Skill	Mon	Tues	Weds	Thurs	Fri	Total

Comments:

Meaningful And Manageable Assessment Through Cooperative Learning, Interaction Book Company, 7208 Cornelia Drive, Edina, MN 55435, (612) 831-9500, FAX (612) 831-9332.

Teacher Observation Form

Name: ______________________________ Date: _______________ Class: __________

Assignment: ____

Groups	Explaining Concepts	Encouraging Participation	Checking For Under-standing	Organizing The Work
1				
2				
3				
4				
5				

Meaningful And Manageable Assessment Through Cooperative Learning, Interaction Book Company, 7208 Cornelia Drive, Edina, MN 55435, (612) 831-9500, FAX (612) 831-9332.

SIMULATIONS, ROLE PLAYING, AND OBSERVATION

There are times when you wish to observe students engaging in a skill or pattern of behavior, but it will take far too much time to wait and observe the behavior occurring naturally. To save time, you create a simulation and observe what students do. Simulations and games are increasingly being used as training and assessment procedures. Simulations can vary widely in complexity of issues and number of participants, ranging from relatively simple simulations for an individual or small group to moderately complex computerized simulations requiring a number of groups to participate. For assessment purposes, students are placed within a simulation and their actions are monitored and observed so that behavioral measures of outcomes can be obtained.

Frequently in simulations, students role play the characters. Initial instructions are given, and the role players determine what happens. Role playing is a tool for:

1. Bringing a specific skill and its consequences into focus so it may be practiced.
2. Experiencing concretely the type of interaction under examination.
3. Setting up an imaginary life situation so students can act and react in terms of the assumptions they are asked to adopt, the beliefs they are asked to hold, and the character they are asked to play.
4. Giving students experience in discussing and identifying effective and ineffective behavior.

You, as the coordinator of the simulated role play:

1. Get students in "role." You help involve the role players in the situation by introducing it in such a way that the players are emotionally stimulated. Using name tags and asking the players questions to help them get a feeling for the part are helpful. Introduce the scene to the role players and the observers.
2. Conduct the simulation. While the students are engaged in the role play, you carefully observe and record the frequency of their effective and ineffective actions.
3. Get students out of "role." Always "de-role" after the role playing has ended.
4. Conduct a processing session in which students reflect on what happened and how to behave more effectively.

Meaningful And Manageable Assessment Through Cooperative Learning, Interaction Book Company, 7208 Cornelia Drive, Edina, MN 55435, (612) 831-9500, FAX (612) 831-9332.

Chapter Nine: Assessing Social Skills

What Are Social Skills

From the standpoint of everyday life...there is one thing we do know; that man is here for the sake of other men--above all, for those upon whose smile and well-being our own happiness depends, and also for the countless unknown souls with whose fate we are connected by a bond of sympathy. Many times a day I realize how much my own outer and inner life is built upon the labors of my fellow men, both living and dead, and how earnestly I must exert myself in order to give in return as much as I have received.

Albert Einstein (scientist & philosopher)

Success in life depends on social skills. An example is Abraham Lincoln. During his four years as President, Lincoln spent most of his time interacting with the people he believed were going to get the job done—the troops. He met with his generals and cabinet members in their homes, offices, and in the field. He toured the Navy Yard and the fortifications in and around Washington and conversed with the troops. He inspected new weaponry and discussed its use with the soldiers in charge. He visited key individuals in government, such as members of Congress, and toured hospitals to visit and interview the sick and the wounded. He virtually lived in the War Department's telegraph office so he could communicate with individuals in every part of the war. Lincoln even went with the troops into several battles, coming under fire at least once (one of the few American Presidents to do so while in office). In establishing human contact with the individuals actually carrying on the war effort, Lincoln was able to provide extraordinary leadership. One-hundred years later, Lincoln's philosophy became part of the revolution in modern leadership and was named MBWA (Management By Wandering Around) by Thomas Peters and Robert Waterman in their 1982 book, **In Search Of Excellence**. Without his valuing relationships and his high level of interpersonal skills, Lincoln may not have been such a success.

Individuals learn social skills to gain social competence. **Social competence** is the extent to which the consequences of a person's actions match his or her intentions. Individuals who are **socially competent** have acquired a broad range of interpersonal and small group skills that they can apply appropriately in interactions with others, thereby creating the joint outcomes they intended. The use of social skills in a fluent and flexible way help people establish positive relationships with others and successfully achieve joint outcomes. Social skills range from simple (i.e., make eye contact with the person to whom you are talking) to complex (i.e., criticizing ideas while confirming the competence of the person). Students' interpersonal and small group skills determine their ability to initiate, develop, and maintain caring and productive relationships and their ability to work effectively with others. There are a number of ways to classify social skills.

What Teamwork Skills To Teach

1. **Forming**: The skills needed to establish a cooperative learning group, such as "stay with your group and do not wander around the room," "use quiet voices," "take turns," and "use each other's names."

2. **Functioning**: The skills needed to manage the group's activities in completing the task and maintaining effective working relationships among members, such as giving one's ideas and conclusions, providing direction to the group's work, and encouraging everyone to participate.

3. **Formulating**: The skills needed to build deeper-level understanding of the material being studied, to stimulate the use of higher-quality reasoning strategies, and to maximize mastery and retention of the assigned material. Examples are explaining step-by-step one's reasoning and relating what is being studied to previous learning.

4. **Fermenting**: The skills needed to stimulate reconceptualization of the material being studied, cognitive conflict, the search for more information, and the communication of the rationale behind one's conclusions. Examples are criticizing ideas (not people) and not changing your mind unless you are logically persuaded (majority rule does not promote learning).

The interpersonal skills individuals "dare" to learn are (Johnson, 1996):

D Disclosing ourselves to and trusting each other. Openness in letting others get to know you is based on self-awareness, self-acceptance, and the willingness to take the risk of trusting others.

A Accurately communicating with each other. You must be able to send messages that are phrased so that the other person can easily understand them and listen in ways that ensure you fully understand the other person.

R Resolving conflicts and relationship problems constructively. The more committed the relationship, the more frequently conflicts tend to occur. When

Meaningful And Manageable Assessment Through Cooperative Learning, Interaction Book Company, 7208 Cornelia Drive, Edina, MN 55435, (612) 831-9500, FAX (612) 831-9332.

conflicts are managed by engaging in problem-solving negotiations or smoothing, the relationship tends to be strengthened.

E Encouraging and appreciating diversity. There is strength in diversity. You encourage others to be themselves and you appreciate the wide variety of attitudes and perspectives brought to the relationship. It takes considerable skill in building and maintaining relationships with individuals from backgrounds and cultures different from yours.

The small group skills students need to master include setting goals, communicating effectively, providing leadership, making effective decisions, managing conflicts constructively, and using power appropriately (Johnson & F. Johnson, 1996). Johnson, Johnson, and Holubec (1993) classify social skills students need to work together in cooperative groups as forming, functioning, formulating, and fermenting skills.

Why Teach And Assess Social Skills

I will pay more for the ability to deal with people than any other ability under the sun.

John D Rockefeller

Social skills are the connections among people. They are key to all aspects of our lives. Any time students talk to, play with, interact with, or work with others, they are using social skills. Increasingly, however, large numbers of children, adolescents, and young adults do not possess the social skills necessary to establish and maintain positive relationships with their peers. Due to changes in the structure of family, neighborhood, and community life, many students have never been taught how to interact effectively with others. Without direct instruction many students may never become socially competent. The severity and persistence of social problems among children, adolescents, and young adults necessitate that schools become more involved in teaching social skills. Yet in many classrooms, social skills are neglected and almost never taught.

Social skills are not a luxury, to be learned when time allows. They are a necessity to all aspects of living. The importance of social skills cannot be overstated, as they are related to (Johnson, 1996; Johnson & F. Johnson, 1996; Johnson & R. Johnson, 1989):

1. **Personal development and identity**: Our identity is created out of relationships with others. As we interact with others we note their responses to us, we seek feedback as to how they perceive us, and we learn how to view ourselves as others view us. Individuals who have few interpersonal skills have distorted relationships with others and tend to develop inaccurate and incomplete views of themselves.

2. **Employability, productivity and career success**: Social skills may be even more important than education and technical skills to employability, productivity, and career success. Recent national surveys found that (a) when hiring new employees, employers value interpersonal and communication skills, responsibility, initiative, and decision-making skills and (b) 90 percent of the people fired from their jobs were fired for poor job attitudes, poor interpersonal relationships, inappropriate behavior, and inappropriate dress. In the real world of work, the heart of most jobs, especially the higher-paying, more interesting jobs, is getting others to cooperate, leading others, coping with complex power and influence issues, and helping solve people's problems in working with others.

3. **Quality of life**: There is no simple recipe for creating a meaningful life, but the research indicates that for almost everyone a necessary ingredient for a high quality of life is some kind of satisfying, close, personal, intimate relationship.

4. **Physical health**: Positive, supportive relationships have been found to be related to living longer lives, recovering from illness and injury faster and more completely, and experiencing less severe illnesses. Physical health improves when individuals learn the interpersonal skills necessary to take more initiative in their relationships and become more constructive in the way they deal with conflict. Loneliness and isolation kill. High quality relationships create and extend life.

5. **Psychological health**: When individuals do not have the interpersonal skills to build and maintain positive relationships with others, psychological illness results. The inability to establish acceptable relationships often leads to anxiety, depression, frustration, alienation, inadequacy, helplessness, fear, and loneliness. The ability to build and maintain positive, supportive relationships, on the other hand, is related to psychological health and adjustment, lack of neuroticism and psychopathology, reduction of psychological distress, coping effectively with stress, resilience, self-reliance and autonomy, a coherent and integrated self-identity, high self-esteem, general happiness, and social competence.

6. **Ability to cope with stress**: Positive and supportive relationships help individuals cope with stress by providing caring, information, resources, and feedback. Supportive relationships decrease the number and severity of stressful events, reduce anxiety, and help with the appraisal of the nature of the stress and one's ability to deal with it constructively. Discussions with supportive peers help individuals perceive the meaning of the stressful event, regain mastery over their lives, and enhance their self-esteem.

Overall, social science research indicates that life without a modicum of social skills is not much of a life. The inability to relate to other people leads to loneliness and isolation. Loneliness and isolation can stunt growth, spark failure, make life seem meaningless, create anxiety and depression, result in an obsession with the past, increase fragility, increase inhumaneness, and even shorten life.

How To Assess Social Skills

To assess students' social skills, you:

1. Review the assumptions underlying the teaching of social skills.
2. Teach the targeted social skills to students.
3. Structure a cooperative learning situation in which the targeted social skills can be observed. Observe students working in cooperative learning groups.
4. Intervene to ensure appropriate use of the social skills.
5. Assess knowledge of social skills.
6. Facilitate self-diagnosis of social skill mastery.
7. Set goals for continuous improvement.
8. Report on students' social skills to interested stakeholders, such as the students, parents, and potential employers.

When We Work In Groups We

G	Give Encouragement
R	Respect Others
O	Stay On Task
U	Use Quiet Voices
P	Participate Actively
S	Stay In Our Group

Basic Assumptions

The assumptions underlying the assessment of students' social skills are as follows (Johnson, Johnson, & Holubec, 1993).

1. **Social Skills Must Be Learned**: Placing socially unskilled students in a group and telling them to cooperate does not guarantee that they will be able to do so. We are not born instinctively knowing how to interact effectively with others. Interpersonal and small group skills do not magically appear when they are needed. You must teach students the social skills required for interacting effectively with others and motivate students to use the skills if students are to become socially competent.

2. **Every Cooperative Lesson Is A Lesson In Social Skills As Well As Academics**: Students must learn both academic subject matter (**taskwork**) and the interpersonal and small group skills required to work with classmates (**teamwork**). Cooperative learning is inherently more complex than competitive or individualistic learning because students have to simultaneously engage in taskwork and teamwork. If group members are inept at teamwork, their taskwork will tend to be substandard. The greater the members' teamwork skills, the higher will be the quality and quantity of their learning. Ways of deciding which interpersonal and small group skills need to be emphasized include:

    a. Observing students at work to determine which social skills they lack.

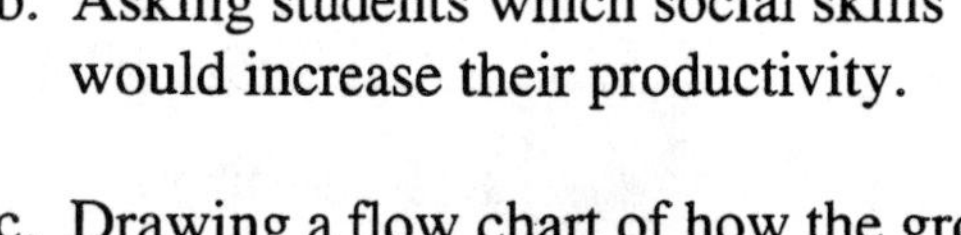

    b. Asking students which social skills would increase their productivity.

    c. Drawing a flow chart of how the group actually completes the assignment. On the basis of the process required, certain social (and cognitive) skills may be suggested or even required.

K	Keep On Task
I	Include Everyone
S	Six-Inch Voices
S	Stay With Your Group
E	Encourage Everyone
S	Share Ideas

3. **Understand What Teamwork Skills To Teach And How To Teach Skills.**

4. **Follow The Three Rules Of Teaching Teamwork Skills**:

    a. **Be specific.** Operationally define each social skill by a T-Chart.

    b. **Start small.** Do not overload your students with more social skills than they can learn at one time. One or two skills to emphasize for a few lessons is enough. Students should not be subjected to information overload.

    c. **Emphasize overlearning.** Having students practice skills once or twice is not enough. Keep emphasizing a skill until the students have integrated it into their behavioral repertoires and do it automatically and habitually.

Teaching Social Skills

When police evaluate potential suspects, they look for the joint presence of three characteristics: opportunity, motive, and means. Engaging in an interpersonal action requires the contact opportunity with other people for the act to occur, a reason sufficient to motivate the act, and access to a method or procedure whereby the act can occur. For students to work as a team, they need (a) an opportunity to work together cooperatively (where teamwork skills can be manifested), (b) a motivation to engage in the teamwork skills (a reason to believe that such actions will be beneficial to them), and (c) some proficiency in using teamwork skills. After providing students with the opportunity to learn in cooperative groups, you must provide students with the motive and means for doing so.

The first step is to ensure that students see the need for the teamwork skill. To establish the need for the teamwork skill, you can:

1. Ask students to suggest the teamwork skills they need to work together more effectively. From the skills suggested, choose one or more to emphasize.

2. Present a case to students that they are better off knowing, than not knowing the chosen skills. You can display posters, tell students how important the skills are,, complement students who use the skills.

3. Setting up a role play that provides a counter-example where the skill is obviously missing in a group is a fun way to illustrate the need for the skill.

The second step is to ensure that students understand what the skill is, how to engage in the skill, and when to use the skill. You:

Encouraging Participation

Looks Like	Sounds Like
Smiles	What Is Your Idea?
Eye Contact	Awesome!
Thumbs Up	Good Idea!
Pat On Back	That's Interesting

1. Operationally define the skill as verbal and nonverbal behaviors so that students know specifically what to do. It is not enough to tell students what skills you wish to see them use during the lesson (*"Please encourage each other's participation and check each other's understanding of what is being learned."*). What is encouraging to one student may be discouraging to another. You must explain exactly what they are to do. One way to explain a social skill is through a T-Chart. You list the skill (e.g., encouraging participation) and then ask the class, *"What would this skill look like (nonverbal behaviors)?"* After students generate several ideas, you ask the class, *"What would this skill sound like (phrases)?"* Students list several ideas. You then display the T-Chart prominently for students to refer to.

2. Demonstrate and model the skill in front of the class and explain it step-by-step until students have a clear idea of what the skill sounds and looks like.

Meaningful And Manageable Assessment Through Cooperative Learning, Interaction Book Company, 7208 Cornelia Drive, Edina, MN 55435, (612) 831-9500, FAX (612) 831-9332.

3. Have students role play the skill by practicing the skill twice in their groups before the lesson begins.

The third step is to set up practice situations and encourage mastery of the skill. To master a skill, students need to practice it again and again. You can guide their practice by:

1. **Assigning the social skill as either a specific role for certain members to fulfill or a general responsibility for all group members to engage in.** You may wish to introduce one or two new skills each week, review previously taught skills, and repeat this sequence until all the skills are taught.

2. **Observing each group and recording which members are engaging in the skill with what frequency and effectiveness.** Utilize student observers as soon as possible. You may wish to begin with a simple observation form that only has two to four skills on it. When you become used to the observation process, you may expand to an intermediate observation form that has six to eight actions listed and then to an advanced observation form that has ten to twelve actions on it. Student observers are trained in the same sequence of simple to intermediate to advanced observation forms. The procedures for observing may be found in Chapter 8.

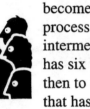

S	Show Need For Skill
T	T-Chart Skill
E	Engage Students In Practice
R	Reflect On Success
N	Practice Until Using Skill Is Natural

3. Cueing the use of the skill periodically during the lesson by asking a group member to demonstrate the skill.

4. Intervening in the learning groups to clarify the nature of the social skill and how to engage in it.

5. Coaching students to improve their use of the skill.

The fourth step is to ensure that each student (a) receives feedback on his or her use of the skill and (b) reflects on how to engage in the skill more effectively next time. Practicing teamwork skills is not enough. Students must receive feedback on how frequently and how well they are using the skill. Organize the observation data into bar graphs and run charts and report the data to the class, groups, and individuals. Help students analyze and reflect on the data. The observer reports the information gathered to the group and group members report their impressions as to how they behaved. The observer shows the observation form to the group, holding it so every group member can see it. He or she then asks the group, "*What do you conclude about (a) your* *participation in the group and (b) the group functioning in general?"* The observer ensures that all group members receive positive feedback about their efforts to learn and help their groupmates learn. After small group processing, there is whole class processing in which the teacher shares his or her feedback to the class as a whole.

Reflection is needed in order to discover what helped and hindered them in completing the academic assignment and whether specific actions had a positive or negative effect. The observer helps group members process how well the group functioned, how frequently and well each member engaged in the targeted skill, and how the interaction among group members should be modified to make it more effective. On the basis of the feedback received and their own assessment of their skill used, the students reflect on how to use the skill more effectively in the future and set improvement goals. Finally, the groups should celebrate their hard work in learning and using the targeted social skills.

Mystery Person

1. Inform the class that you will be focusing on one student whose name will be kept secret.
2. Select a student randomly or select a student who will be a positive role model or who could benefit from some recognition.
3. Observe during the lesson without showing whom you are observing.
4. Describe to the whole class what the person did (frequency data) without naming the person.
5. Ask students to guess who the mystery person is.

The fifth step is to ensure that students persevere in practicing the skill until the skill seems a natural action. With most skills there is a period of slow learning, then a period of rapid improvement, then a period where performance remains about the same, then another period of rapid improvement, then another plateau, and so forth. Students have to practice teamwork skills long enough to make it through the first few plateaus and integrate the skills into their behavioral repertoires. There are stages most skill development goes through:

1. Self-conscious, awkward engaging in the skill.
2. Feelings of phoniness while engaging in the skill. After a while the awkwardness passes and enacting the skill becomes more smooth. Many students, however,

Meaningful And Manageable Assessment Through Cooperative Learning, Interaction Book Company, 7208 Cornelia Drive, Edina, MN 55435, (612) 831-9500, FAX (612) 831-9332.

feel inauthentic or phony while using the skill. Students need teacher and peer encouragement to move through this stage.

3. Skilled but mechanical use of the skill.

4. Automatic, routine use where students have fully integrated the skill into their behavior repertoire and feel like the skill is a natural action to engage in.

Encourage students to improve continuously their teamwork skills by refining, modifying, and adapting them.

Teaching Social Skills

Steps In Teaching A Skill	Teacher Actions
Step 1: Establish The Need For The Skill	1. Students choose needed skills. 2. You choose and persuade. 3. Role play the absence of skill.
Step 2: Define The Skill	1. Define with T-chart. 2. Demonstrate, model, explain.
Step 3: Guide Practice Of The Skill	1. Assign the social skill as a role. 2. Record frequency & quality of use. 3. Periodically cue the skill.
Step 4: Guide Feedback And Reflection	1. Structure feedback sessions. 2. Structure reflection (processing).
Step 5: Repeat Steps 3 & 4 Repeatedly	Emphasize continued improvement while proceeding through the stages of skill development.

Ensuring Every Group Member Receives Positive Feedback

1. Each group focus on one member at a time. Members tell the target person one thing he/she did that helped them learn or work together effectively. The focus is rotated until all members have received positive feedback.

2. Members write a positive comment about each of the other member's participation on an index card. The students then give their written comments to each other so that every member will have, in writing, positive feedback from all the other group members.

3. Members comment on how well each other member used the social skills by writing an answer to one of the following statements. The students then give their written statements to each other.

    a. *I appreciated it when you...*

    b. *I liked it when you...*

    c. *I admire your ability to...*

    d. *I enjoy it when you...*

    e. *You really helped out the group when you...*

This procedure may also be done orally. In this case students look at the member they are complimenting, use his or her name, and give their comments. The person receiving the positive feedback makes eye contact and says "*thank you.*" Positive feedback should be directly and clearly expressed and should **not** be brushed off or denied.

Create Cooperative Situations Where Skills Can Be Used

In order to assess students' social skills, a situation must be created where students work together to achieve a common goal. Cooperative learning situations are structured so that students can learn social skills and demonstrate the level of their mastery of the skills. While the students learn together, you observe to assess the quality and quantity of their use of the targeted social skills.

Meaningful And Manageable Assessment Through Cooperative Learning, Interaction Book Company, 7208 Cornelia Drive, Edina, MN 55435, (612) 831-9500, FAX (612) 831-9332.

Ideas For Monitoring And Intervening

Check For	If Present	If Absent
Members seated closely together	*Good seating.*	*Draw your chairs closer together*
Group has right materials and are on right page	*Good, you are all ready.*	*Get what you need--I will watch.*
Students who are assigned roles are doing them	*Good! You're doing your jobs.*	*Who is supposed to do what?*
Groups have started task	*Good! You've started.*	*Let me see you get started. Do you need any help?*
Cooperative skills being used (in general)	*Good group! Keep up the good work!*	*What skills would help here? What should you be doing?*
A specific cooperative skill being used	*Good encouraging! Good paraphrasing!*	*Who can encourage Edye? Repeat in your own words what Edye just said.*
Academic work being done well	*You are following the procedure for this assignment. Good group!*	*You need more extensive answers. Let me explain how to do this again.*
Members ensuring individual accountability	*You're making sure everyone understands. Good work!*	*Roger, show me how to do #1. David, explain why the group chose this answer.*
Reluctant students involved	*I'm glad to see everyone participating.*	*I'm going to ask Helen to explain #4. Get her ready and I will be back.*
Members explaining to each other what they are learning and their reasoning processes	*Great explanations! Keep it up.*	*I want each of you to take a problem and explain to me step-by-step how to solve it.*
Group cooperating with other groups.	*I'm glad you're helping the other groups. Good citizenship!*	*Each of you go to another group and share your answer to #6.*
One member dominating	*Everyone is participating equally. Great group!*	*Helen, you are the first to answer every time. Could you be the accuracy checker?*
Groups that have finished	*Your work looks good. Now do the activity written on the board.*	*You are being very thorough. But time is almost up. Let's speed up.*
Group working effectively	*Your group is working so well. What behaviors are helping you?*	*Tell me what is wrong in the way this group is working. Let's make three plans to solve the problem.*

Meaningful And Manageable Assessment Through Cooperative Learning, Interaction Book Company, 7208 Cornelia Drive, Edina, MN 55435, (612) 831-9500, FAX (612) 831-9332.

Intervene To Improve Use Of Social Skills

While observing students engage in learning activities, you may see patterns of behavior interfering with learning or teamwork. You may then wish to intervene for the following reasons:

1. To correct misunderstandings or misconceptions about task instructions and the academic concepts and procedures being learned.

2. To correct the absence, incorrect use, or inappropriate use of interpersonal, small group, and cognitive skills.

3. To reinforce, encourage, and celebrate the appropriate or competent use of skills and procedures.

Teachers decide when and at what level they wish to intervene:

1. **Should I intervene now or wait for the group processing time?** You may wish to stop the group's work and intervene immediately, or you may wish to wait until the processing time and then intervene.

2. **Should I intervene in this group or should I have the entire class focus on the issue?** Sometimes the problem is specific to a group and sometimes it is a generic problem that all groups may be experiencing.

Teachers have to decide how to intervene effectively. Ineffective or weak interventions include (a) telling students how to be more effective, (b) solving the problem for the group, (c) rescuing floundering groups. Instead, you should highlight the problem for the group to solve and guide them to a solution that they themselves discover and implement. You teach students how to diagnose and solve their problems in group functioning by:

1. Using the language or terms relevant to the learning. Instead of saying, *"Yes, that is right,"* you will wish to say something more specific to the assignment, such as, *"Yes, that is one way to find the main idea of a paragraph."* The use of the more specific statement reinforces the desired learning and promotes positive transfer by helping the students associate a term with their learning.

2. Interview members of a cooperative learning group about their reasoning processes by asking:

   a. *What are you doing?*

   b. *Why are you doing it?*

c. *How will it help you*?

3. Show the group members the observation data and ask them to identify the problem. Often just the awareness of the recorded information (for example, showing the data indicating that group members are not sharing or helping) will get group members back on the right track.

4. If the group members cannot identify a clear procedure to correct the problem, guide them towards several alternative courses of action. Highlighting a problem may only create helplessness, demoralization, and frustration if students believe there is nothing they can do to solve it. In such a case, giving them several strategies will empower them.

5. Join the group and:

   a. Have group members set aside their task ("*pencils down, close your books*").

   b. Point out the problem ("*here is what I observed*").

   c. Ask them to create three possible solutions.

   d. Ask them to decide which solution they are going to try first.

6. Have students role play the situation and practice new behaviors that would solve the problem.

Intervening In Cooperative Learning Groups

O = Observe

IDQ = Intervene, by sharing data and/or asking a question.

SP = Have students process and plan how they will take care of issue.

BTW = Tell students to go back to work.

Assess Knowledge Of Social Skills

To assess students' knowledge about the social skills being taught, objective tests may be given. Such a test on leadership skills is provided at the end of this chapter.

Meaningful And Manageable Assessment Through Cooperative Learning, Interaction Book Company, 7208 Cornelia Drive, Edina, MN 55435, (612) 831-9500, FAX (612) 831-9332.

Self-Assessment Of Social Skills Mastery

A self-diagnosis questionnaire for leadership skills is given at the end of this chapter. Students complete a checklist or questionnaire about their actions in the group in order to assess how often and how well they individually performed the targeted social skill and other small group skills. There are at least two ways you may have students diagnosis the level of their social skills. You may have students complete a self-diagnosis questionnaire or engage in a learning activity as a participant-observer to diagnosis their social skills. Each group member can complete a checklist or questionnaire. The focus of the questions could be what the member did (I, me), what other members did (you, they), or what all members did (we). Self-assessments ("I" statements) are gathered from group members about how often and how well they individually performed the targeted social skills and other expected behaviors. The "you" statements give students an opportunity to give other group members feedback about which actions were perceived as helpful or unhelpful. The "we" statements provide an opportunity for group members to reach consensus about which actions helped or hurt the group's work.

Then the results are used to help analyze how well group members worked together. For each question the frequencies can be summed and divided by the number of members in order to derive an average. Or, each group member can publicly share his or her answers in a "whip." The group whips through members' answers, one question at a time, by giving each group member 30 seconds to share his or her answer to each question with no comment allowed from other group members. A third procedure is having each group member name actions he or she performed that helped the group function more effectively, and then name one action the member to his/her right (or left) performed that also helped the group. Another procedure is to have students (a) complete the self-assessment, (b) engage in a cooperative learning activity in which they have the opportunity to use the skills (the activity is observed and feedback is given to each student), and (c) compare their self-perceptions of how they used the skills with the data gathered by the observer on how they actually behaved in the situation.

Setting Goals For Continuous Improvement

The group members set goals for improving their competence in engaging in the social skills during the next group meeting. Members discuss the goals and publicly commit to achieving them. The observer helps the group set a growth goal by asking, "*What could you add to be even a better group tomorrow than you were today?*" The continuous improvement of students' competencies and group effectiveness is emphasized. The procedures for setting goals detailed in Chapter 2. A goals setting form is included in the end of this chapter.

Meaningful And Manageable Assessment Through Cooperative Learning, Interaction Book Company, 7208 Cornelia Drive, Edina, MN 55435, (612) 831-9500, FAX (612) 831-9332.

Report On Students' Social Skills

Besides reporting the results on assessing students' social skills to students during and immediately following the lesson in order to help students improve their skills, periodic summaries of students' social skills may need to be reported to other interested stakeholders, such as parents and potential employers. Students, for example, will wish to include data on their social and teamwork skills in their portfolios and discuss them in student-led conferences and employment interviews. Teachers may summarize social skill data in charts and graphs, write a narrative on each student's social skills, or complete a checklist for a parent conference or report card. An example of a social skills report card is given at the end of this chapter.

Summary

One of the most important student performances to assess is students' social competence. **Social competence** is having the consequences of your actions match your intentions. Your social competence is determined by your ability to use social skills appropriately in interactions with others. One of the most useful ways of classifying social skills is to divide them into forming, functioning, formulating, and fermenting skills. Assessing social skills is important as they largely determine personal development and identity, employability and career success, quality of life, physical health, psychological health, and ability to cope with stress. The inability to relate to others stunts growth, sparks failure, makes life meaningless, kills, creates anxiety and depression, and makes one more fragile, lost in the past, and inhumane.

The assessment of social skills consists of several steps. **First**, you review the assumptions underlying the teaching of social skills. Social skills must be learned. Every cooperative lesson is a lesson in social skills as well as academics. You must understand what social skills to teach and how to teach them. When teaching social skills be specific, start small, and emphasize overlearning. **Second**, you teach students each social skill. You show the need for the skill, define it with a t-chart, set up practice situations in which students can use the skill, ensure that students receive feedback on their use of the skill and reflect on how to improve, and ensure that students persevere in practicing the skill until it becomes automatic. **Third**, as part of teaching students social skills you structure cooperative learning situations so students can use the social skills and you can observe their doing so. **Fourth**, you intervene in the cooperative learning groups to ensure that members are using the social skills appropriately and to reinforce them for doing so. **Fifth**, you facilitate the self-diagnosis by students of the level of their mastery of the targeted social skills. Students can complete checklists or questionnaires to do so. **Sixth**, you assign students in setting improvement goals to increase their social competence. **Seventh**, you assess students' knowledge of social skills. **Finally**, you report on the level of students' social skills to interested stakeholders, such as the students, parents, and potential employers.

Other T-Charts

CHECKING FOR UNDERSTANDING

Looks Like	Sounds Like
Eye contact	Explain that to me please.
Leaning forward	Can you show me?
Interested expression	Tell us how to do it.
Open gestures and posture	How do you get that answer?
	Give me an example please.
	How would you explain it to the teacher?

Contributing Ideas

Looks Like	Sounds Like
Leaning forward	My idea is...
Open gestures and posture	I suggest...
Taking turns	We could...
Member talking with others listening	I suggest we...
	This is what I would do.
	What if we...

SUMMARIZING

Looks Like	Sounds Like
Leaning forward	Our key ideas seem to be...
Pleasant expression	Let's review what we have said so far.
Open gestures and postures	At this point, we have...
	The points we have made so far are...
	Our thinking is ...

Meaningful And Manageable Assessment Through Cooperative Learning, Interaction Book Company, 7208 Cornelia Drive, Edina, MN 55435, (612) 831-9500, FAX (612) 831-9332.

Observing Social Skills

	Jose	Tia	Helen	Total
Who Talks				

	Dale	Frank	Edythe	Total
Contributing Ideas				
Encouraging Participation				
Total				

	FRANCES	JUAN	GIA	TOTAL
Contributes Ideas				
Checks For Understanding				
Encourages Participation				
Supporter, Praiser				
Total				

Meaningful And Manageable Assessment Through Cooperative Learning, Interaction Book Company, 7208 Cornelia Drive, Edina, MN 55435, (612) 831-9500, FAX (612) 831-9332.

TEST FOR UNDERSTANDING OF FUNCTIONING (LEADERSHIP) SKILLS

The task and maintenance leadership skills are listed in column 1 and statements reflecting expressing the skills are in column 2. For each task or maintenance action, indicate which statement ("*a*" through "*l*") expresses it.

Task Actions	
_____ 1. Information and opinion giver	a. *"Helen, my understanding of you is that you are suggesting that we define the problem before we try to solve it."*
_____ 2. Information and opinion seeker.	b. *"How about giving our report on yoga while standing on our heads?"*
_____ 3. Direction and role definer	c. *"Dale thinks we should play football, Jose thinks we should go to lunch, and Tai believes we should write a story."*
_____ 4. Summarizer	d. *"I think we should help resolve the conflict between David and Linda."*
_____ 5. Energizer	e. *"George Washington was the first President of the United States and in my opinion, the best one."*
_____ 6. Checker for understanding.	f. *"Francene has not said anything for the past five minutes. Is there a problem?"*
Maintenance Actions	
_____ 7. Encourager of participation	g. *"That is an important insight Roger. It indicates you have really worked hard on the homework."*
_____ 8. Communication facilitator	h. *"Fire up! We can find a good solution. Let's put a little more effort into it."*
_____ 9. Tension reliever	i. *"Frank, explain to us step-by-step how to solve question 12."*
_____ 10. Process observer	j. *"We should first define the problem and second suggest solutions. We can then decide which solution to adopt."*
_____ 11. Interpersonal problem solver	k. *"Roger, do you know who the fourth President of the United States was and what he is famous for?"*
_____ 12. Supporter and praiser	l. *"Helen, I would like to hear what you think about this; you have good ideas."*

Answers: 1. e, 2. k, 3. j, 4. c, 5. h, 6. i, 7. l, 8. a, 9. b, 10. f, 11. d, 12. g.

Meaningful And Manageable Assessment Through Cooperative Learning, Interaction Book Company, 7208 Cornelia Drive, Edina, MN 55435, (612) 831-9500, FAX (612) 831-9332.

UNDERSTANDING YOUR LEADERSHIP ACTIONS QUESTIONNAIRE

A group member provides **leadership** any time he or she engages in an action that (a) helps the group complete its task or (b) helps the group maintain effective working relationships among its members. When you are a member of a group, which leadership actions do you engage in? How do you influence other group members to complete the task and work together effectively?

Each of the following items describes a leadership action. For each question mark:

5 *if you always behave that way*

4 *if you frequently behave that way*

3 *if you occasionally behave that way*

2 *if you seldom behave that way*

1 *if you never behave that way*

WHEN I AM A MEMBER OF A GROUP:

1. I offer facts and give my opinions, ideas, feelings, and information in order to help the group discussion.

2. I warmly encourage all members of the group to participate. I am open to their ideas. I let them know I value their contributions to the group.

3. I ask for facts, information, opinions, ideas, and feelings from the other group members in order to help the group discussion.

4. I help communication among group members by using good communication skills. I make sure that each group member understands what the others say.

5. I give direction to the group by planning how to go on with the group work and by calling attention to the tasks that need to be done. I assign responsibilities to different group members.

6. I tell jokes and suggest interesting ways of doing the work in order to reduce tension in the group and increase the fun we have working together.

7. I pull together related ideas or suggestions made by group members and restate and summarize the major points discussed by the group.

Meaningful And Manageable Assessment Through Cooperative Learning, Interaction Book Company, 7208 Cornelia Drive, Edina, MN 55435, (612) 831-9500, FAX (612) 831-9332.

8. I observe the way the group is working and use my observations to help discuss how the group can work together better.

9. I give the group energy. I encourage group members to work hard to achieve our goals.

10. I promote the open discussion of conflicts among group members in order to resolve disagreements and increase group cohesiveness. I mediate conflicts among members when they seem unable to resolve them directly.

11. I ask others to summarize what the group has been discussing in order to ensure that they understand group decisions and comprehend the material being discussed by the group.

12. I express support, acceptance, and liking for other members of the group and give appropriate praise when another member has taken a constructive action in the group.

Your Leadership Actions

In order to obtain a total score for task actions and maintenance actions, write the score for each item in the appropriate column and then add the columns.

Task Actions	Maintenance Actions
_____ 1. Information and opinion giver	_____ 2. Encourager of participation
_____ 3. Information and opinion seeker	_____ 4. Communication facilitator
_____ 5. Direction and role definer	_____ 6. Tension reliever
_____ 7. Summarizer	_____ 8. Process observer
_____ 9. Energizer	_____ 10. Interpersonal problem solver
_____ 11. Comprehension checker	_____ 12. Supporter and praiser
_____ Total For Task Actions	_____ Total For Maintenance Actions

Meaningful And Manageable Assessment Through Cooperative Learning, Interaction Book Company, 7208 Cornelia Drive, Edina, MN 55435, (612) 831-9500, FAX (612) 831-9332.

Continuously Improving My Social Skills

Skills Targeted	Checklist	Questionnaire	Observed Behavior
1.			
2.			
3.			
4.			

Conclusions:

PLAN FOR IMPROVING MY SOCIAL SKILLS:

The Time-Line For Achieving My Goals Is:

Meaningful And Manageable Assessment Through Cooperative Learning, Interaction Book Company, 7208 Cornelia Drive, Edina, MN 55435, (612) 831-9500, FAX (612) 831-9332.

Report Form: Social Skills

Student: ______________________ **Date:** _________ **Grade:** ____________

N = Needs Improvement P = Making Progress S = Satisfactory E = Excellent

Shows Cooperative Attitude (Forming Skills)

_____ Moves Into Group Quietly

_____ Stays With Group; No Wandering

_____ Uses Quiet Voice In Group Work

_____ Takes Turns

_____ Uses Others' Names

_____ Respects Rights Of Others

_____ Positive About Working In Group

_____ Is Willing To Help Others

_____ Follows Directions

_____ Shows Courtesy Toward Others

Leadership (Functioning) Skills

_____ Clarifies Goals

_____ Gives Direction To Group's Work

_____ Contributes Ideas, Opinions

_____ Requests Others' Ideas, Opinions

_____ Summarizes, Integrates

_____ Encourages Others' Participation

_____ Supports; Gives Recognition, Praise

_____ Paraphrases

_____ Facilitates Communication

_____ Relieves Tension

Facilitates Understanding (Formulating) Skills

_____ Summarizes, Integrates

_____ Seeks Accuracy (Corrects)

_____ Relates New Learning To Old

_____ Helps Group Recall Knowledge

_____ Checks For Understanding

_____ Makes Covert Reasoning Overt

Intellectual Challenge (Fermenting) Skills

_____ Criticizes Ideas, Not People

_____ Differentiates Members' Ideas

_____ Integrates Members' Ideas

_____ Asks For Rationale, Justification

_____ Extends Others' Reasoning

_____ Probes, Asks Complex Questions

Meaningful And Manageable Assessment Through Cooperative Learning, Interaction Book Company, 7208 Cornelia Drive, Edina, MN 55435, (612) 831-9500, FAX (612) 831-9332.

REPORT FORM: WORK HABITS AND PERSONAL DEVELOPMENT

Student: ____________________________ Date: __________ Grade: ______________

N = Needs Improvement P = Making Progress S = Satisfactory E = Excellent

	October	February	May	Total
____ Completes Work On Time				
____ Uses Time Wisely				
____ Checks Work				
____ Welcomes Challenges				
____ Listens Carefully				
____ Takes Risks In Learning				
____ Makes Effort Needed				
____ Meets Responsibilities				
____ Strives For High Quality Work				
____ Appropriately Asks For Help				
____ Appropriately Uses Materials				
____ Participates In Discussions				
_____ Seeks Extra Credit, Extensions				
____ Follows Rules				

Meaningful And Manageable Assessment Through Cooperative Learning, Interaction Book Company, 7208 Cornelia Drive, Edina, MN 55435, (612) 831-9500, FAX (612) 831-9332.

Chapter Ten: Assessing Student Attitudes

Importance Of Student Attitudes

W. Edwards Deming was fond of saying, *"The primary responsibility of a teacher is to create a love of learning."* If he visited your class, he would ask, "*Do your students like or dislike your class? Do they like the subject you teach? If given a chance, would they give up some of their free time to study further the topics you discuss in class? Or do they perceive your class as being boring, uninteresting, and filled with busy work?*"

All learning has affective components. Whenever a student masters knowledge or skills, she or he develops an attitude toward subject area and the processes of learning. Because students' attitudes influence future behavior, the development of positive attitudes may be more important than the mastery of specific knowledge and skills. It does little good to teach a student to read if she or he ends up disliking and avoiding reading whenever possible.

Since the overall purpose of schools is to develop each student to maximum capacity as a productive and happy member of society, an important measure of success is not the degree to which students master knowledge and skills, but whether the students voluntarily use such knowledge and skills in their daily life outside of school and in their lives after they have finished school. Besides positive attitudes toward subject areas and skills such as reading, writing, and math, schools are supposed to inculcate positive attitudes toward (a) self, (b) diverse others, (c) potential careers, and (d) positive attitudes toward being "role responsible" (having the capacity to live up to general expectations of appropriate role behavior such as promptness and cleanliness) and "role readiness" (having the ability to meet the demands of many organizational settings with the proper cooperation). Perhaps most important of all, schools are supposed to ensure students develop positive attitudes toward our pluralistic, democratic society, freedom of choice, equality of opportunity, self-reliance, and free and open inquiry into all issues.

To achieve instructional objectives such as creating life-long learners or a commitment to scholarship, the development of positive attitudes may be more important than the actual mastery of facts and knowledge. An **attitude** is a positive or negative reaction to a person, object, or idea. It is a learned predisposition to respond in a favorable or unfavorable manner to a particular person, object, or idea. They are important determinants of behavior. When instruction creates interest and enthusiasm, learning will be easier, more rapid, and result in higher achievement than when instruction promotes disinterest and negativism (Bloom, 1976; Johnson, 1970).

Meaningful And Manageable Assessment Through Cooperative Learning, Interaction Book Company, 7208 Cornelia Drive, Edina, MN 55435, (612) 831-9500, FAX (612) 831-9332

Students should regard learning as an enduring quest for meaning and understanding, not as credit accumulation or a bureaucratic requirement. Students may only learn effectively when they are open to instruction, desire to learn the material being taught, and have sufficient confidence in themselves to put forth the necessary energy and resources to overcome difficulties and obstacles. A strong desire to learn science leads to science achievement, a strong liking for Shakespeare leads to frequent reading of his plays, and a strong dislike for school leads to absentees, refusal to do homework, and withdrawal. The attitudes students develop toward a class, subject area, learning, and school determine academic achievement, educational aspirations, and academic self-esteem. Life-long learners who desire to investigate, explore new fields of thought, and gain new insights, are created more through the development of positive attitudes than through mastery of material.

Reading Objectives

1. Students should use reading as a tool for acquiring information.

2. Students should develop a life-long habit of reading good books of fiction and non-fiction.

3. Students should find relaxation and enjoyment in reading good books.

Assessing Students' Attitudes

Because of their importance on so many educational outcomes, student attitudes toward the subject area you teach, the instructional activities you use, school personnel (including you), other students, and their ability to complete assignments successfully should be assessed regularly. The information can then be used to modify and improve instructional programs so that they influence students to adopt positive attitudes toward learning. Attitudes, of course, should usually have no effect on students' grades. Components of instructional programs such as teaching strategies and curriculum materials, however, can be modified on the basis of students' attitudes.

A teacher, school, or school system can assess student attitudes through observational procedures, questionnaires (standardized or teacher-made), and interviews. Since observing and interviewing are discussed in other chapters, this chapter will focus on using questionnaires to assess students' attitudes. In planning how to use questionnaires (or observations and interviews) to measure student attitudes, the procedure you may wish to use is as follows:

1. **Decide on which attitudes to measure**. Minimally, you may wish to measure attitudes toward the subject area, the instructional methods used, and learning in general. You may also wish to determine attitudes toward classmates, academic self-esteem, and so forth.

2. **Construct a questionnaire by writing specific questions to measure the targeted attitudes**. In constructing your own questionnaires and writing your own questions:

   a. Decide on what types of questions to use.

   b. Decide which forms of response to elicit.

   c. Write well-worded questions.

   d. Arrange the questions into the optimal sequence.

   e. Ensure the physical layout is appealing and facilitates the ease with which the questionnaire may be completed and scored.

3. **Select the standardized attitude measures you wish to use if any**. Whether you use a standardized attitude measure depends on your instructional goals and expertise in using the results to improve instruction.

4. **Give your questionnaire near the beginning and then near the end of an instructional unit, semester, or year**. From such a spacing, you will be able to calculate whether attitudes have improved or deteriorated. If you use the same questions for a few years, you will be able to build norms as to how most students respond. Such multi-year comparisons are helpful in interpreting the positiveness of students' attitudes.

   a. **Use more than one question and use different types of questions in measuring student attitudes toward any one aspect of your class**. A combination of observations and questionnaires is often helpful.

   b. **Ensure and protect student anonymity**--do not ask students to put their names on the questionnaires. This increases the likelihood of getting honest responses. You can crease a system of identification that will allow you to compare pre- and post-attitudes for each student by having students make up a number combination at the beginning of the course and put it on the questionnaires. Since you do not know which student is using which number combination, students anonymity is protected. You may also wish to have each cooperative learning group decide on a number combination. Each student then writes his or her group number and his or her personal number on each questionnaire. This allows you to analyze the pre and post data for each group as well as for each individual. If trust is high, names can be used.

c. **Emphasize that you are asking students to indicate their attitudes in order to improve instruction and not to evaluate students.** Make it clear that students' attitudes will have no impact on their grades. Ask for student cooperation in giving honest reactions.

Music Objectives

1. Students appreciating music as an important part of our cultural heritage.

2. Students cultivating a taste for good music.

3. Students developing a lasting joy for good music.

5. **Analyze and organize the data for feedback to interested stake-holders and to make instructional decisions.** Calculate the means and standard deviations for each question and scale and place the results in bar and run charts.

6. **Give the feedback in a timely and orderly way and facilitate the stake-holders' use of the data.** Establish a rapid feedback system so that students (and other stake-holders) see the results (a) portrayed in an easily understandable way and (b) used in ways that clearly change the course. The data gathered are only as good as the motivation of students to give accurate information. The care and honesty with which students complete attitude questionnaires is influenced heavily by the ways in which they see the data being used. Sharing the results indicates that their cooperation is appreciated. The major flaw with most large testing programs is the failure to provide feedback concerning results and uses of the information, which decreases respondents' motivation to provide accurate and valid information. Much care and attention must be given to the delivery of testing results to interested stake-holders.

7. **Use the data on student attitudes to modify and improve the course and your teaching.** Vary your instructional methods and curriculum materials to inculcate more positive attitudes toward the subject area and learning in general.

Deciding On Which Attitudes To Measure

Which attitudes you wish to measure depends on your instructional goals and the subject matter you teach. Minimally, however, you may wish to measure attitudes toward the subject area, the instructional methods used, and learning in general. You may also wish to determine attitudes toward social support, academic self-esteem, and class cohesion.

Meaningful And Manageable Assessment Through Cooperative Learning, Interaction Book Company, 7208 Cornelia Drive, Edina, MN 55435, (612) 831-9500, FAX (612) 831-9332

Constructing Your Own Questionnaire

For most classes, you will want to construct your own questionnaire to use to measure specific aspects of the course and your success in getting students to love learning and love learning your subject area. In preparing your own questionnaire, three types of questions can be used: open-ended questions, closed-ended questions, and semantic-differential questions. **Open-ended questions** call for the student to answer by writing a statement that may vary in length. They may require respondents to give a free response or supply a word or phrase to fill-in-the-blank. Examples of open-ended questions are:

My general opinion about English is ______________________________.

My teachers are ______________________________________.

If someone suggested I take up American history as my life's work, I would reply

____.

History is my ________________ *subject.*

Such open-ended questions provide the teacher with interesting samples of student attitudes. Open-ended questions are a good way to obtain new ideas about what to ask to measure student attitudes and values. Student responses are scored by counting the number of times a word or phrase occurs. A mean and standard deviation may then be calculated. Open-ended questions, however, tend to be hard to analyze and often are not fully answered.

Closed-ended questions require the student to indicate the alternative answer closest to his or her internal response. The response they require can be dichotomous, multiple-choice, ranking, or scale. Here are some examples:

English is my favorite school subject. ___ *True* ___ *False*

Do you intend to take another course in English? ___ *Yes* ___ *No* ___ *Don't Know*

Circle each of the words that tell how you feel about English: interesting very important worthless difficult dull weird exciting boring useful

Rank these subject areas from most interesting (1) to least interesting (6) to you:

_____ *Social Studies* _____ *English*

_____ *Science* _____ *Mathematics*

_____ *Physical Education* _____ *Foreign Language*

Meaningful And Manageable Assessment Through Cooperative Learning, Interaction Book Company, 7208 Cornelia Drive, Edina, MN 55435, (612) 831-9500, FAX (612) 831-9332

How interested are you in learning more about English?

Very Uninterested 1:2:3:4:5:6:7 Very Interested

The questions are scored by counting the frequencies of each response and then calculating the mean response and the standard deviation.

Perhaps the most general method for the measurement of attitudes is **the semantic differential** (Osgood et. al., 1957). This type of question allows the teacher to present any attitude object (be it a person, issue, practice, subject area, or anything else) and obtain an indication of student attitudes toward it. A semantic-differential question consists of a series of rating scales of bipolar adjective pairs underneath the concept the teacher wishes to obtain student attitudes toward. An example is:

Poetry

Ugly 1:2:3:4:5:6:7 Beautiful

Bad 1:2:3:4:5:6:7 Good

Worthless 1:2:3:4:5:6:7 Valuable

Negative 1:2:3:4:5:6:7 Positive

The teacher then sums the response to obtain an overall indication of attitudes toward the concept. Almost any concept of interest can be used in this type of question. Each concept is listed separately with the same sets of adjectives underneath. If a teacher does not use adjective pairs that are generally evaluative, such as those given above, he or she may wish to score the responses to each adjective pair separately instead of summing them.

How Good Are Your Questions?

Writing good closed-ended and open-ended questions takes some expertise and practice. Write a series of questions to measure students' attitudes toward one of the classes you teach. Then evaluate each of the question by considering the following points:

______ *1. Is the question worded simply with no abbreviations and difficult words?*

______ *2. Are all the words in the question familiar to the respondents?*

______ *3. Is the question worded without slang phases, colloquialisms, and bureaucratic words?*

Meaningful And Manageable Assessment Through Cooperative Learning, Interaction Book Company, 7208 Cornelia Drive, Edina, MN 55435, (612) 831-9500, FAX (612) 831-9332

______ 4. *Are any words emotionally loaded, vaguely defined, or overly general?*

______ 5. Does the question have unstated assumptions or implications that lead respondents to give a certain response? (Is it desirable to rewrite the syllabus for this course?)

______ 6. Does the question presuppose a certain state of affairs? (Has your instructor improved the format of assignments?)

______ 7. Does the question ask for only one bit of information? (Rate the quality and relevance of this class.)

______ 8. Is only one adjective or adverb used in the question? (Is the teacher helpful and sensitive?)

______ 9. *Does the wording of the question imply a desired answer?*

______ 10. Do any words have a double meaning that may cause misunderstandings? (liberal, conservative, traditional)

______ 11. Are the response options mutually exclusive and sufficient to cover each conceivable answer?

______ 12. Does the question contain words that tend not to have a common meaning, such as significant, always, usually, most, never, and several?

If you are satisfied that your questions pass this test, they are ready to be pretested. A well-conducted pretest will disclose any further problems that may exist with a question.

Decisions Regarding Form Of Responses To Questions

There are two general types of responses: Open-ended responses or closed-ended responses. The types of open-ended responses are fill-in-the-blank and free responses. The types of closed-ended responses include dichotomous, multiple choice, ranking, or scale.

1. Is the question best asked as an open-ended or closed-ended question?
2. For open-ended questions, should respondents give a free response or fill-in-the-blank?

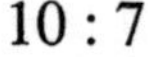

Meaningful And Manageable Assessment Through Cooperative Learning, Interaction Book Company, 7208 Cornelia Drive, Edina, MN 55435, (612) 831-9500, FAX (612) 831-9332

3. For closed-ended questions, should the response be dichotomous, multiple choice, ranking, or scale?

4. If a multiple choice or scale check response is used, does it (s) cover adequately all the significant alternatives without overlapping, (b) are the choices in a defensible order, and (c) are the response alternatives of uniform value (distance)?

One of the most common approaches for writing closed-ended questions with a scaled response is the **Likert method of summated ratings**. The procedure for developing a Likert scale is to ask several questions about the topic of interest. For each question a response scale is given with anywhere from three to nine points. Questions with five alternatives are quite common. Two ways of presenting the alternatives are:

_____*Strongly Disagree (1)*

_____*Disagree (2)*

_____*Undecided (3)*

_____*Agree (4)*

_____*Strongly Agree (5)*

Strongly Disagree 1--2--3--4--5 Strongly Agree

A student's responses for all the questions are summed together to get an overall scale indicating the student's attitudes toward the issue being measured. The results for an entire class or school may be factor analyzed to build an attitude scale consisting of more than three items.

Questionnaire Exercise: Wording Of Questions

Given below are a number of poorly written questions. Your **task** is to identify the fault in each question. Find a partner and **cooperatively** decide on answers. Both of you must agree and be able to explain why each question is poorly written.

1. Is the science text informative and interesting?

   No 1--2--3--4--5--6--7 Yes

2. Good health habits are a good thing, aren't they?

   No 1--2--3--4--5--6--7 Yes

3. Do you still fail examinations?

   No 1--2--3--4--5--6--7 Yes

Meaningful And Manageable Assessment Through Cooperative Learning, Interaction Book Company, 7208 Cornelia Drive, Edina, MN 55435, (612) 831-9500, FAX (612) 831-9332

4. Does the teacher give you instructions parsimoniously?

No 1--2--3--4--5--6--7 Yes

5. Is it desirable to teach history?

No 1--2--3--4--5--6--7 Yes

6. Does learning good health habits usually prolong one's life?

No 1--2--3--4--5--6--7 Yes

7. Are history classes too liberal?

No 1--2--3--4--5--6--7 Yes

8. Is mathematics a communist plot?

No 1--2--3--4--5--6--7 Yes

9. Don't you believe that all high school students should not take advanced math courses?

No 1--2--3--4--5--6--7 Yes

10. Does your math class stress competition?

No 1-2-3-4-5-6-7 Yes

11. Think of the English class you have taken that stands out as being the worst class you have even attended (do not identify the class). Very briefly and frankly describe what made the class so bad. ____

____

12. Which area of the country has the best health education program?

______ Midwest ______ Northeast ______ West

13. Which of the following do you like the best?

______ Quebec ______ Manitoba

______ British Columbia ______ Canada

14. Are science classes taught in a way that is:

_____ poor _____ good _____ satisfactory _____ excellent

Meaningful And Manageable Assessment Through Cooperative Learning, Interaction Book Company, 7208 Cornelia Drive, Edina, MN 55435, (612) 831-9500, FAX (612) 831-9332

15. Do you like math?

_____No _____Yes

16. What is your age? ______

Questionnaire Exercise: Answers

1. The first question is, in measurement terms, "double- barreled'; it asks for two bits of information at once. The problem arises when the respondent thinks the science text was informative but boring or interesting and uninformative.

2. The wording of this question implies a desired answer.

3. This question presupposes a certain state of affairs, mainly that the respondent has previously failed examinations.

4. Many respondents may not know the definition of "parsimoniously." The question is ambiguous because the word parsimonious is obscure.

5. The word "desirable" is overly general.

6. The word "usually" is too vague and does not have a common meaning.

7. The word "liberal" has a double meaning. It could mean political liberal or it could be too generous.

8. The words "communist plot" are too emotionally loaded to obtain a valid response. Emotionally loaded words bias answers and slant the respondent for a particular answer.

9. This question has a double negative that is confusing.

10. This is a leading question that suggests competition is a possible emphasis of math courses.

11. This question contains long and difficult sentences that are likely to be misunderstood. It also is loaded with unstated assumptions. This question presupposes previous states of affairs. It presupposes that the respondent has attended several English classes and presupposes that one or more were "bad." The respondents may not have the information needed to answer the question.

12. The responses for this question are incomplete. All areas of the country need to be listed. It does not allow for every possible response.

13. The responses are not equal. Canada includes all of the above.

14. The responses are not balanced.

15. The problem with this question is response restriction. What if you do not care one way or the other?

16. This question is too private, may embarrass the respondent, lead to resistance, evasion, or deception.

Decisions On Question Content (Apart From Wording)

1. Define your goals for the questionnaire. Your goals will point towards the information you wish to obtain (that is, the domains of information you wish to sample).

2. Write questions relevant to the domains. Then assess the quality of your questions against the following criteria.

3. **Criterion 1: Is the question necessary?** The question may ask for information that is (a) already covered in another question or (b) more detailed than necessary.

4. **Criterion 2: Does the question cover too much?**

   a. Should the question be sub-divided?

   b. Does the question adequately cover the ground intended?

   c. Is additional related material needed to interpret the answers?

   d. Is further information needed on respondents' intensity of feelings?

   e. Is further information needed on how important the respondent considers the issue?

5. **Criterion 3: Do respondents have the information necessary to answer the question?**

   a. Does the questions call for answers that the respondent either cannot give at all or cannot give reliably?

   b. Is the focus of the question such that it should be answered by some respondents and not others?

c. Are alternative questions required to fit the content of the question with different types of respondents.

6. **Criterion 4: Does the question need to be more concrete, specific, and closely related to the respondent's personal experience?** Does it ask about specific recent events rather than what the respondent "usually" does?

7. **Criterion 5: Is the question content sufficiently general and free from spurious concreteness and specificity?** Do the replies express general attitudes and only seem to be specific?

8. **Criterion 6: Is the question content biased or loaded in one direction without accompanying questions to balance the emphasis?** Would the content be accepted as fair by an informed person with opposite views?

9. **Criterion 7: Will the respondents give the information sought?**

   a. Is the material too private, of an embarrassing nature, or otherwise likely to lead to resistance, evasion, or deception?

   b. Is the question likely to encounter emotional influences and desires that will lead to falsification of answers?

Question Sequence

A questionnaire (or interview) consists of a series of question sequences. The order of the sequences must be arranged so that responses are unbiased. In ordering your questions, you may wish to use the "funnel" sequence with various "filter" questions. The **funnel sequence** starts off with broad questions and then progressively narrows down the scope of the questions until very specific questions are asked at the end. Suppose, for example, you wanted to know whether some students avoided English because of the demands to learn grammar. You would not want to begin your questionnaire with questions that directly asked what you wanted to know, such as:

Q1: Do you believe that English classes are too hard because of having to learn grammar?

Q2: Do you avoid taking English classes because you do not want to learn grammar?

These are grossly leading questions that rule out the possibility that there may be other reasons why a student does not wish to take an English class. It would be more

Meaningful And Manageable Assessment Through Cooperative Learning, Interaction Book Company, 7208 Cornelia Drive, Edina, MN 55435, (612) 831-9500, FAX (612) 831-9332

valuable if students spontaneously stated they avoided English because it involves grammar before the students realized what the questions are really about. Therefore, you may wish to start off with very broad questions, such as:

Q3: What is your opinion of English as a course of study?

Q4: What do you think of students who take lots of English classes?

Each question provides the respondent with an opportunity to mention the issue of grammar spontaneously. Next, you may wish to ask more restricted questions, such as:

Q5: What English classes are you taking this year?

Q6: How many English classes have you taken in previous years?

Q7: Do you recommend English classes to your friends?

Each question should be followed up by "Why?" if the reply is negative, thus providing further opportunities for the grammar issue to emerge spontaneously. After that, you may narrow the questions still further:

Q8: Do you believe that English classes are undesirable in any way?

Q9: What are some of the difficulties in taking English classes?

Q10: Why do some students avoid taking English classes?

Note that the grammar issue still have not be mentioned directly. Finally, you being up the issue as nondirectively as possible:

Q11: Some students believe that English classes are too hard because you have to learn grammar, but others believe that learning grammar does not take away from the overall interesting and useful things you learn in English classes. What do you believe?

Q12: Do you believe that English classes are too hard because you have to learn grammar or do you believe that learning grammar does not take away from the interesting and useful things you learn in English?

By proceeding in this way you not only increase your chances of obtaining what you are seeking through a spontaneous reply, you also place the whole issue of grammar and English classes in the context of some of the other factors that determine whether students take English. This context is very important; it may be that other reasons for not taking English are mentioned far more frequently than grammar.

A **filter question** is used to exclude a respondent from a particular sequence of questions if the questions are not relevant to him or her. Thus, in the above example, you might wish to ask for some factual information about enrollment in English classes. Obviously, if the student is taking English then there is no point in asking him or her about why English classes are avoided.

Q1: Are you currently enrolled in an English class?

Q2: Have you taken an English class in the last year?

If the answer is yes, then the student can skip the next few questions and proceed to the beginning of the next question sequence.

In a questionnaire (or interview), try to avoid (a) putting ideas into respondents' minds and (b) suggesting that they have attitudes when they do not. With any issue, you will want to start with open questions and only introduce more structured or precoded questions in a later stage.

Frequently, questions are grouped either by content or by response form. All questions dealing with attitudes toward English may be grouped together, or all multiple-choice items may be grouped together. If all questions are of equal importance and specificity, and no logical grouping is apparent, the standard procedure is to arrange the questions in random order.

The following criteria may help in deciding where to place a question in a sequence:

_____ 1. Did you begin the questionnaire with a few non-threatening questions?

_____ 2. Is the answer to the question likely to be influenced by the content of the preceding questions?

_____ 3. Is the question sequenced in correct psychological order?

_____ 4. Does the question come too early or too late from the point of view of arousing interest, receiving sufficient attention, and avoiding resistance?

_____ 5. Are items grouped logically either by content or response form?

_____ 6. If all questions are of equal importance and no sequence is necessary, did you arrange the questions in random order.

_____ 7. Are filter questions used when appropriate?

_____ 8. Are questions arranged like a funnel with the most general questions first and the most specific questions last?

_____ 9. Are all personal questions placed last?

Physical Layout Of Questionnaire

_____ 1. Did you identify the nature of the questionnaire with a title in bold type on the first page?

_____ 2. Did you include brief but clear instructions?

_____ 3. Are the pages numbered?

_____ 4. Does the appearance of the questionnaire encourage respondents to spend the time and effort needed to complete it?

_____ 5. Is the layout of the questionnaire such that it will be easy to tabulate and summarize responses?

_____ 6. If you are using a long checklist, did you group the items in threes to help respondents keep their place?

Overall Format Of Your Questionnaire?

After you have built the questions, they need to be placed in a questionnaire. The overall format of the questionnaire will have important effects on whether students complete it truthfully. Some general guidelines for evaluating your questionnaire as a whole are:

_____ *1. Have you begun the questionnaire with interesting and easy to answer questions?*

_____ *2. Does the questionnaire look as professional as possible?*

_____ *3. Will the questionnaire appeal to students and motivate them to complete it?*

_____ *4. Does the questionnaire contain brief and precise instructions where they are needed?*

_____ *5. Is the format conducive to your chosen method of summarization (tabulating, key punching)?*

_____ *6. Are students able to complete the questionnaire?*

Meaningful And Manageable Assessment Through Cooperative Learning, Interaction Book Company, 7208 Cornelia Drive, Edina, MN 55435, (612) 831-9500, FAX (612) 831-9332

My View Of This Class Is

Answer each question below with your best opinion. Do not leave any questions blank.

1. My general opinion about history is ______________________________.

2. History is my ______________ subject.

3. If someone suggested I take up history as my life's work, I would reply ______________________________.

4. History is my favorite school subject. ___ True ___ False

5. Do you intend to take another course in history? __Yes __No __I'm not sure

6. How interested are you in learning more about history?

Very interested 1:2:3:4:5:6:7 Very uninterested

History

Ugly 1:2:3:4:5:6:7 Beautiful

Bad 1:2:3:4:5:6:7 Good

Worthless 1:2:3:4:5:6:7 Valuable

Negative 1:2:3:4:5:6:7 Positive

Standardized Attitude Measures: Classroom Life

To evaluate the impact of educational strategies and programs on student attitudes and values at the school and school district level, an instrument with established validity and reliability is needed. The **Classroom Life Measure** (Johnson & Johnson, 1983) contains 85 Likert-type questions on which respondents indicate on a 5-point scale the truth of the statement where a rating of "1" indicates that the statement is very untrue and a rating of "5" indicates that the statement is very true. It contains 15 factors that have been identified both theoretically and through previous factor analysis (Johnson & Johnson, 1983; Johnson, Johnson, & Anderson, 1983). The factors, their descriptions, their number of items, and their reliability coefficients may be found in Table 1. This survey was used to gather descriptive information about student interaction and perception of their evening study environment.

Meaningful And Manageable Assessment Through Cooperative Learning, Interaction Book Company, 7208 Cornelia Drive, Edina, MN 55435, (612) 831-9500, FAX (612) 831-9332

Table 1: Scales Included in the Classroom Life Instrument

Scale	Description	Items	Reliability
Cooperative Learning	Liking for and positive attitudes toward working cooperative with other students	7	0.83
Positive Goal Interdependence	Perceptions of joint outcomes and ensuring that all group members learn the assigned material	6	0.61
Resource Interdependence	Perceptions of sharing materials, having a division of labor, and jigsawing materials	5	0.74
Teacher Academic Support	Belief teacher cares about how much one learns & wishes to help one learn	4	0.78
Teacher Personal Support	Belief teacher cares about and likes one as a person	4	0.80
Student Academic Support	Belief classmates care about how much one learns and wish to help one learn	4	0.67
Student Personal Support	Belief classmates care about and like one as a person	5	0.78
Class Cohesion	Belief students in class are friends and like each other	5	0.51
Academic Self-Esteem	Belief one is a good student and is doing a good job of learning	5	0.61
Fairness Of Grading	Belief students get the grades they deserve & hard work leads to success	5	0.61
Achieving For Social Approval	Belief one achieves to please teachers, parents, and peers	5	0.72
Alienation	Belief one is estranged from school, peers, and classroom activities	11	0.68
Learning With Heterogeneous Peers	Belief working with diverse peers is interesting and beneficial	4	0.51
Competitive Learning	Liking for and positive attitudes toward competing with classmates	8	0.80
Individualistic Learning	Liking for and positive attitudes toward learning alone	7	0.80

Making Decisions On The Basis Of Attitudes

If the school does not teach values, it will have the effect of denying them.

Gordon Allport, 1961, p. 215

The attitudinal data collected by teacher-constructed questionnaires and standardized attitudinal measures is organized to facilitate decisions about how to improve student learning and instruction. Once students have filled out the questionnaire(s), you:

_____ 1. Score the questionnaires.

_____ 2. Calculate a mean for the class as a whole and for each learning group.

_____ 3. Organize feedback for the class, each cooperative learning groups, and each student.

_____ 4. Give individual feedback to students and help plan how to increase the positiveness of their attitudes toward the subject area, the instructional experience, and learning.

_____ 5. Give groups feedback and help them plan how to increase the positiveness of members' attitudes toward the subject area, the instructional experience, and learning.

_____ 6. Give teachers feedback and help them plan how to improve the quality of (a) instruction and (b) specific interventions to increase the positiveness of students' attitudes toward the subject area, the instructional experience, and learning.

Summary

Attitudes are learned positive or negative reactions to a person, object, or idea. They are one of the most important outcomes of instruction, as they largely determine whether students continue to study the subject area, become uninterested, or wish to avoid it in the future. In assessing student attitudes, you (a) decide which attitudes to measure, (b) construct a questionnaire, (c) select a standardized measure if it is appropriate, (d) give the measures near the beginning and end of each instructional unit, semester, or year, (e) analyze and organize the data for feedback to interested stakeholders, (f) give the feedback in a timely and orderly way, and (g) use the results to make decisions about improving the instructional program.

In deciding on which attitudes to assess, include attitudes toward the subject area, the instructional methods used, and learning in general. Then construct a questionnaire that may contain open-ended, closed-ended, or semantic differential questions. Each question needs to be well-worded and requiring either an open-ended (fill-in-the-blank or free response) or closed-ended (dichotomous, multiple choice, ranking, or scale) responses. The questions are then arranged in an appropriate sequence and given an attractive format. A standardized questionnaire, such as the Classroom Life instrument may be used to measure a broader range of attitudes.

Classroom Life

Directions: On the answer sheet, next to each statement, write the number which tells how true each of these statements is of you.

False All The Time	False Some Of The Time	Neither False Nor True	True Some Of The Time	True All The Time
1	**2**	**3**	**4**	**5**

1. Other students in this class want me to do my best school work.
2. My best friends are in this class.
3. I am not doing as well in school as I would like to.
4. I find it hard to speak my thoughts clearly when I am in this class.
5. In this class, the other students like to help me learn.
6. Schoolwork is fairly easy for me.
7. Other students in this class think it is important to be my friend.
8. When we work together in small groups, we try to make sure that everyone in the group learns the assigned material.
9. I learn more from students who are similar to me.

10. I do schoolwork to make my teacher happy.
11. In this class it is important that we learn things by ourselves.
12. I like to work with other students in this class.
13. I should get along with other students better than I do.
14. I do schoolwork because my classmates expect it of me.
15. My teacher really cares about me.
16. When we work together in small groups, our job is not done until everyone in the group has completed the assignment.
17. In this class, we work together.

Meaningful And Manageable Assessment Through Cooperative Learning, Interaction Book Company, 7208 Cornelia Drive, Edina, MN 55435, (612) 831-9500, FAX (612) 831-9332

False All The Time	False Some Of The Time	Neither False Nor True	True Some Of The Time	True All The Time
1	2	3	4	5

18. In this class, we spend a lot of time working at our own desks.

19. I learn new things from arguing with other students.

20. My teacher thinks it is important to be my friend.

21. In this class, everyone has an equal chance to succeed if they do their best.

22. In this class, other students care about how much I learn.

23. Whenever I take a test I am afraid I will fail.

24. When we work together in small groups, we all receive bonus points if everyone scores above a certain criteria.

25. In this class, other students like me the way I am.

26. When we work together in small groups, we all receive the same grade.

27. My teacher cares about how much I learn.

28. I do schoolwork to make my parents happy.

29. I would rather work alone than argue.

30. In this class, everybody is my friend.

31. Other students in this class want me to come to class every day.

32. I do schoolwork to keep my teacher from getting mad at me.

33. In this class, students check answers with other students.

34. In this class, we do not talk to other students when we work.

35. When we work together in small groups, our grade depends on how much all members learn.

36. My teacher likes to see my work.

Meaningful And Manageable Assessment Through Cooperative Learning, Interaction Book Company, 7208 Cornelia Drive, Edina, MN 55435, (612) 831-9500, FAX (612) 831-9332

False All The Time	False Some Of The Time	Neither False Nor True	True Some Of The Time	True All The Time
1	2	3	4	5

37. Other students in this class care about my feelings.

38. I often get discouraged in school.

39. Other students in this class like me as much as they like others.

40. In this class, we help each other with our schoolwork.

41. I like being in a group where students often disagree with each other.

42. If a student works hard, he or she can definitely succeed in this class.

43. My teacher likes to help me learn.

44. When we work together in small groups, I have to make sure that the other members learn if I want to do well on the assignment.

45. In this class, we work by ourselves.

46. In this class, other students really care about me.

47. I have a lot of questions I never get a chance to ask in class.

48. I do schoolwork to be liked by other students.

49. In this class, we learn more when we work with others.

50. My teacher wants me to do my best schoolwork.

51. When we work together in small groups, we cannot complete an assignment unless everyone contributes.

52. My teacher likes me as much as he or she likes other students.

53. I am often lonely in this class.

54. In this class, students get the scores they deserve, no more and no less.

55. My teacher cares about my feelings.

Meaningful And Manageable Assessment Through Cooperative Learning, Interaction Book Company, 7208 Cornelia Drive, Edina, MN 55435, (612) 831-9500, FAX (612) 831-9332

False All The Time	False Some Of The Time	Neither False Nor True	True Some Of The Time	True All The Time
1	2	3	4	5

56. All the students in this class know each other well.

57. I deserve the scores I get in this class.

58. I am a good student.

59. When we work together in small groups, the teacher divides up the material so that everyone has a part and everyone has to share.

60. I like being in a learning group with students who are different from me.

61. I often feel upset in school.

62. Arguing with other students makes me feel unhappy.

63. I have more fun when I work with students who are different from me.

64. I learn more from students who are different from me.

65. Sometimes I think the scoring system in this class is not fair.

66. When we work together in small groups, we have to share materials in order to complete the assignment.

67. I like to share my ideas and materials with other students.

68. It bothers me when I have to do it all myself.

69. I like my work better when I do it all myself.

70. I like the challenge of seeing who's best.

71. I don't like to be second.

72. When we work together in small groups, everyone's ideas are needed if we are going to be successful.

73. I am happiest when I am competing with other students.

74. Competing with other students is a good way to work.

Meaningful And Manageable Assessment Through Cooperative Learning, Interaction Book Company, 7208 Cornelia Drive, Edina, MN 55435, (612) 831-9500, FAX (612) 831-9332

False All The Time 1	False Some Of The Time 2	Neither False Nor True 3	True Some Of The Time 4	True All The Time 5

75. I do not like working with other students in school.

76. I can learn important things from other students.

77. I work to get better grades than other students do.

78. I like to help other students learn.

79. I like to compete with other students to see who can do the best work.

80. Working in small groups is better than working alone.

81. I try to share my ideas and materials with other students when I think it will help them.

82. When we work together in small groups, I have to find out what everyone else knows if I am going to be able to do the assignment.

83. It is a good idea for students to help each other learn.

84. I like to do better work than other students.

85. I like to cooperate with other students.

86. I like to work with other students.

87. I do better work when I work alone.

88. Students learn a lot of important things from each other.

89. I would rather work on schoolwork alone than with other students.

90. I like to be the best student in the class.

91. I am doing a good job of learning in class.

Meaningful And Manageable Assessment Through Cooperative Learning, Interaction Book Company, 7208 Cornelia Drive, Edina, MN 55435, (612) 831-9500, FAX (612) 831-9332

Classroom Life: Scales

Teacher Academic Support

27. My teacher cares about how much I learn.

36. My teacher likes to see my work.

43. My teacher likes to help me learn.

50. My teacher wants me to do my best schoolwork.

Teacher Personal Support

15. My teacher really cares about me.

20. My teacher thinks it is important to be my friend.

52. My teacher likes me as much as he or she likes other students.

55. My teacher cares about my feelings.

Student Academic Support

1. Other students in this class want me to do my best schoolwork.

5. In this class, other students like to help me learn.

22. In this class, other students care about how much I learn.

31. Other students in this class want me to come to class every day.

Student Personal Support

7. Other students in this class think it is important to be my friend.

25. In this class, other students like me the way I am.

39. Other students in this class like me as much as they like others.

46. In this class, other students really care about me.

37. Other students in this class care about my feelings.

Cooperation

67. In this class, I like to share my ideas and materials with other students.

76. In this class, I can learn important things from other students.

Meaningful And Manageable Assessment Through Cooperative Learning, Interaction Book Company, 7208 Cornelia Drive, Edina, MN 55435, (612) 831-9500, FAX (612) 831-9332

78. In this class, I like to help other students learn.

81. In this class, I try to share my ideas and materials with other students when I think it will help them.

83. In this class, it is a good idea for students to help each other learn.

85. In this class, I like to cooperate with other students.

88. In this class, students learn a lot of important things from each other.

Cooperation, Scale Two

17. In this class, we work together.

33. In this class, students check answers with other students.

40. In this class, we help each other with our schoolwork.

49. In this class, we learn more when we work with others.

Positive Goal Interdependence

8. When we work together in small groups, we try to make sure that everyone in our group learns the assigned material.

16. When we work together in small groups, our job is not done until everyone in our group has finished the assignment.

24. When we work together in small groups, we all receive bonus points if everyone scores above a certain criteria.

66. When we work together in small groups, we have to share materials in order to complete the assignment.

72. When we work together in small groups, everyone's ideas are needed if we are going to be successful.

82. When we work together in small groups, I have to find out what everyone else knows if I am going to be able to do the assignment.

Resource Interdependence

51. When we work together in small groups, we cannot complete an assignment unless everyone contributes.

59. When we work together in small groups, the teacher divides the material so that everyone has a part and everyone has to share.

66. When we work together in small groups, we have to share materials in order to complete the assignment.

72. When we work together in small groups, everyone's ideas are needed if we are going to be successful.

82. When we work together in small groups, I have to find out what everyone else knows if I am going to be able to do the assignment.

Alienation

3. I am not doing as well in school as I would like to.

4. I find it hard to speak my thoughts clearly when I am in this class.

6. *Schoolwork is fairly easy for me.

13. I should get along with other students better than I do.

23. Whenever I take a test I am afraid I will fail.

38. I often get discouraged in school.

47. I have a lot of questions I never get a chance to ask in class.

53. I am often lonely in this class.

58. I am a good student.

61. I often feel upset in school.

65. Sometimes I think the scoring system in this class is not fair.

Extrinsic Motivation, Social Support

10. I do schoolwork to make my teacher happy.

14. I do schoolwork because my classmates expect it of me.

28. I do schoolwork to make my parents happy.

32. I do schoolwork to keep my teacher from getting mad at me.

48. I do schoolwork to be liked by other students.

Cohesion

2. My best friends are in this class.

12. I like to work with other students in this class.

30. In this class everybody is my friend.

53. *I am often lonely in this class.

56. All the students in this class know each other well.

Academic Self-Esteem

3. *I am not doing as well in school as I would like to.

6. Schoolwork is fairly easy for me.

91. I am doing a good job of learning in this class.

58. I am a good student.

23. Whenever I take a test I am afraid I will fail.

Fairness Of Grading

21. In this class, everyone has an equal chance to succeed if they do their best.

42. In this class, if a student works hard, he/she can definitely succeed.

57. In this class, I deserve the scores I get.

65. *In this class, sometimes I think the scoring system is not fair.

54. In this class, students get the scores they deserve, no more and no less.

Individualistic Learning

11. In this class it is important that we learn things by ourselves.

18. In this class, we spend a lot of time working at our own desks.

34. In this class, we do not talk to other students when we work.

45. In this class, we work by ourselves.

68. *It bothers me when I have to do it all myself.

75. I don't like working with other students in school.

80. *Working in small group is better than working alone.

86. *I like to work with other students.

87. I do better work when I work alone.

89. I would rather work on school work alone than with other students.

69. I like my work better when I do it all myself.

Competitive Learning

70. I like the challenge of seeing who's best.

71. I don't like to be second.

73. I am happiest when I am competing with other students.

74. Competing with other students is a good way to work.

77. I work to get better grades than other students do.

79. I like to compete with other students to see who can do the best work.

84. I like to do better work than other students.

90. I like to be the best student in the class.

Controversy

19. I learn new things from arguing with other students.

29. *I would rather work alone than argue.

41. I like being in a group where students often disagree with each other.

62. *Arguing with other students makes me feel unhappy.

Valuing Heterogeneity

9. *I learn more from students who are similar to me.

60. I like being in a learning group with students who are different from me.

63. I have more fun when I work with students who are different from me.

64. I learn more from students who are different from me.

Meaningful And Manageable Assessment Through Cooperative Learning, Interaction Book Company, 7208 Cornelia Drive, Edina, MN 55435, (612) 831-9500, FAX (612) 831-9332

Chapter Eleven: Interviewing

What Is An Interview

Very closely related to giving questionnaires is conducting interviews. An **interview** is a personal interaction between the interviewer (the teacher) and one or more interviewees (students) in which verbal questions are asked and verbal or linguistic responses are given. An interview may involve one student or a small group of students. The personal interaction between interviewer and the interviewee(s) and the verbal or linguistic nature of the data are what constitutes the major strengths and weaknesses of the interview procedure. Interviews may take place before, during, and after a lesson or instructional unit. Interviews can focus on a book read, a project completed, a research paper written, a film or video made, a field trip taken, a guest speaker heard, a composition written, a work of art seen, a piece of music heard, foreign language learned, a problem solved, a scientific experiment conducted, a portfolio completed, or even the procedure used to fix a car.

The key difference between a questionnaire and an interview is that in an interview, the interviewer and the respondent are both present as the questions are asked and answered. Questions and answers can thus be clearly communicated and misunderstandings can be identified and immediately clarified. The interviewer has the opportunity to observe both the student and the total situation to which the student is responding. The key problem with interviewing is the subjective nature of asking questions and recording student responses.

Interviews are often structured according to what type of question they contain. There are two types of questions: fixed-alternative (closed-ended) and open-ended questions. **Fixed-alternative** or closed-ended questions are used when possible alternatives are known, limited, and clear cut (*English class is lots of fun.* _____ *Yes* _____ *No*). They are well suited to obtaining factual information and knowledge. The advantages of closed-ended questions are that they (a) are easy to understand, (b) are easy to administer, (c) require the respondent, not the interviewer, to make judgments, (c) quick and inexpensive to analyze, and (d) eliminates the possibility of irrelevant answers. Their disadvantages include (a) they force respondents' to give an answer that does not reflect their true knowledge or opinion, (b) important alternative responses may not be included, and (c) the alternatives may be interpreted differently by various respondents.

Open-ended questions are used when issues are complex, when relevant dimensions are not known, or when the purpose of the interview is exploration of students' knowledge and reasoning processes. Perhaps the best way to determine whether a student understands a subject or problem is simply to ask the student to explain what he or she knows. The advantages of open-ended questions are that they (a) provide information on students' reasoning, (b) do not bias responses by suggesting alternatives, and (c) provide the opportunity to clarify and probe a response. Disadvantages include that they (a) are difficult to administer, (b) require extensive training of the interviewer as well as competence, and (c) elicit responses that are complex and difficult to analyze.

Why Interview Students

Interviewing is an important assessment and teaching procedure. For **assessment**, interviewing students provides information concerning students' learning, level of understanding, reasoning processes, meta-cognitive thought processes, and retention. Any student of any age or ability level can be interviewed. The learning of preschool and primary students who cannot read or write can be assessed in an interview. The learning of unmotivated students who do not express what they know on tests can be assessed in an interview. **Oral examinations**, in which students are interviewed about what they have learned, are especially useful for students who have certain learning disabilities (such as dyslexia) that impair their ability to read or write. Paper and pencil tests may seriously understate such students' actual understanding of the material being studied. Through oral interviews, the students' true level of achievement may be identified.

For **teaching**, interviewing helps students (a) clarify their thinking, (b) reflect on their learning, (c) achieve new levels of understanding, (d) believe their ideas are valued, (e) appreciate their progress, and (f) set future goals. **Socratic interviewing**, for example, is a historical procedure of using an interview to lead students to deeper and deeper insights about what they know.

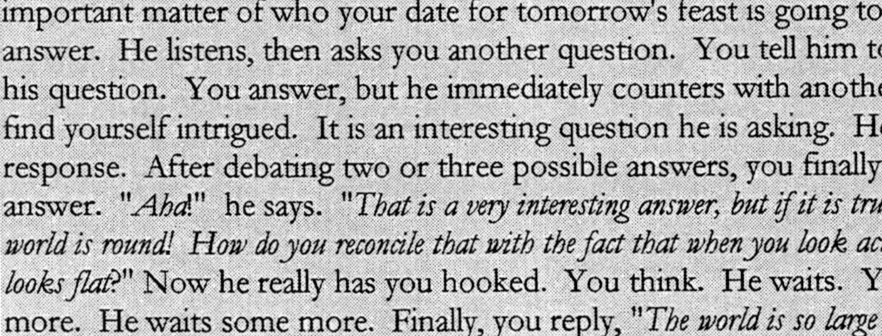

Image yourself standing on a street corner in Athens about 390 BC. You're thinking about how you're going to get a date for tomorrow's feast when along comes Socrates. Socrates asks you a question. To get rid of him so you can go back to the more important matter of who your date for tomorrow's feast is going to be, you give a short answer. He listens, then asks you another question. You tell him to leave. He repeats his question. You answer, but he immediately counters with another question. You find yourself intrigued. It is an interesting question he is asking. He waits for your response. After debating two or three possible answers, you finally give your best answer. "*Aha!*" he says. "*That is a very interesting answer, but if it is true, it implies that the world is round! How do you reconcile that with the fact that when you look across a field, the world looks flat?*" Now he really has you hooked. You think. He waits. You think some more. He waits some more. Finally, you reply, "*The world is so large that when you look across a field you see too small a segment of the world to perceive a noticeable curve.*" "*That is a brilliant hypothesis,*" Socrates tells you, "*why don't you skip the feast tomorrow and develop it so it can be tested?*" You find yourself agreeing to do just that. Figuring out this problem is far more interesting than going to a feast. As Socrates walks away you yell, "*Why didn't you*

Meaningful And Manageable Assessment Through Cooperative Learning, Interaction Book Company, 7208 Cornelia Drive, Edina, MN 55435, (612) 831-9500, FAX (612) 831-9332.

just tell me the world was large and round?" "I don't believe in putting 'ready made' ideas into students' minds," says Socrates. *"The only true way students can learn is to be led by questioning to their own 'discoveries'!"*

While this example fictionalizes what Socrates actually did, it does reflect that Socrates (470 - 339 BC) believed that direct questioning students face-to-face was the means of inducing thinking and thereby leading the student to discover his or her own wisdom. Through questioning he would induce cognitive conflict within the student, which in turn would motivate the student toward further inquiry. In essence, the Socratic method of teaching is an oral interview in which the inconsistencies and conflicts in a student's reasoning are highlighted to motivate the student to engage in a deeper level of thinking.

Being A Socrates

1. Choose a topic being studied.

2. Develop two or three general questions on what the student knows about the topic to begin an interview.

3. After asking the opening questions, probe what the student knows while looking for inconsistencies, contradictions, or conflicts in what the student is saying.

4. Ask follow-up questions that highlight the conflicts within the student's reasoning and makes the contradictions focal points for the student's attention.

5. Continue the interview until the student has resolved the conflicts by moving towards deeper-level analysis of what he or she knows and arriving at greater and greater insights into the material being studied.

6. Conclude the interview with pointing the student toward further resources to read and study.

This combination of assessing what students know and understand while teaching students "*their own wisdom*" by leading them into deeper insights and better conceptualized frameworks makes interviewing one of the most important assessment tools. The direct interaction in an interview provides more opportunity to motivate

Meaningful And Manageable Assessment Through Cooperative Learning, Interaction Book Company, 7208 Cornelia Drive, Edina, MN 55435, (612) 831-9500, FAX (612) 831-9332.

students to do their best, motivate students to supply accurate and complete information immediately, probe for attitudes and beliefs, reveal the complexity of students' reasoning, clarify communication, and guide students in their interpretations of the questions. Interviewing may provide the most flexibility in assessing and teaching students while at the same time giving teachers the most control over the assessment situation.

Perhaps the greatest strength of the interview is the opportunity it provides to build positive relationships between you (the teacher) and your students. Through the direct, face-to-face interaction, you can create a more personal, positive, supportive, and trusting relationship with the student. Supportive relationships improve the learning climate of the class and school. You can establish norms about the relationship, build rapport and closeness, and generally get acquainted with the student.

How To Interview Students

The simplest way to interview students is to develop a questionnaire with closed-ended questions and read the questionnaire to the student while marking down their responses. While this guarantees that students answer each question, this procedure does not capitalize on the flexibility and strengths of interviewing.

The **focused interview** arranges questions like a funnel so that the initial questions are broad and general and subsequent questions require the student to be more and more precise and specific in his or her answers. The interviewer has the freedom to explore and probe in directions that are unanticipated. Only the initial questions are planned, as the subsequent questions are built on the statements made by the student being interviewed. Each student receives a different interview as each follow-up question is idiosyncratic to the student's previous response. You (the teacher), for example, may ask for the student's analysis of King Lear by Shakespeare and, according to what the student says in response, ask a series of questions that require the student to reveal more and more of his or her impressions of and reasoning about the play.

The primary purpose of a **small-group interview** is to assess whether all group members have mastered and understood the assigned material. Conducting a small group interview begins with assigning students to cooperative learning groups. The groups should be heterogeneous. Give a set of questions to the groups on Monday. Instruct the students to prepare all group members to respond to the questions. Give time during each class period for the groups to practice their responses to the questions. On Thursday and Friday conduct an oral examination with the students, using the following procedure.

You meet with a group and randomly select one member to explain the answer to a randomly selected question. When that member finishes responding to the question, other group members can add to the answer. Judge the answer to be "adequate" or "inadequate." Then ask another member a different question. Repeat this procedure until all questions have been answered or until you (the teacher) judge the group to be inadequately prepared. In this case, you ask the group to return to the assignments until members are better prepared. Give some guidance by identifying particular weaknesses and strengths in the member's answers. All group members are given equal credit for successfully passing the test. Among the many advantages of small group interviews are that you can quickly sample students' level of learning while making personal contact with each student. The disadvantages of the group interview are that (a) there may be a chaining effect that biases responses and (b) the group may inhibit some individuals.

Guidelines For Interviewing

1. Word and organize the questions so that the relationship between you and the student becomes more positive and trusting. A positive, trusting relationship encourages both you and the student to feel at ease, be spontaneous, respond honestly, and communicate effectively.

2. Phrase questions so that (a) students do not become defensive, (b) students' thoughts are clarified, (c) students have the opportunity to expand or modify, (d) you do not put ideas into the student's mind, and (e) you do not suggest that students should have attitudes when they have none.

3. Begin the interview with simple, non-threatening questions and save the move complex and threatening questions for the end of the interview.

4. Move from general to specific questions.

5. Make nonverbal cues helpful to eliciting full and complete responses from the student. Avoid smiling too much and excessive affirmative nodding of the head.

6. Be quiet. What the student needs is a skillful, empathetic listener.

7. Allow sufficient wait-time for students to formulate their thoughts and answer. Do not rush students' responses.

Types Of Interview Questions To Ask Students

1. Questions intended to prompt students to give information previously learned or to present information collected.

2. Questions that prompt students to add to their answers.

3. Questions aimed at prompting students to put together a sequence of at least two ideas.

4. Questions that encourage students to describe the sequence of their procedures.

5. Questions that prompt discussion and encourage students to listen to one another.

6. Questions aimed at prompting students to use evidence as a basis for stating relationships among variables.

7. Questions aimed at encouraging students to interpret new experiences using concepts they already have or to apply concepts they have just learned in a new situation.

Summary

An **interview** is a personal interaction between a teacher and either one or a small group of students in which verbal questions are asked and verbal responses are given. Students may be interviewed before, during, and after a lesson or instructional unit. Interviews can contain fixed-alternative or open-ended questions. It is a highly flexible procedure that can be used for both assessment and teaching purposes. Students can be interviewed to assess their learning, cognitive reasoning, meta-cognitive thought, and retention. Students can also be interviewed to clarify their thinking, achieve new levels of understanding, reflect on their learning, believe their ideas are valued, appreciate their progress, and set future goals. Socrates is an example of a teacher who used oral interviews as the major instructional strategy. Interviews can also be used to build a more positive, supportive, and trusting relationship with each student.

Individual interviews may range from highly structured reading of a questionnaire with closed-ended questions to a focused interview in which the teacher unfolds the students' knowledge by progressively asking students to be more precise and specific in their answers. Small groups can be interviewed to assess their success in ensuring that all members have mastered the assigned material. The guidelines for interviewing include creating a supportive, nonthreatening climate, move from simple to complex questions, move from general to specific questions, and allow sufficient wait-time for students to formulate their thoughts and answer. The questions asked should prompt students to give information previously learned or collected, add to their answers, put a sequence of ideas together, provide evidence for their conclusions, and apply known concepts to new situations.

Interviewing Students To Assess Reasoning

Class: ______________________________ Date: __________

	Group One	Group Two	Group Three	Group Four
What Are You Doing?				
Why Are You Doing It?				
How Will It Help You?				
Total				

Meaningful And Manageable Assessment Through Cooperative Learning, Interaction Book Company, 7208 Cornelia Drive, Edina, MN 55435, (612) 831-9500, FAX (612) 831-9332.

INTERVIEW ON "PERSONAL BEST" IN HELPING A CLASSMATE LEARN

1. Describe a situation in which you demonstrated a "personal best" in helping a classmate learn something important and valuable. Include Who, When, Where, and What your classmate learned.

2. Opportunities And Challenges:

   a. What made the learning difficult for your classmate?

   b. How were you being innovative in your helping?

3. Costs And Gains:

   a. What did it cost you to help? (time, energy, resources)

   b. What did you gain by helping? (satisfaction, pride, skills)

4. Involvement:

   a. How did you energize to the learning situation?

   b. What did you do to empower your classmate?

   c. How did you keep your classmate involved in the learning?

5. Celebration: How did you celebrate your classmates' success and recognize the hard work the two of you put into the learning?

6. What did you learn about helping another person learn?

7. How would you sum up your experience in your own words? How did it represent your personal best?

Conflict Report Form: Interview

Date:________ Name:________________________________ ____Male ____Female

Grade:______ Teacher:__________________________ Subject Area:____________

Who Was Involved In The Conflict:____

Relationship With Other: ____Friend ____Non-Friend ____Stranger ____Adult

_____ Brother/Sister Other:____

What Was The Conflict About?____

____

____

Where Did The Conflict Take Place:____

What Strategies Were Used To Try To Solve The Conflict?______________________

____

____

____

Was The Conflict Resolved? _____Yes _____No

What Was The Solution:____

____

____

How Did You Feel About The Way The Conflict Was Resolved?

1	2	3	4	5
Very Unhappy	**Unhappy**	**OK**	**Happy**	**Very Happy**

Conclusions:

Meaningful And Manageable Assessment Through Cooperative Learning, Interaction Book Company, 7208 Cornelia Drive, Edina, MN 55435, (612) 831-9500, FAX (612) 831-9332.

NAEP Scoring Scales: Mathematics

Level 200: Beginning Skills And Understanding

Learners at this level have considerable understanding of two-digit numbers. They can add two-digit numbers but are still developing an ability to regroup in subtraction. They know some basic multiplication and division facts, recognize relations among coins, use simple measurement instructions...

Level 250: Basic Operations And Beginning Problem Solving

Learners have an initial understanding of the four basic operations. They are able to apply whole number addition and subtraction skills to one-step work problems and money situations, in multiplication, they can find the product of a two-digit and a one-digit number. They can compare information from graphs and charts, and are developing an ability to analyze logical relations.

Level 300: Moderately Complex Procedures And Reasoning

Learners are developing an understanding of number systems. They can compute with decimals, simple fractions and commonly encountered percents. They can identify geometric figures, measure lengths and angles, and calculate areas of rectangles. They are also able to interpret simple inequalities, evaluate formulas and solve simple linear equations. They can find averages...and are developing the skills to operate with signed numbers, exponents, and square roots.

Level 350: Multistep Problem Solving And Algebra

Learners can solve routine problems involving fractions and percents, recognize properties of geometric figures, and work with exponents and square roots. They can solve a variety of two-step problems using variables, identify equivalent algebraic expressions and solve linear equations and inequalities...

Meaningful And Manageable Assessment Through Cooperative Learning, Interaction Book Company, 7208 Cornelia Drive, Edina, MN 55435, (612) 831-9500, FAX (612) 831-9332.

Chapter Twelve: Learning Logs And Journals

WHAT ARE LOGS AND JOURNALS

Learning logs and journals are key tools for having students document and reflect on their learning experiences. **Logs** are a self-report procedure in which students record short entries concerning the subject matter being studied. Log entries may be questions about material covered in lectures and readings, observations of science experiments, mathematics problem-solving entries, lists of outside readings, homework assignments, or anything else that lends itself to keeping records. **Journals** are a self-report procedure in which students record narrative entries concerning the subject matter being studied. Journal entries may be personal observations, feelings, and opinions in response to readings, events, and experiences. A journal is a personal collection of writing and thoughts that have value for the writer about what the writer is learning and its personal relevance. These entries often connect what is being studied in one class with other classes or with life outside of the classroom. Journal entries are usually more descriptive, longer, and free-flowing than logs.

Why Should We Use Logs And Journals

Logs and journals are useful assessment tools for:

1. Keeping track of the number of problems solved, books read, or homework assignments completed.

2. Recording from lectures, movies, presentations, field trips, experiments, or reading assignments (a) key ideas, (b) questions, and (c) reflections.

3. Responding to questions posed by the teacher or other students.

4. Following the progress of an experiment, the weather, or in school, national, or world events or even a story and (a) monitoring change over time or (b) making predictions about what will happen next.

5. Connecting the ideas presented to other subject areas.

6. Brainstorming ideas about potential projects, papers, or presentations.

7. Identifying problems and recording problem-solving techniques.

Meaningful And Manageable Assessment Through Cooperative Learning, Interaction Book Company, 7208 Cornelia Drive, Edina, MN 55435, (612) 831-9500, FAX (612) 831-9332.

8. Applying what is learned in the course to one's own personal life.

9. Using what is learned in the course to clarify, update, and refine one's action theories (e.g., what actions are needed to achieve a desired consequence in a given situation).

How To Use Logs And Journals

Learning logs and journals are usually considered formative assessment methods. It is difficult to assign point values or letter grades, but it can be done.

1. Assign students the task of keeping a journal (or a log) related to the content of the course. Explain what a journal is. Highlight the cooperative goal of ensuring that all group members keep journals that meet the specified criteria.

2. Inform students of when their entries should start, how often they are to write an entry, how long an entry should be, how often they will share their entries with groupmates and you, the teacher, how the entries will be assessed, and when the final journal or log is due.

3. Show students samples or models of completed journals or logs, ranging from excellent to poor. Students need to develop a frame of reference as to what is and is not an acceptable journal or log.

4. Have students develop (a) specific criteria to assess the quality of the completed journals or logs and (b) indicators of excellent, medium, and poor quality for each criteria. Teach students a standardized rubric if you, the school, the district, or the state has one.

5. Have students construct their journal or log. To help students make entries into their log or journal you may wish to give them a prompt or lead-in. In the first class session structure the first entry. In each subsequent class session, give a prompt, lead-in, or a procedure for an entry. Examples of daily prompts or lead-ins are:

An interesting part is...	I want to know more about...
I predict...	I wonder...
Three important ideas are...	The ways I helped others learn are...
I need to work more on...	I am excited about...
A connecting idea is...	I believe...

6. Have students share their journal or log entries with the other members of their cooperative learning group on a regular basis (e.g., daily, twice a week, once a week).

7. Have students turn in their journals or logs to you (the teacher) on a periodic basis for feedback and/or a grade based on the number of entries and their quality.

8. Have students complete a self-assessment on their journal or log entries based on the predetermined criteria.

9. Have students, with the help of their cooperative learning group and you (the teacher), select a few of the journal entries to be rewritten and placed in their portfolios.

How To Assess Logs And Journals

There are two ways to assess the quality of logs and journals. The first is rate entries against criteria of excellence. The four steps in doing so are to (a) specify a number of criterion of quality, (b) develop indicators of high, medium, and low performance on that criterion, (c) rate a student's log or journal on each of the criterion, and (d) add the ratings for each criterion together to determine a total score. An example of rating sheet is given below.

The second method for assessing journals or logs is to assign point values to each criteria. This allows you to give different criteria different weight. An example is given below.

ASSIGNING POINT VALUES TO ENTRIES

Points	Criteria
20	Completeness Of Entries
10	Entries Recorded On Time
15	Originality Of Entries
15	Higher-Level Reasoning Demonstrated
15	Connections Made With Other Subject Areas
25	Personal Reflection
100	Total

Meaningful And Manageable Assessment Through Cooperative Learning, Interaction Book Company, 7208 Cornelia Drive, Edina, MN 55435, (612) 831-9500, FAX (612) 831-9332.

RATING THE QUALITY OF ENTRIES

Number Of Entries

1———2———3———4———5

No Entries | Few Entries | All Required Entries

Length Of Entry

1———2———3———4———5

Less Than 1 Page | One Page | Several Pages

Depth And Personalization

1———2———3———4———5

Surface, impersonal | partial, personal | Deep, Very Personal

Thoughtfulness

1———2———3———4———5

Response Only | Response, Examples | Response, Examples, Reflections

Originality

1———2———3———4———5

Straight-Forward | Some Metaphor, Images | Highly Creative

Comments:

Score: ______

22 - 25 Points = A

18 - 21 Points = B

13 - 17 Points = C

8 - 12 Points = D

Meaningful And Manageable Assessment Through Cooperative Learning, Interaction Book Company, 7208 Cornelia Drive, Edina, MN 55435, (612) 831-9500, FAX (612) 831-9332.

Problem Solving Log

Name: ______________________________

Date: _________ Class: ______________

1. My problem is…
2. The best way to analyze the problem is…
3. Something that is similar to the problem is…
4. Three ways to solve the problem are…
5. A question I still have about the problem is…
6. I need help with…

Reading Log

Name:

Date:

1. Key Ideas:
2. Connections:
3. Questions:
4. Liked Best:

Keeping A Journal For A Course

As you complete this course you will be asked to keep a journal in which you record what you are learning about the subject matter covered and yourself as a person. A journal is a personal collection of writing and thoughts that have value for the writer about what you have learned in the course and its personal relevance to you. It has to be kept up on a regular basis. The journal is an important part of this course. It is not an easy part. The entries should be important to you in your effort to make this course useful, and since this is a cooperative course, useful to your fellow students. You may be surprised how writing sharpens and organizes your thoughts. The journal will be of great interest to you after you have finished this course.

Purposes

1. To keep track of the activities related to this course (what you are doing to make the material useful in your teaching).
2. To answer in writing some of the questions that are important for a clear understanding of the course content (these will often be suggested, but others can be selected by you).
3. To collect thoughts that are related to the course content (the best thinking often occurs when you are driving to or from school, about to go to sleep at night, and so forth).
4. To collect newspaper and magazine articles and references that are relevant to the topics covered in the course.

5. To keep summaries of conversations and anecdotal material that are unique, interesting or illustrate things related to the content of the course.

6. To collect interesting thoughts, articles, and conversations not especially related to the course, but important to you.

(Note: If you publish your journal as did John Holt, Hugh Prather, and others, all we ask is a modest 10 percent of the royalties.)

Action Theories And Journals

One procedure for using journals in a course is to use it specifically to:

1. Increase students' awareness of their action theories.

2. Make judgments about the effectiveness of their action theories.

3. Update or refine their action theories on the basis of what is learned in the course.

To do so, students have to understand what an action theory is and how they are to use a journal to examine and modify their action theories.

Action Theory

All humans need to become competent in taking action and simultaneously reflecting on their action in order to learn from it. Integrating thought with action requires that we plan our behavior, engage in it, and then reflect on how effective we were. When we learn a pattern of behavior that effectively deals with a recurrent situation, we tend to repeat it over and over until it functions automatically. Such habitual behavioral patterns are based on theories of action. An **action theory** is a theory as to what actions are needed to achieve a desired consequence in a given situation. All theories have an "if...then..." form. An action theory states that in a given situation, if we do "x," then "y" will follow. Our theories of action are normative; they state what we "ought" to do if we wish to achieve certain results. Examples of action theories can be found in almost everything we do. If we smile and say "hello," then others will return our smile and greeting. If we apologize, then the other person will excuse us. If we steal, then we will be punished. If a person shoves us, then we should shove back. All our behavior is based on theories that connect our actions with certain circumstances.

As children we are taught action theories by parents, teachers, and other socializing agents. As we grow older we learn how to modify our action theories and develop new ones. We learn to try to anticipate what actions will lead to what consequences, to try out and experiment with new behaviors, to experience the consequences, and then to reflect on our experiences to determine whether our action is valid or needs modification. Education is based on the systematic development and modification of action theories.

We all have many action theories, one for every type of situation in which we regularly find ourselves. This does not mean that we are aware of our action theories. An action is usually based on tacit knowledge--knowledge that we are not always able to put into words. Since most of our action theories function automatically, we are rarely conscious of our assumed connections between actions and their consequences. One of the purposes of this course is to help you become more conscious of the action theories that guide how you behave in certain situations, test your theories against reality, and modify them to make them more effective.

Journal

1. Write a journal that includes at least one entry per week.

2. Summarize what you are learning in the course for the current week.

3. Describe how you behaved during an important experience you have had during the week. You should describe:

   a. The nature of the situation.

   b. The people involved.

   c. The relationships among participants.

   d. The strategies you used to manage the situation.

   e. The feelings experienced.

   f. The outcomes that resulted from your actions.

4. From the description, summarize the implicit action theories that were directing your behavior.

5. Use what you have learned in the course to describe how you could have behaved in a more effective and constructive way. This includes describing how you would modify your action theories.

Learning Logs And Informal Cooperative Learning

One of the most useful ways to use learning logs in a class is with informal cooperative learning. Whenever a lecture, demonstration, presentation, guest speaker,

Meaningful And Manageable Assessment Through Cooperative Learning, Interaction Book Company, 7208 Cornelia Drive, Edina, MN 55435, (612) 831-9500, FAX (612) 831-9332.

film, or video is used, the combination of learning logs and informal cooperative learning will enhance the quality of instruction and ensure high quality assessment of learning. In this section that nature of informal cooperative learning is explained and the procedure for using informal cooperative learning with learning logs is discussed.

Informal Cooperative Learning

Reflective logs can be used very productivity with informal cooperative learning (Johnson, Johnson, & Smith, 1991; Johnson, Johnson, & Holubec, 1992). **Informal cooperative learning groups** are temporary, ad hoc groups that last for only one discussion or one class period. Their purposes are to (a) focus student attention on the material to be learned, (b) set a mood conducive to learning, (c) help organize in advance the material to be covered in a class session, (d) ensure that students cognitively process the material being taught, and (e) provide closure to an instructional session. Informal cooperative learning groups also ensure that misconceptions, incorrect understanding, and gaps in understanding are identified and corrected, and learning experiences are personalized. They may be used at any time, but are especially useful during a lecture or direct teaching.

In order for lecturing to be successful students must be cognitively active, not passive. What is proclaimed to be the major problem with lecturing is: "*The information passes from the notes of the professor to the notes of the student without passing through the mind of either one.*" During lecturing and direct teaching the instructional challenge is to ensure that students, not the faculty, do the intellectual work of conceptualizing and organizing material, explaining it, summarizing it, and integrating it into existing conceptual networks. Students are intellectually active the more they do the advance organizing, process cognitively what they are learning, and provide closure to the lesson.

The following procedure will help you plan a lecture that keeps students more actively engaged intellectually. It entails having focused discussions before and after the lecture (i.e., bookends) and interspersing pair discussions throughout the lecture.

1. **Introductory Focused Discussion**: Assign students to pairs. The person seated next to them will do. You may wish to require different seating arrangements each class period so that students will meet and interact with a number of other students in the class. Then give the pairs the cooperative assignment of completing the initial (advance organizer) task. Give them only four or five minutes to do so. The discussion task is aimed at promoting advance organizing of what the students know about the topic to be presented and establishing expectations about what the lecture will cover.

2. **Lecture Segment One**: Deliver the first segment of the lecture. This segment should last from 10 to 15 minutes. This is about the length of time an adult can concentrate on a lecture.

Meaningful And Manageable Assessment Through Cooperative Learning, Interaction Book Company, 7208 Cornelia Drive, Edina, MN 55435, (612) 831-9500, FAX (612) 831-9332.

3. **Pair Discussion 1**: Give the students a discussion task focused on the material you have just presented. The discussion must be completed in three or four minutes. Its purpose is to ensure that students are actively thinking about the material being presented. The discussion task may be to (a) give an answer to a question posed by the instructor, (b) give a reaction to the theory, concepts, or information being presented, or (c) relate material to past learning so that it is integrated into existing conceptual frameworks. Discussion pairs use the "*formulate-explain-listen-create*" procedure:

   a. Each student formulates his or her answer.

   b. Students explain their answer with their partner.

   c. Students listen carefully to partner's answer.

   d. Pairs create a new answer that is superior to each member's initial formulation through the process of association, building on each other's thoughts, and synthesizing.

   Randomly choose two or three students to give 30 second summaries of their discussions. **It is important that students are randomly called on to share their answers after each discussion task**. Such **individual accountability** ensures that the pairs take the tasks seriously and check each other to ensure that both are prepared to answer.

4. **Lecture Segment 2:** Deliver the second segment of the lecture.

5. **Pair Discussion 2:** Give a discussion task focused on the second part of the lecture.

6. Repeat this sequence of lecture segment and pair discussion until the lecture is completed.

7. **Closure Focused Discussion**: Give an ending discussion task to summarize what students have learned from the lecture. Students should have four or five minutes to summarize and discuss the material covered in the lecture. The discussion should result in students integrating what they have just learned into existing conceptual frameworks. The task may also point students toward what the homework will cover or what will be presented in the next class session. This provides closure to the lecture.

Learning Log Procedure

Require that students keep a learning log for the course. They are to bring their log to every class session. The log entries are completed as follows.

Meaningful And Manageable Assessment Through Cooperative Learning, Interaction Book Company, 7208 Cornelia Drive, Edina, MN 55435, (612) 831-9500, FAX (612) 831-9332.

1. **Introductory Focused Discussion**: To prepare students for the class session you have them complete a short initial focused discussion task. Plan your lecture around a series of questions that the lecture answers. Prepare the questions on an overhead transparency or write them on the board so that students can see them. In their pairs students (a) come to agreement on their initial answers to the questions and record the answers in their learning logs and (b) record in their logs questions they wish to have answered about the topic. Doing so helps students organize in advance what they know about the topic to be studied and establish expectations about what the class session will focus on.

2. **Pair Discussions Interspersed Throughout The Lecture**. You ask students to engage in a three-minute discussion with their partner and write their conclusions in their learning log. Pairs use the **formulate-explain-listen-create procedure**. The conclusions students write in their logs enables teachers to track students' reasoning and identify which parts of the material covered were and were not comprehended.

3. **Closure Focused Discussion**: You ask students to engage in a five-minute discussion with their partner and write in their learning logs (a) a summary of what they have learned in the class session, (b) how it relates to what was covered the previous class sessions and the assigned reading, (c) any questions about the material covered today, and (d) how it relates to the material that will be covered in the next class session.

4. Partners read each others log sheets and ensure that they are complete, readable, and reflect what was discussed. They sign their names to verify that they have checked the log entry.

5. Students hand in their log sheets. You (the teacher) read them to assess what students learned, what students did not comprehend accurately or completely, and what questions students still have about the material covered.

6. You return the entry sheets the next day and students place them in their logs.

Double Entry Journal

Initial Entry	*Upon Reflection*

Meaningful And Manageable Assessment Through Cooperative Learning, Interaction Book Company, 7208 Cornelia Drive, Edina, MN 55435, (612) 831-9500, FAX (612) 831-9332.

Informal Cooperative Learning Log

Name:____________________ **Class:**______________ **Date:**____________

Task: Your task is to work with your partner in completing this log entry during the class session. At the end of the session, your partner will check your log page to ensure it is completed; you will check his or hers. You then hand in your entry for the teacher to read. The teacher will give it back to you tomorrow and you will add it to your learning log.

1. **Introductory Discussion**: The teacher has presented one to three questions for you to answer. You have five minutes to do so. Work cooperatively with your partner using the formulate, explain, listen, create procedure. Use what you know from the assigned readings and from your general knowledge to answer the questions.

   a. ____

   b. ____

   c. ____

2. **Pair Discussions**: Use the formulate, explain, listen, create procedure to answer each question posed by the teacher during the class session.

   a. ____

   My Answer: __________________________________

   Your Answer: ________________________________

   Our Answer: _________________________________

   b. ____

   My Answer: __________________________________

   Your Answer: ________________________________

   Our Answer: _________________________________

   c. ____

   My Answer: ____________________________

   Your Answer: __________________________

Meaningful And Manageable Assessment Through Cooperative Learning, Interaction Book Company, 7208 Cornelia Drive, Edina, MN 55435, (612) 831-9500, FAX (612) 831-9332.

Our Answer: ____

d. ____

My Answer: ____

Your Answer: ____

Our Answer: ____

3. **Closure Focused Discussion**: In the space below and on the back of this page (you and your partner have five minutes):

    a. Summarize what you have learned during the class session.

    b. Relate your new learning with what the previous class sessions and the assigned reading have covered.

    c. List any questions you still have about the material covered today.

    d. Predict what will be covered next.

Read And Verified By:____

Meaningful And Manageable Assessment Through Cooperative Learning, Interaction Book Company, 7208 Cornelia Drive, Edina, MN 55435, (612) 831-9500, FAX (612) 831-9332.

Self And Other Rating

Thomas Mann (1875-1955), a German writer, once said, *"No one remains quite what he was when he recognizes himself."* Having students rate themselves and their groupmates is an important addition to most instructional units (Johnson, Johnson, & Holubec, 1993). **First**, students rate the quality and quantity of their learning. **Second**, students rate the quality and quantity of the learning of each of their groupmates. **Third**, students discuss and reflect on their learning experiences (under the guidance of an observant teacher), comparing their self-ratings with the ratings they receive from groupmates. Such self and other ratings allow students to see how the quality of their work has evolved.

There are a number of factors that teachers need to assess besides test scores. Students need to arrive at class on time and be prepared to learn (have the essential materials, resources, and attitudes). Students need to provide academic help and assistance to groupmates and ask groupmates for help when they need it. In using a rating form students need to understand clearly the purpose of the form and how it will be used, the number of points (if any) the form will count in evaluating students, and the questions on the form.

Meaningful And Manageable Assessment Through Cooperative Learning, Interaction Book Company, 7208 Cornelia Drive, Edina, MN 55435, (612) 831-9500, FAX (612) 831-9332.

Student Self And Peer Evaluation Form

This form will be used to assess the members of your learning group. Fill one form out on yourself. Fill one form out on each member of your group. During the group discussion, give each member the form you have filled out on them. Compare the way you rated yourself with the ways your groupmates have rated you. Ask for clarification when your rating differs from the ratings given you by your groupmates. Each member should set a goal for increasing his or her contribution to academic learning of all group members.

Rating Your Self And Groupmates

Person Being Rated: ______________________ Date: __________ Group: ______

Write the number of points earned by the group member (4 = Excellent, 3 = Good, 2 = Poor, 1 = Inadequate)

_____ *On time for class.*

_____ *Arrives prepared for class.*

_____ *Reliably completes all assigned work on time.*

_____ *Work is of high quality.*

_____ *Contributes to groupmates' learning daily.*

_____ *Asks for academic help and assistance when it is needed.*

_____ *Gives careful step-by-step explanations (not just tell answers).*

_____ *Builds on others' reasoning.*

_____ *Relates what is being learned to previous knowledge.*

_____ *Helps draw a visual representation of what is being learned.*

_____ *Voluntarily extends a project.*

Meaningful And Manageable Assessment Through Cooperative Learning, Interaction Book Company, 7208 Cornelia Drive, Edina, MN 55435, (612) 831-9500, FAX (612) 831-9332.

Chapter Thirteen: Total Quality Learning And Student Management Teams

Continuous Improvement Of Quality Of Learning

We don't seek to be one thousand percent better at any one thing. We seek to be one percent better at one thousand things.

Jim Carlzon, President, Scandinavian Air Systems

In the Bible there is a parable about a person of high rank who was going on a journey. Before he left, he gathered his sons together and gave each a talent. On his return, he asked his sons what they had done with their talents. Each son who had increased his talents pleased him. The son who had buried his talent angered the father so much that he took that single talent away and gave it to the son who had increased his talents the most. The moral of this parable is that those who develop and continuously improve what they have will receive even more; those who do nothing with what they have will lose even that.

Focusing on continuous improvement makes assessment the centerpiece of schools. Continuous assessment is needed to make small, incremental, daily improvements in learning and instruction. A teacher dedicated to continuous improvement of instruction will find some way to improve every day the quality of the way he or she teaches. A student dedicated to continuous improvement of learning will find some way to improve the quality of the way he or she learns each day. Changes do not have to be dramatic. Small, incremental changes are fine. Ideally, everyone in the school will dedicate themselves to continuous improvement of the quality of the processes of learning, instructing, and administrating. In Japan, this mutual dedication is called **kaizen**, a society-wide covenant of mutual help in the process of getting better and better, day by day. **Continuous improvement** is the ongoing search by everyone involved for changes that can increase the quality of the process. A **process** is all the tasks, organized in a sequence, that contribute to the accomplishment of one particular outcome, such as learning a math procedure, teaching a lesson, or conducting a faculty meeting.

Continuous improvement of the processes of learning, teaching, and administrating begins with changing the organizational structure of the class and school. There are two types of organizational structures: (a) mass-production and (b) team-based, high performance. In a **mass-production organizational structure**, the quality of students' learning is determined by inspecting the final outcome to see if it is adequate or needs improvement. Examples are final examinations or competency tests. This is known as inspecting quality in. In a **team-based, high-performance organizational structure**, the quality of students' learning is determined by examining the process of learning to determine if students can improve it. This is known as continuous improvement or total quality learning.

Historical Origins Of Continuous Improvement

The name most closely associated with the continuous improvement of organizational processes is W. Edwards Deming. Deming was born in Sioux City, Iowa. During World War II he taught members of industry how to use statistical methods to improve the quality of military production. Following World War II, Deming taught the Japanese his theories of quality control and continuous improvement. Many experts credit him (along with Joseph Juran and others) with laying the groundwork for Japan's economic boom. Deming's thesis was that in most organizations, management tends to view what goes wrong as the fault of individual people, not the organizational structure, while in fact the opposite tends to be true. Deming and Juran formulated the **85/15 rule**: 85 percent of the problems can only be corrected by changing the organizational structure (largely determined by management) and less than 15 percent of the problems can be solved by changing individual workers. When problems arise, therefore, management should look for causes in the organizational structure and work to remove them, before casting blame on workers.

Continuous improvement in learning occurs when a cooperative learning group plans how to complete an assignment, does the assignment, assesses their effectiveness in doing so, reflects on how team members can improve the process of learning, and then modifies members' behavior in completing the next assignment. If students continuously improve their process of learning for twelve years, so that each assignment is completed more effectively than the one before, great learning would be occurring every hour! This chapter focuses on the continuous improvement of the processes of learning. The same principles can be used to continuous improve teaching and administrating.

Continuous Improvement Procedure

The steps to improving continuously the learning and instructing that takes place in a school are:

1. Form Teams
2. Select A Process For Improvement
3. Define The Process

4. Engage In The Process
5. Gather Information About Process, Display It, And Analyze It
6. Plan For Improvement
7. Repeat Learning Process In A Modified Way
8. Institutionalize Changes That Work

Step One: Form Teams

The first step in continuous improvement is to form teams. In a high-performance organizational structure, teams do all the important work. Continuous improvement of the process of learning is not possible without teams. Students, therefore, are assigned to cooperative learning groups and given the responsibilities of continuously improving the quality of their own and their groupmates' learning. To fulfill these responsibilities, students need to be trained in how to organize their work, assess its quality daily, and place the results in a quality chart.

Step Two: Analyze Assignment And Select A Learning Process For Improvement

The second step is to analyze the current assignment and select a process of learning for improvement. The team selects a specific, definable process to work on, such as members' ability to read with comprehension, write, present, or reason scientifically. Deming believed that if students concentrated on the continuous improvement of the processes of learning, the outcomes of learning (how much they learn and their scores on achievement and retention measures) would take care of themselves. One of the most profound changes educators can make is to focus on processes of learning rather than on examination of what students know.

Step Three: Define The Process

The third step is to define the process clearly. The definition of the process guides the assessment of student efforts. The team cannot improve a process until it defines the process, preferably by drawing a picture of it. Two common ways to picture a process are the flow chart and the cause and effect diagram.

Meaningful And Manageable Assessment Through Cooperative Learning, Interaction Book Company, 7208 Cornelia Drive, Edina, MN 55435, (612) 831-9500, FAX (612) 831-9332.

Flow Charts

The **Flow Chart** is a pictorial/visual representation showing all the steps of a process or procedure and how they relate to each other. A flow chart describes the flow of people, material, and information within a designated workspace. The level of detail will vary based on the needs of the team. Even without significant detail, flow charts can help identify gaps, duplication, and other potential problems. Easily recognizable symbols are used in flow charts to represent the type of activity performed (see Figure .2). A flow chart is created by:

1. Clearly defining where the process begins and ends and what are the inputs and the outputs. This is defining the boundaries.

2. Identifying all the steps the process actually follows (what are the key steps, who does what, when). There is usually only one output arrow out of a process box. Otherwise, it may require a decision diamond.

3. Drawing the steps in sequence.

4. Observing what team members actually do.

5. Comparing actual performance with the flow chart and either revising the flow chart or planning how to increase the quality with which group members engage in each step.

A variation on the above procedure is to (a) draw a flow chart of what steps the process actually follows, (b) draw a flow chart of what steps the process should follow if everything worked right, and (c) compare the two charts to find where they are different because this is where the problems arise. This is sometimes called **imagineering**.

Cause And Effect Diagrams

A **Cause-And-Effect Diagram** represents the relationship between some effect (the problem being studied) and all its possible causes (see Figure 13.3). The effect or problem is stated on the right side of the diagram and the major causes or influences are listed on the left. A cause-and-effect diagram is drawn to (a) illustrate clearly the various causes affecting a process by sorting out and relating the causes and (b) explore systematically cause and effect relationships so that the most likely causes of a problem or effect can be identified. For every effect there are likely to be several major categories of causes. A team uses any category that emerges from the discussion or that helps team members think creatively. This charting technique is also referred to as a fishbone diagram due to its appearance when completed.

Flow Charts

Composition

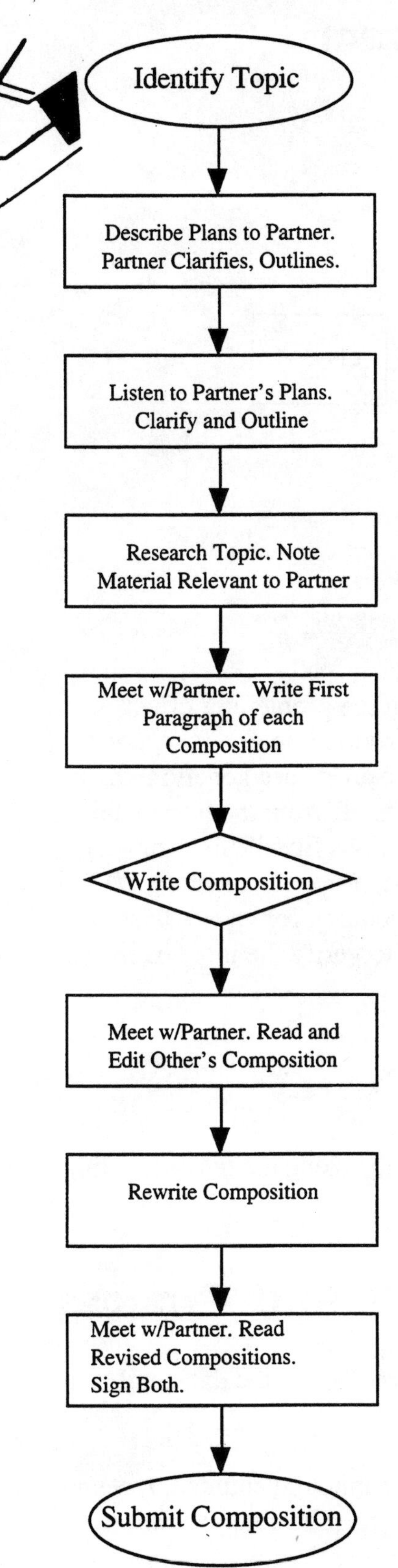
Identify Topic
Describe Plans to Partner. Partner Clarifies, Outlines.
Listen to Partner's Plans. Clarify and Outline
Research Topic. Note Material Relevant to Partner
Meet w/Partner. Write First Paragraph of each Composition
Write Composition
Meet w/Partner. Read and Edit Other's Composition
Rewrite Composition
Meet w/Partner. Read Revised Compositions. Sign Both.
Submit Composition

Math Problems

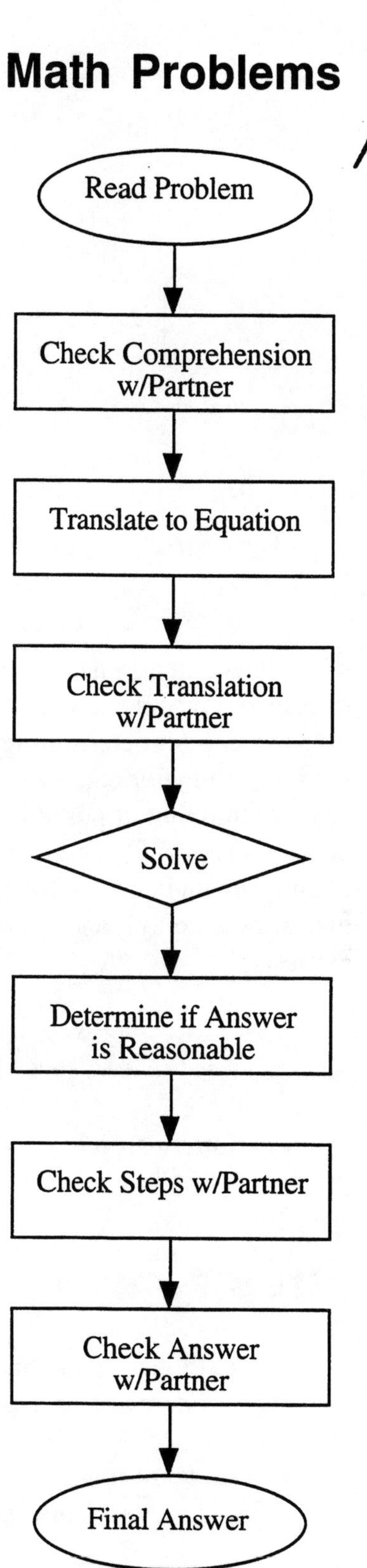
Read Problem
Check Comprehension w/Partner
Translate to Equation
Check Translation w/Partner
Solve
Determine if Answer is Reasonable
Check Steps w/Partner
Check Answer w/Partner
Final Answer

Cause And Effect Diagram

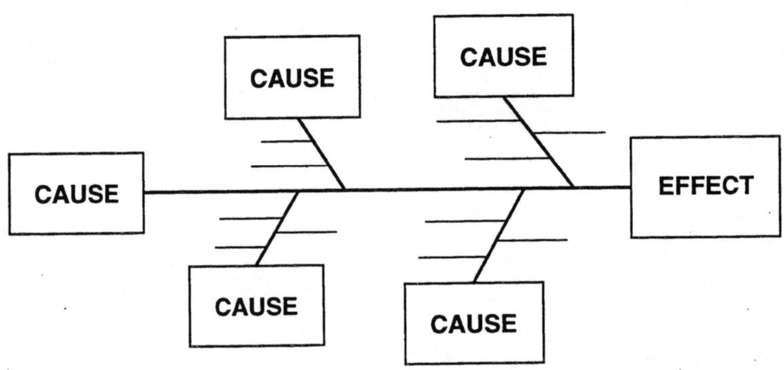

A team creates a cause-and-effect diagram by (a) defining the problem or effect clearly and placing it in a box on the right, (b) drawing a horizontal line or arrow, pointing to the effect, (c) determining the major categories of possible causes (use generic terms), (d) for each major category, drawing a single line that branches off from the horizontal line, (e) thinking of possible causes in each category (ask questions like "Why?" or "Why does this happen?") and adding each cause as a branch of the appropriate category, (f) identifying and circling the most basic (root) causes (start by looking for causes that appear repeatedly), and (g) using a check sheet to gather data to verify the most likely root causes(s).

Step Four: Engage In The Process

The fourth step is to engage in the process. Team members engage in the learning process so they can measure each step.

Step Five: Gather Information About Process

The fifth step is to gather information about the process, display the data, and analyze it. There are three parts to this step.

1. **The team identifies quantifiable factors.** If a factor cannot be counted, it cannot be improved (conversely, to be able to improve it, you must be able to count it).

Meaningful And Manageable Assessment Through Cooperative Learning, Interaction Book Company, 7208 Cornelia Drive, Edina, MN 55435, (612) 831-9500, FAX (612) 831-9332.

2. **The team develops a design for gathering the relevant data**. This includes specifying what data will be collected, who will collect it, when it will be collected, and how it will be collected. A check sheet or observation form is a common way to gather objective data to answer the question, "*How often are certain events happening?*" A team uses the observation form to tally and count the number of times an event is observed in a specified time period (such as the number of times a social skill was used during a 50-minute period) or the amount of product (such as the progress in writing a composition).

3. **The team analyzes and portrays the data in ways that help members understand it easily**. Common ways to portray data are the Pareto chart, run chart, scatter diagram, and histogram.

Pareto Charts

The **Pareto Chart** is a form of vertical bar chart that helps teams separate the vital few problems and causes from the trivial many. It takes its name from the Italian economist Vilfredo Frederico Damaso Pareto (1548-1623). While studying the unequal distribution of income, Pareto found that 80 percent of the wealth was controlled by only 20 percent of the population. In the late 1940s, Joseph Juran generalized Pareto's findings into the **Pareto Principle (80/20 Rule)**--80 percent of the trouble comes from 20 percent of the problems (the "*vital few*" should be separated from the "*trivial many*"). The Pareto chart is used to display the frequency and relative importance of problems, causes, or conditions in order to choose a starting point for process improvement, monitor progress, or identify root causes of a problem. Pareto analysis allows the team to take data from basic tools (like check sheets and interviews) and present it in a simple bar graph format. The steps in developing a Pareto chart are as follows:

1. List the actions, conditions or causes you wish to monitor.

2. Collect the data on the number of times the actions conditions, or causes occurred in a predetermined period of time.

3. Rank the various actions, conditions or causes from highest to lowest by:

   a. Computing a total for each action, condition, or cause.

   b. Computing the total number of actions, conditions, or causes.

   c. Ranking the action, condition, or cause from most frequently occurring to least frequently occurring.

4. On the right-hand vertical axis, note the percentage scale (0 to 100 percent).

Meaningful And Manageable Assessment Through Cooperative Learning, Interaction Book Company, 7208 Cornelia Drive, Edina, MN 55435, (612) 831-9500, FAX (612) 831-9332.

5. On the left-hand axis, list the measurement scale by:

    a. Recording the total number of actions, conditions, or causes on the left vertical axis at the point that corresponds to 100 percent.

    b. Multiple the total number of actions, conditions, or causes by 0.75 to determine the number that corresponds to 75 percent.

    c. Multiple the total number of actions, conditions, or causes by 0.50 to determine the number that corresponds to 50 percent.

    d. Multiple the total number of actions, conditions, or causes by 0.25 to determine the number that corresponds to 25 percent.

6. Under the horizontal axis, write the actions, conditions, or causes in descending order (the most frequently occurring action to the left and the least occurring to the right):

    a. Identify the action, condition, or cause with the largest total. Working from left to right, (1) label the first bar on the horizontal axis of the chart with the action, condition, or cause, (2) record the total in the blank space, and (3) draw a vertical bar stretching from 0 to the total frequency of occurrence using the measurement scale on the left-hand axis as a guide.

    b. Identify the action, condition, or cause with the second largest total. Label the second bar on the horizontal axis of the chart with the action, condition, or cause. Record the total in the blank space. Draw a vertical bar stretching from 0 to the total frequency of occurrence using the measurement scale on the left-hand axis as a guide.

    c. Continue this procedure until every action, condition, or cause has been recorded on the chart in sequence from most to least frequently occurring.

7. Plot the cumulative frequencies of the data in a line graph:

    a. For the most frequent action, condition, or cause draw a point at its total frequency using the left-vertical axis measurement scale as a guide (the point will be at the top of the bar graph).

    b. Add the frequency of the first and second most frequent actions, conditions, or causes, together for a cumulative total. Plot that point on the chart using the left-vertical axis as a guide.

c. Add the frequency of the first, second, and third most frequent actions, conditions, or causes together for a cumulative total. Plot that point on the chart using the left-vertical axis as a guide.

d. Continue this procedure until the cumulative total for all actions, conditions, or causes have been plotted on the chart. Draw a line connecting the cumulative points.

8. Make an action plan by:

   a. Noting how many of the actions, conditions, or causes account for 80 percent of the total.

   b. Planning the actions required to either increase or decrease the frequency of the actions, conditions, or causes accounting for 80 percent of the total.

   c. Planning the actions required to either increase or decrease the frequency of the actions, conditions, or causes accounting for 20 percent of the total.

A Pareto Diagram is an extension of the cause-and-effect diagram in that the causes are not only identified but also listed in order of their occurrence. Once team members gain some experience in making Pareto Diagrams, members construct them very quickly. The advantages of the Pareto Diagram are that it can be used to analyze almost anything, it is easy to do, and easy to understand. The disadvantage is that only quantifiable data can be used in constructing it.

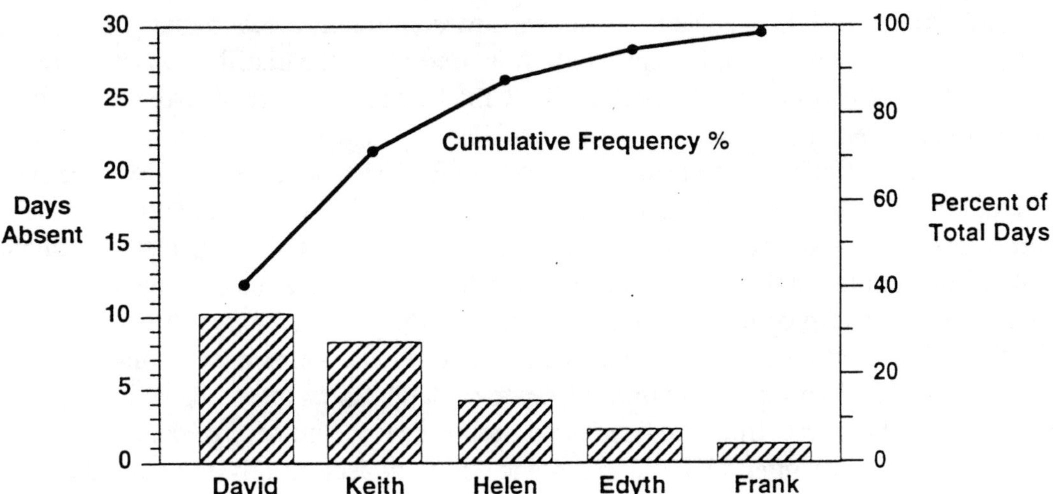

Meaningful And Manageable Assessment Through Cooperative Learning, Interaction Book Company, 7208 Cornelia Drive, Edina, MN 55435, (612) 831-9500, FAX (612) 831-9332.

Run Chart

A **Run Chart** is used to monitor the process over time to see whether or not the long-range average is changing. It was discussed in Chapter 8.

Scatter Diagram

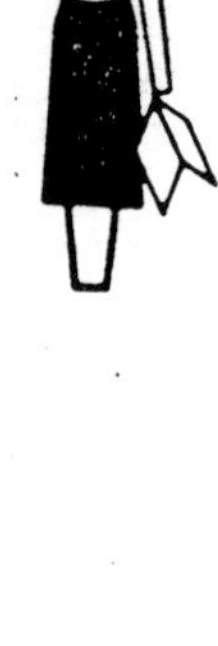

A **Scatter Diagram** displays the relationship between two actions, conditions, or causes (see Figure 10.7). A team uses a scatter diagram to display what happens to one variable when another variable changes, that is, to indicate the strength of a possible relationship between two variables. Usually, a team constructs a scatter diagram so that the horizontal axis represents the measurement values for the possible cause variable and the vertical axis represents the measurement values for the possible effect variable. A team creates a scatter diagram by (a) collecting paired samples that may be related (the more data points the better--50 to 100 are good), (b) constructing a data sheet that lists the values of variable 1 in one column and the values of variable 2 in another column, and (c) plotting the data on the chart by placing an x on the chart at each point the paired data intersects (circle repeated data points). The ways the points are scattered about the chart indicate the relationship between the two variables. A randomly scattered pattern suggests they are unrelated. If the pattern moves from bottom left to top right, a positive correlation most likely exists. If the pattern moves from top left to bottom right, a negative correlation most likely exists. The more the cluster of data points resembles a straight line, the stronger the relationship.

Histogram

A **Histogram** (History Diagram) shows how continuous measurement data are clustered and dispersed (see Figure 10.8). It is used when the distribution and spread of data needs to be displayed. Histograms show the frequency of an occurrence and the dispersion between the highest and lowest values. By displaying measurement data across a range of values (spread) the team learns about the process's ability to meet specifications, whether the distribution is centered in the right place, and whether the data points are evenly balanced or skewed. Histograms are useful when the team collects large quantities of data and simple tabulation does not provide easy analysis. A histogram consists of a series of equal-width columns of varying height. The horizontal axis represents the range of data and the vertical axis represents the number of data points in each interval. Each column represents an interval within the range of data. Since interval size is constant, so are the column widths. Since column height represents the number of data points that occur within a given interval, column heights will vary accordingly. The number of intervals (columns) determines how much of a pattern will be visible. A team creates a histogram by:

1. Collecting the data to be analyzed.

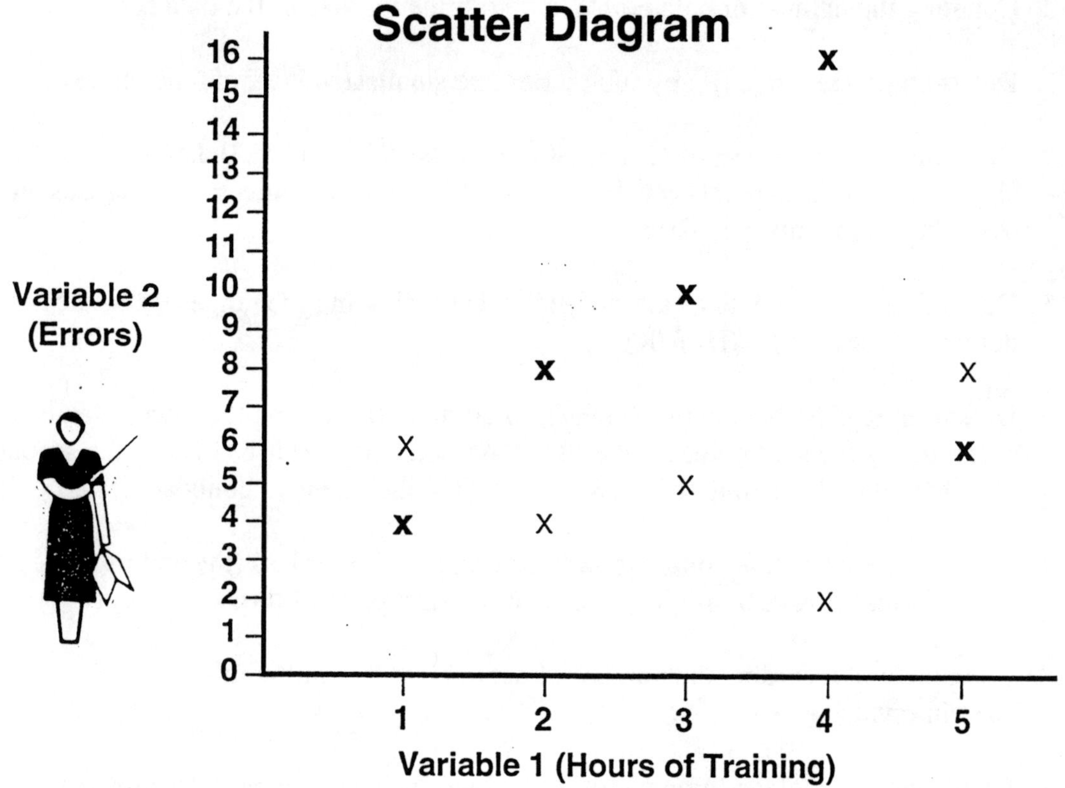
Scatter Diagram
Variable 2
(Errors)
16
15
14
13
12
11
10
9
8
7
6
5
4
3
2
1
0
1
2
3
4
5
Variable 1 (Hours of Training)

Histogram

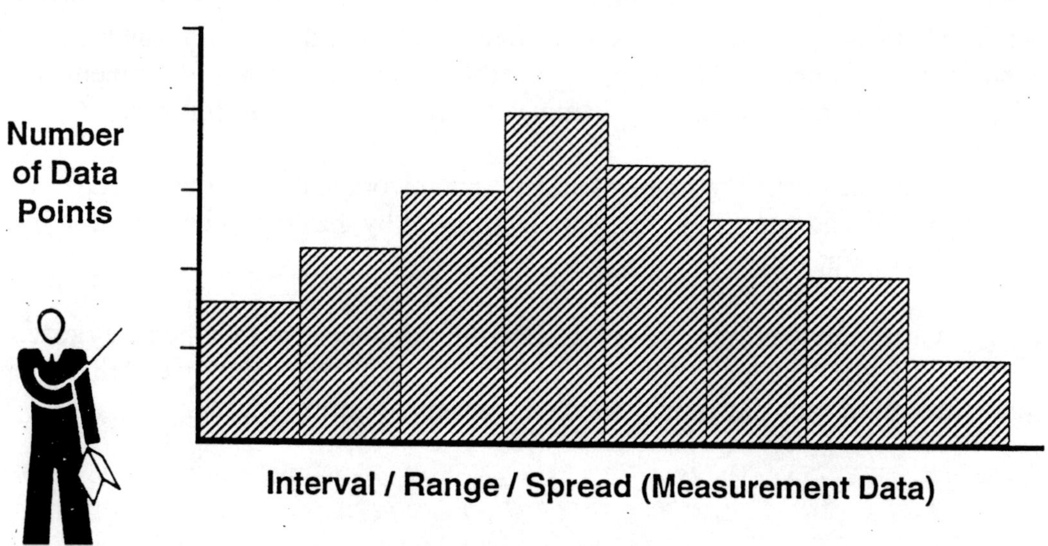
Number
of Data
Points
Interval / Range / Spread (Measurement Data)

2. Counting the number of data points to determine the size of the data set (n).

3. Determining the range (R) by subtracting the smallest value from the largest.

4. Determining the number of classes (K) to use (such as under 50 data points = 5-7 classes, 50-100 data points = 6-10 classes, 100-250 data points = 7-12 classes, and over 250 data points = 10-20 data points).

5. Determining class width or interval size (H) by dividing the range (R) by the number of classes (K) (H=R/K).

6. Determining class boundaries for each interval by (a) finding the lowest value data point (this is the start point for the first class boundary) and (b) finding the second class boundary by adding the class width (H) to the previous boundary's start point.

7. Making sure each data point can fit in one and only one class (the end point of each interval must always be slightly less than the start point of the next class).

8. Counting and recording the number of data points that fall within each class/interval.

9. Drawing a rectangle/column above each class (horizontal axis) reflecting the appropriate frequency of occurrences.

10. Analyzing the distribution and its implications.

Quality Chart Procedure

Using quality charts is the heart of the continuous improvement process (Johnson & Johnson, 1994). Each day (or week) the cooperative learning group rates the extent to which each member is meeting the learning criteria. The results are then charted each week to help the group (a) determine the frequency and fidelity with which each group member is implementing the targeted procedures and (b) set goals for implementation efforts for the coming week. An example of a quality chart is as follows:

1. Each member shows his or her daily homework and work during class. The quality and quantity of the work is assessed by the criteria contained in the appropriate rubrics.

2. Group members receive points according to the extent to which they reached each criterion. The individual student may keep a quality chart by entering the points received each day or the total points received during a week.

3. The points earned by group members are added together and divided by the number of members. The result is the group score. The score is plotted on the group's quality chart.

4. The group discusses the results and the long-term trend for each member and the group as a whole and plans either how to improve the quality and quantity of their learning efforts during the coming week or how to maintain their high level of learning.

5. Group members celebrate how hard they are working and how successful they are.

Data Summary Chart

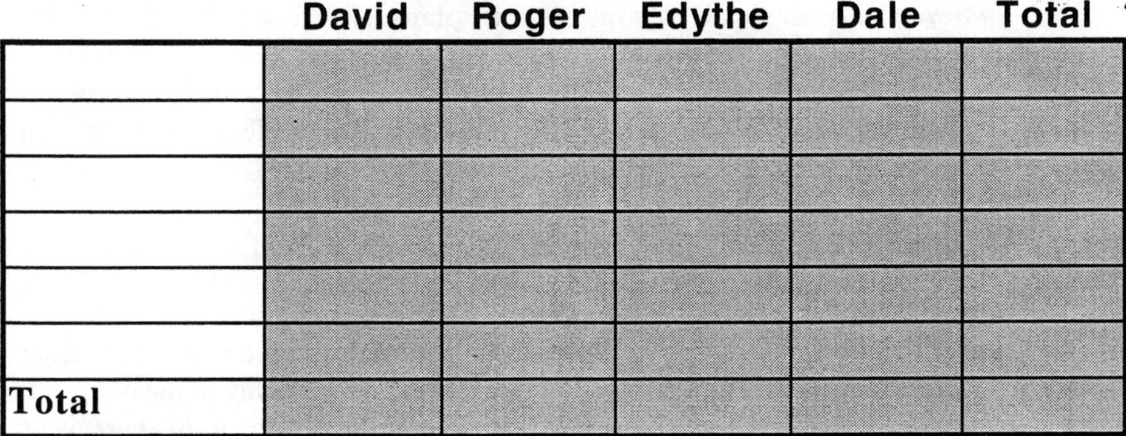

	David	Roger	Edythe	Dale	Total
Total					

(0 Points=Did not do, 1 Point=Half did, 2 Points=Did)

Quality Chart

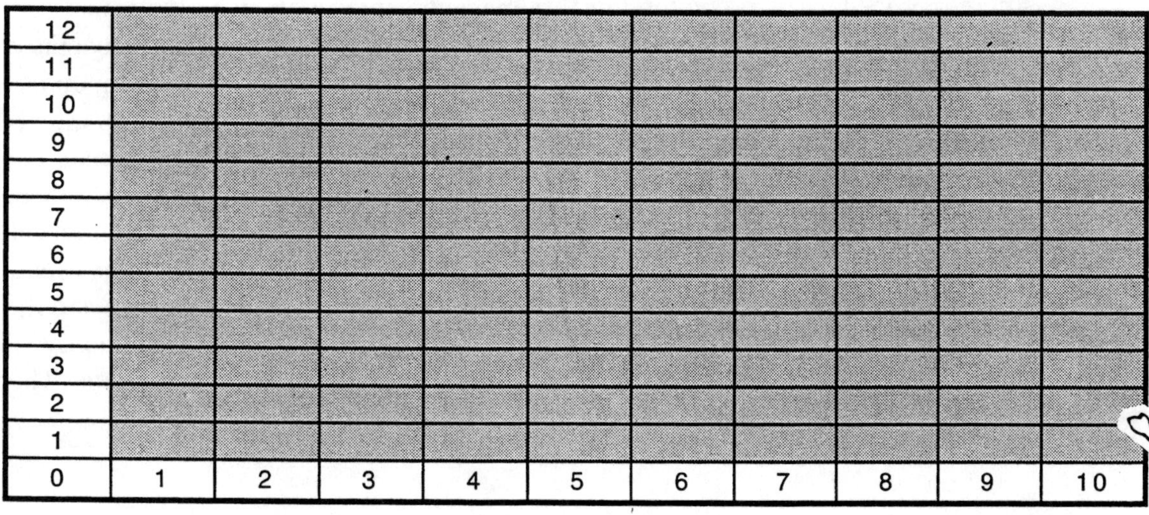

12										
11										
10										
9										
8										
7										
6										
5										
4										
3										
2										
1										
0	1	2	3	4	5	6	7	8	9	10

Meaningful And Manageable Assessment Through Cooperative Learning, Interaction Book Company, 7208 Cornelia Drive, Edina, MN 55435, (612) 831-9500, FAX (612) 831-9332.

Step Six: Plan For Improvement

The sixth step is to generate an improvement theory/plan based on the analysis of the data collected. The theory/plan specifies how the team plans to modify or replace the process in order to improve the quality of the team's work. The results of the current quality chart and the long-term trend of increasing or decreasing quality of work is examined. Plans are made to improve the processes of learning and thereby improve the quality and quantity of members' learning.

Step Seven: Repeat Learning Process In A Modified Way

Step Seven is for the team to implement its plans. The focus is on making small, incremental improvements in a process day after day after day. The team carefully evaluates the implementation (members gather more data). If the modified process works, the team adopts it. If it does not work, the team redesigns it and tries it out again on a small basis.

STEP EIGHT: INSTITUTIONALIZE CHANGES

The eighth step is to institutionalize the changes that work and the continuous improvement process. Ensure that there is no backsliding (reverting to the old practices) by taking new data samples forever, analyzing them, revising the theory/plan, revising the process, and so forth.

Student-Management Teams

Another procedure based on total quality management principles is student management teams. A **student management team** consists of three or four students plus the instructor who assume responsibility for the success of the class by focusing on how to improve either the instructor's teaching or the content of the course. The group members monitor the course through their own experience and the comments of classmates. They then make recommendations as to how the course could be improved. The group meets weekly. The quality of the course is analyzed, suggestions for improving the course are developed, and plans are made for implementing the suggestions. The meetings usually last for about one hour and occur on neutral territory, away from the classroom and the instructor's office.. The group maintains a journal of suggestions on how to improve the course, the actions taken, and the success or failure of the implementation efforts. There are four stages in implementing a student management team:

Stage One: Forming. The instructor asks for students to volunteer to be on the committee and selects three of four members from the pool of volunteers.

Stage Two: Team Building. The instructor meets with the team and presents the team goal of ensuring the course's success by continuously improving the instruction and course content. The initial task needs to be easy for the group to achieve and should highlight the interdependence between the instruction and the student members. In other words, the initial task should be such that the instructor cannot complete it without the help of the student members. Members should be accountable to contribute their share of the work, learn the teamwork skills required, and regularly process how effectively the team is functioning. The instruction's receptivity to feedback and criticism and encouragement for student members to improve the course at this point either builds or destroys the group's trust.

Stage Three: Improving The Course.

a. To improve instruction, the instructor and the student members may wish to (a) examine specific aspects of instruction the instructor wishes feedback on, (b) conduct a survey of previous classes to discover which aspects of instruction they should focus their attention on, and (c) conduct formative surveys of the effectiveness of instruction at various points throughout the semester, plot the data in quality charts, systematically implement the team's suggestions for change, and track the impact of the changes on the quality of instruction.

b. To improve the content of the course, the team may focus on improving the clarity and organization of the course material, evaluate the effectiveness of the texts, and do a time-benefit analysis of course assignments.

Stage Four: Reaping Long-Term Gains. The team keeps a written log on the progress of the class with notes of insights and changes they have implemented. This written log provides guidelines for the instructor on how to revise the instruction and content of the course for the next semester.

Summary

Faculty empower students by placing them in teams and assigning them the task of continuously improving the quality of the processes of learning. **Continuous improvement** is the ongoing search (made by everyone from students to school board members) for incremental changes that can be made to increase the quality of the processes of learning, instructing, and administrating. Each time students write a composition, for example, they should find at least one way to improve their writing skills. The change does not have to be dramatic. Small, incremental changes are fine.

To improve continuously the process of learning, students need to engage in eight steps. First, they must form teams. Quality learning is not possible without cooperative learning groups. Second, team members analyze the assignment and select a learning process for improvement. Third, members define the process to improve, usually by drawing a flow chart or cause-and-effect diagram. Fourth, team members engage in the process. Fifth, students gather data about the process, display the data, and analyze it. Tools to help them do so include observation forms, Pareto charts, run charts, scatter diagrams, and histograms. Sixth, on the basis of the analysis, team members make a plan to improve the process. Seventh, students implement the plan by engaging in the learning process in a modified and improved way. Finally, the team institutionalizes the changes that do in fact improve the quality of the learning process.

Total quality learning may also be promoted through the use of student management teams. A **student management team** consists of three or four students plus the instructor who assume responsibility for the success of the class by focusing on how to improve either the instructor's teaching or the content of the course. The group members monitor the course through their own experience and the comments of classmates. There are four stages of using student management teams: forming the team by recruiting and choosing members, building a cooperative team by structuring the five basic elements, improving the instruction and content of the course, and reaping the long-term gains from the process by carrying on the improvements to the next course.

The process of continuous improvement needs to be placed in the context of improving the quality of learning. For students, this starts with cooperative learning groups. A constancy of purpose is created among students by structuring strong positive goal interdependence. Students adopt the new philosophies of quality learning (each group member completes perfectly done assignments every time) and continuous improvement (each day students improve their learning abilities). Students spend less time focused on test scores and more time on examining the process of learning and continuously improving it. Ongoing training in teamwork and academic skills is made an essential part of daily school life. Leadership is distributed among all group members. Fear is driven out of the classroom by eliminating all competition among students and increasing social support. Barriers among students are reduced by ensuring that the cooperative learning groups are heterogeneous and strong relationships are built among students.

Meaningful And Manageable Assessment Through Cooperative Learning, Interaction Book Company, 7208 Cornelia Drive, Edina, MN 55435, (612) 831-9500, FAX (612) 831-9332.

Chapter Fourteen: Teaching Teams And Assessment

Colleagial Teaching Teams

Assessment and reporting practices of schools have become so labor intensive and complex that one teacher cannot expect to do them alone. Realistically, colleagial teaching teams are needed to coordinate and continuously improve the instruction, assessment, reporting process (Johnson & Johnson, 1994). **Colleagial teaching teams** consist of two to five faculty members who work together to implement instructional, assessment, and reporting procedures with fidelity and flexibility as well as solve any implementation problems that may arise. The activities of a colleagial teaching team include (a) professional discussions in which faculty conceptually clarify the instructional, assessment, and reporting procedures, (b) coplanning, codesigning, and copreparing lessons, assessment procedures, and reporting procedures, and (c) co-implementing the instructional, assessment, and reporting procedures, and (d) co-assessing how successful the lessons and procedures were. The reasons for conducting assessments in teaching teams include the fact that in general, team efforts are more productive than individual efforts (Johnson & Johnson, 1989) and the labor intensive nature of many of the new assessment procedures is significantly reduced when teachers coordinate their assessment efforts.

Colleagial teaching teams focus on assessing the (a) quality and quantity of student learning and (b) quality of the overall instructional program. **First, teacher teams are needed to assess the quality and quantity of student learning and communicate the results to interested audiences**. Using a variety of alternative assessment methods allows you to know your students better and to provide them and other interested stakeholders such as their parents with more precise and descriptive information about the students' progress. The more intensive and varied the assessment procedures, however, the more time and effort it takes to implement them and, therefore, the more help teachers need from colleagues.

Second, teacher teams are needed to assess the quality of instructional programs. Instructional programs consist of curriculum materials and instructional procedures. Pressures to assess and reform curricula and instructional methods come form many areas, not the least of which is the establishment of ambitious content knowledge standards at the district, state, and national levels. In order to ensure that students reach those content standards, new assessment procedures congruent with the standards are needed. Instructional programs extend beyond any one individual teacher and, therefore, teacher teams (not individual teachers) should be responsible for collecting, organizing, and

Meaningful And Manageable Assessment Through Cooperative Learning, Interaction Book Company, 7208 Cornelia Drive, Edina, MN 55435, (612) 831-9500, FAX (612) 831-9332.

communicating the data about the quality of instruction in a school and district. In assessing the effectiveness of instruction programs, teacher teams have to be concerned with such issues as (a) the use of national standards to evaluate the quality of schooling, (b) comparisons being made among schools, school districts, and states, (c) accountability to a wider variety of audiences (such as business and industry, state legislators, and foreign companies who are considering locating a facility in the community), (d) accountability to achieve more diverse outcomes (such as ability to work effectively in teams and with diverse teammates), (e) broader definitions of achievement, and (f) the need to compete with schools in other countries.

Conducting The Assessment And Reporting Process

Once colleagial teaching teams are organized and focused on the continuous improvement of student learning and the quality of instruction, the next step is to conduct the assessment and reporting process. The assessment and reporting process includes (a) developing rubrics, (b) applying the rubric in a reliable way, and (c) communicating the results to interested audiences.

In order to conduct a valid and reliable assessment, teachers need clearly defined rubrics that contain the criteria used in evaluating a student's work or the quality of the instructional program. In developing rubrics, two heads are better than one, especially if a number of teachers plan to use the same rubric in a reliable way. Whoever is going to use the rubric should have their say in developing it.

Developing rubrics is usually hard, time consuming work. It is, however, one of the most important professional conversations that teachers can have. Developing rubrics requires teachers to think very clearly and come to consensus about what is "quality" work. The best way to craft rubrics is for a team of teachers and others to meet regularly to decide on the relevant dimensions of a performance and draft possible criteria, try them out with their students, and revise them as needed.

Developing the rubrics in teams increases teachers' co-orientation and ability to apply the same rubric in the same way. Students may be confused, for example, if one teacher scores compositions with a heavy emphasis on writing mechanics while another teacher scores compositions with a heavy emphasis on ideas and creativity. Teachers need to become co-oriented as to the criteria used to evaluate and communicate about students' work.

In assessing students' learning and skills, there are a number of problems that require teacher teams to solve.

1. **Generalizability of Scores**: We know very little about the number of performances necessary to estimate a student's ability accurately. Shavelson, Gao, and Baxter (1991), for example, concluded that in order to estimate accurately a student's problem-solving ability in mathematics and science, eight to twenty performances are needed. Such estimates, however, vary considerably by content areas, specific curriculum, and grade level. The circumstances under which the performances are made, furthermore, effect how reflective they are of what the students can do.

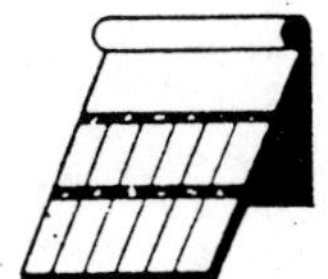

2. **Lack of Inter-Student Comparisons**: Comparing the performances of one student with those of another can be very subjective.

3. **Student Self-Ratings**: It is unclear how student self-ratings contribute to assessments of academic or behavioral development.

4. **Score Aggregation**: For each student performance, there may be a series of criteria used in assessment. The resulting ratings are aggregated for any one performance and across all the student's performances to obtain a summary overall rating. What results is similar to a grade.

5. **Score Reliability**: In order for scores to be reliable, (a) different teachers must give the student performance the same score or (b) the same teacher must give the student performance the same score at two different times. To achieve reliability, (a) criteria have to be anchored in observable and objective characteristics of a performance and (b) simple rubrics must be developed and used to guide assessment. The more complex the criteria and rubrics, the lower the reliability tends to be. High interrater reliability may be achieved when a team of teachers score student performances together and discuss why each performance does or does not meet the criteria. Such discussions allow teachers to become co-oriented as to what the criteria mean and how they may be applied to student performances.

6. **Time And Other Costs Required For Assessment Activities**: There is very little data on the value of the new assessment procedures weighed against the cost in teacher time and other resources required to implement them.

7. **Teacher Training Required**: Teachers need training in how to conduct valid and reliable assessments. Even when clear scoring standards have been developed, teachers may not apply the standards consistently without direct, systematic, ongoing training. This training has to be ongoing--just because teachers achieve a high-level of interrater reliability at one time does not mean it will continue forever. Even experienced teachers are often guilty of "scoring criteria drift" by developing idiosyncratic scoring rules or discontinuing to use the recommended scoring criteria.

8. **Continual refining and upgrading**. Once established, a rubric is not written in stone. The criteria used in the rubrics need to go through a continuous improvement process where teachers regularly discuss them and refine, upgrade, and improve the criteria and the words/phrases used to describe them.

Communicating the results of assessments may involve helping others understand what is and is not quality work. The more thoroughly students understand the criteria and rubrics, the more able they will be to produce it. Well-defined criteria and rubrics, furthermore, point students toward (a) what they need to do next to improve and (b) the support they need to do so. The more thoroughly parents understand the criteria and rubrics, the more able they are to help students produce quality work. Potential employers will be more able to recognize the quality work students have done as their understanding of the criteria and rubrics increases. The use of charts and graphs to explain student performance over time is especially helpful in the communication process.

Continuous Improvement Of Instruction, Assessment, Reporting

The colleagial teaching team uses the continuous improvement procedure to improve learning, instruction, assessment, and reporting. The team (a) defines the process it is using to instruct, assess, and report the results by drawing a picture of it as a flow chart or cause-and-effect diagram, (b) engage in the process, (c) measure each of its steps, display the data, and analyze it, (d) create and implement an improvement plan that focuses on making small, incremental improvements in the process day after day after day, (e) and repeat steps b, c, and d over and over again (Johnson & Johnson, 1994). This continuous improvement process needs to be institutionalized in the daily ebb and flow of school life.

A procedure for creating the criteria to assess the implementation of the targeted procedures is benchmarking (Johnson & Johnson, 1994). **Benchmarking** is establishing criteria based on best known practices. First, you identify criteria by (a) surveying the research to see what has proven to be effective and (b) locating the schools where it is most successfully implemented. If you can, visit the schools. Second, you set a goal to achieve that level of performance in your classroom and school as a minimum. Third, you plan how you will modify the processes of learning, instructing, and reporting to achieve the goals. Fourth, you assess the effectiveness of what you are doing and adapt the procedures and strategies to your specific situation. Finally, you continue to move your benchmark higher as you reach your initial goals.

For colleagial teaching teams to continuously improve instruction and student learning, members must collect data on a regular basis, portray the data in quality charts, and use benchmarking to determine the criteria for effectiveness.

Low-Cost Arrangements For Working Together

Given below are a number of low cost arrangements for giving teachers time to coplan and coteach in their colleagial support groups. Give the pluses and minuses for using each arrangement.

1. Administrator taking one or more classes to free teachers to meet or coteach.

   a. Pluses:

   b. Minuses:

2. A teacher round-robin where one teacher takes more than one class in order to free colleagues to meet or coteach.

   a. Pluses:

   b. Minuses:

3. Send classes to the library for study and research so teachers can meet or coteach.

   a. Pluses:

   b. Minuses:

4. Have aides, parents, or student teachers take one or more classes so teachers can meet or coteach.

   a. Pluses:

   b. Minuses:

5. Have gym or music teachers take several classes at the same time so teachers can meet or coteach.

   a. Pluses:

   b. Minuses:

Meaningful And Manageable Assessment Through Cooperative Learning, Interaction Book Company, 7208 Cornelia Drive, Edina, MN 55435, (612) 831-9500, FAX (612) 831-9332.

Summary

The days are gone when a teacher, working in isolation from colleagues, could instruct, assess, and report results by him- or herself. The practices have become so labor intensive and complex that one teacher cannot expect to do them alone. Realistically, colleagial teaching teams are needed to coordinate and continuously improve the instruction, assessment, and reporting process. Teachers need to begin their instruction, assessment, and reporting efforts with forming a colleagial teaching team. This allows them to capitalize on the many ways teams enhance productivity. The team focuses its efforts on continuously improving both student learning and the quality of instruction. The team as a whole conducts the assessment and reporting process by developing rubrics, applying the rubrics effectively, and reporting results to interested audiences. The team then establishes a continuous improvement process focusing on maximizing the quality of instruction of each member. While engaging in the continuous improvement process, the team establishes a parallel continuously retraining process whereby team members learn how to use the instruction, assessment, and reporting procedures more effectively and to adapt and refine them as conditions in the school change. The team enlist the aid of all other school faculty in ensuring that the school's ecology supports and enhances learning and instruction. Finally, teachers have to remember that establishing and maintaining effective colleagial teaching teams is not easy. It takes continual effort.

Colleagial Teaching Teams

1. **What is a colleagial teaching team?**

2. **What are the two purposes of the colleagial teaching team?**

   a.

   b.

Colleagial teaching teams focus on continuously improving the assessment of the (a) quality and quantity of student learning and the communication the results to interested audiences and (b) quality of instructional program.

3. **Who will be the members of your colleagial teaching team?** List the names of the teachers in your school who are most competent. Then list the names of the teachers in your building who are most committed to assessment. Then choose those teachers who are on both lists and who like each other the most (committed to each other as friends). These are probably the teachers who you will want to be in your colleagial teaching team. Include at least five teachers on the list as one or more may be unwilling or unable to volunteer the time needed (at least one formal meeting a week and daily hallway meetings).

Most Competent	Most Committed	Like Each Other	Teaching Team

Meaningful And Manageable Assessment Through Cooperative Learning, Interaction Book Company, 7208 Cornelia Drive, Edina, MN 55435, (612) 831-9500, FAX (612) 831-9332.

4. **When, where, and how often will the colleagial support group meet?** Regular meetings are necessary if team members are to create and operate assessment systems. Daily quick discussions between classes will supplement formal meetings.

a. When:

b. Where:

c. How often (at least once a week is recommended):

5. **What are the resources the colleagial teaching team needs?** Team members may need further training, more practice, or visits to other schools to see various assessment systems in action. Plan what resources the team will need to ensure members continually grow in expertise in conducting high quality assessments.

a.

b.

c.

d.

6. **List the ways you will structure the five basic elements of cooperation into the teaching team**:

a. Positive Interdependence:

b. Individual Accountability:

c. Promotive (Face-To-Face) Interaction:

d. Social Skills:

e. Processing:

Creating Rubrics To Assess Student Learning

Step One: Define the assessment procedure. Indicate on the checklist below the procedures the team will use to assess students' learning.

_____ Quizzes, Tests, Examinations

_____ Compositions

_____ Presentations

_____ Projects, Experiments, Surveys, Historical Research

_____ Homework, Extra-Credit

_____ Other:

_____ Other:

Step Two: Develop a set of criteria to use in evaluating the performance produced by students. The steps for doing so are:

______ a. Brainstorm a potential list of criteria

______ b. Rank order the criteria from most important to least important.

______ c. Construct a rubric for each criterion. Begin with the criterion ranked most important by listing indicators of very poor, poor, middle, good, and very good levels of performance.

______ d. Find some exemplary and very poor student performances and analyze them to help develop a set of indicators that accurately measures their strengths and weaknesses.

______ e. Apply the rubrics to a set of sample performances.

Step Three: Construct rubrics. Rubrics are needed to assess the quality and quantity of each student's performance for each criterion.

______ a. Begin with the criterion ranked most important.

______ b. List indicators of very poor, poor, middle, good, and very good levels of performance.

______ c. Find some exemplary and very poor student performances and analyze them to help develop a set of indicators that accurately measures their strengths and weaknesses.

Meaningful And Manageable Assessment Through Cooperative Learning, Interaction Book Company, 7208 Cornelia Drive, Edina, MN 55435, (612) 831-9500, FAX (612) 831-9332.

Step Four: Train the teachers in using the rubric so that they are co-oriented, consistent, and reliable in their use of the rubric. Teachers have to be able to apply the same rubric in the same way at different times. Different teachers have to be able to apply the same rubric in the same way. One procedure for training is:

_____ a. Score a student performance together as a group, discussing how the performance should be assessed on each criterion.

_____ b. Score a set of student performances separately, with each team member scoring the performances on his or her own. Then compare the scoring to see if team members are using the rubrics in the same way.

_____ c. Score all student performances with at least two team members scoring each performance. Any differences in the scoring are then discussed until two or more team members agree on the scoring of each student performance.

Step Five: On the basis of the assessment, plan how to improve the instructional program. Suggestions are:

1.

2.

3.

Step Six: Continually improve the criteria, the indicators for each criterion, and the team members' skills in using the rubrics to assess the quality and quality of student learning. Beware of scoring criteria drift. Remember the need to periodically recalibrate team members' use of the scoring rubrics. Search for exemplary rubrics and scoring procedures in other teams and schools and use them as benchmarks to improve your team's assessment practices.

Assessment Rubric

Student: ______________________ **Date:** __________ **Class:** ______________

Type Of Performance: ____

Write the indicators for each of the five levels of performance for each criterion.

VERY POOR	POOR	MIDDLE	GOOD	VERY GOOD
Criterion One				
♦	♦	♦	♦	♦
♦	♦	♦	♦	♦
♦	♦	♦	♦	♦
Criterion Two				
♦	♦	♦	♦	♦
♦	♦	♦	♦	♦
♦	♦	♦	♦	♦
Criterion Three				
♦	♦	♦	♦	♦
♦	♦	♦	♦	♦
♦	♦	♦	♦	♦
Criterion Four				
♦	♦	♦	♦	♦
♦	♦	♦	♦	♦
♦	♦	♦	♦	♦
Criterion Five				
♦	♦	♦	♦	♦
♦	♦	♦	♦	♦
♦	♦	♦	♦	♦

Comments:

Assessment Rubric

Student: ______________________ **Date:** _________ **Class:** ______________

Type Of Performance: ____

Write the indicators for each of the five levels of performance for each criterion.

INADEQUATE	MIDDLE	EXCELLENT
Criterion One		
♦	♦	♦
♦	♦	♦
♦	♦	♦
Criterion Two		
♦	♦	♦
♦	♦	♦
♦	♦	♦
Criterion Three		
♦	♦	♦
♦	♦	♦
♦	♦	♦
Criterion Four		
♦	♦	♦
♦	♦	♦
♦	♦	♦
Criterion Five		
♦	♦	♦
♦	♦	♦
♦	♦	♦

Comments:

Meaningful And Manageable Assessment Through Cooperative Learning, Interaction Book Company, 7208 Cornelia Drive, Edina, MN 55435, (612) 831-9500, FAX (612) 831-9332.

Chapter Fifteen: Giving Grades

What Is Grading?

"The Committee On Grading was called upon to study grading procedures. At first, the task of investigating the literature seemed to be a rather hopeless one. What a mass and a mess it all was! Could order be brought out of such chaos? Could points of agreement among American educators concerning the perplexing grading problem actually be discovered? It was with considerable misgiving and trepidation that the work was finally begun."

Warren Middleton, 1933

While the quality of student learning and the instructional program can be assess in many different ways, periodically teachers are asked to give an overall summation of the learning achieved by each of the students. This grading is not necessary for the instructional or the learning processes. Teachers can teach without grades and students can and do learn without grades. Giving grades does not improve teaching and receiving grades does not increase learning. Most teachers, however, are required by their school districts to give students grades at regular intervals. This requirement is not new. The issues of grading and reporting on student learning have been with us a long time. Many great minds have tried to resolve the difficulties of grading. Yet the difficulties persist. What Middleton struggled with 60 years ago, we struggle with today.

Grades are given because they are perceived as being the most effective way of communicating summative evaluations. **Grades** are symbols (letters, numbers, words) that represent a value judgment concerning the relative quality of a student's achievement during a specified period of instruction. In giving grades you summarize and combine each student's performances on a variety of assignments. You may even add in bonus points for other aspects of achievement, such as effort, attendance, and participation in class.

Why Grades Must Be Fair

"The real voyage of discovery consists not in seeking new landscapes, but in having new eyes."

Marcel Proust, 1871-1922, French novelist

Grades are important. A student's grades may determine whether he or she is admitted into gifted education and advanced placement classes. A student's grades

Meaningful And Manageable Assessment Through Cooperative Learning, Interaction Book Company, 7208 Cornelia Drive, Edina, MN 55435, (612) 831-9500, FAX (612) 831-9332

determine which educational and career opportunities are available to him or her. A student's grades determine whether he or she receives certain honors and recognition (such as being a National Merit Scholar). In the 1960s, grades were used to determine which male college students were drafted by the military. Since drafted males were often sent to Vietnam and in Vietnam many were killed, college grades literally determined in some cases who lived and who died. The power of grades to determine a student's educational and career opportunities as well as future earnings makes giving grades perhaps the most serious responsibility teachers have. This may be why giving grades is frequently cited as the most difficult and least desirable task teachers face.

The fairness of grading depends largely on the basis on which they are distributed. There are three possible bases for distributing grades to students: **equity** (the person who contributes the most or scores the highest receives the greatest reward), **equality** (every person receives the same reward), and **need** (those who have the greatest need receive the greatest reward). All three systems operate within our society and all three systems have ethical rationales. Typically, the equality system assures persons that their basic needs will be met and that diverse contributions will be equally valued. The need system assures persons that in moments of crisis others will provide support and assistance. The equity system assures members that if they strive for excellence, their contributions will be valued and rewarded. Educators who wish to give rewards in the classroom merely on the basis of equity may be viewing "fairness" from too limited a perspective.

Whether grades are perceived as fair may depend on several factors (Johnson & Johnson, 1989):

1. Students who "lose" in a competitive learning situations commonly perceive the grading system as unjust and, consequently, dislike the class and the teacher.

2. Before a task is performed, group members generally perceive a competitive grading system as being the most fair, but after a task is completed, having all members receive the same grade or reward is viewed as the fairest.

3. The more frequently students have experienced long-term cooperative learning experiences, and the more cooperative learning was used in their classes, the more students believed that (a) everyone who tries has an equal chance to succeed in class, (b) students get the grades they deserve, and (c) the grading system is fair.

History Of Grading

Pre-1850:	Throughout human history, assessment of what students have learned has always occurred. The Ancient Greeks, for example, had students orally explain what they knew so teachers could determine which topics the student had yet to master. Summative evaluation with the use of grades, on the other hand, is relatively new.
1850s:	Summative grades were introduced in the United States. Before this time, grading was virtually unknown.
Late 1880s:	Teachers were asked to issue progress evaluations on each student by writing down the skills the student had mastered. Students who completed the requirements for one level could move up to the next level.
Early 1900s:	With the dramatic increase in secondary education, high school teachers introduced percentages as a way to certify students' accomplishments in specific subject areas. Elementary teachers continued to use written descriptions to document student learning.
1912	The use of percentage grades was challenged as being unreliable by studies that demonstrated that different teachers would give markedly different percentile grades to the same English, history, or geometry papers.
1918:	Many teachers adopted grading scales with fewer and larger categories. A three-point scale used the categories Excellent, Average, and Poor. A five-point scale used the categories Excellent, Good, Average, Poor, and Failing with the corresponding letters of A, B, C, D, and F.
Early 1930s:	Norm-referenced grading became popular as a way to reduce the subjectivity of grading. Some advocates specified that 6 percent of students in a class should receive an A, 22 percent a B, 44 percent a C, 22 percent a D, and 6 percent a F. The rationale was that since scores on intelligence tests in the United States approximated a normal probability curve, the achievement scores of students within any class would also.
Late 1930s:	The debate over grading became so intense that a number of schools abolished formal grades altogether and returned to using verbal descriptions of student achievement. Other districts adopted pass-fail grading systems, while others adopted a mastery approach where students had to master a skill or content area before they moved on to other areas of study.
1950s:	Researchers focused on how best to use grades concluded that a combination of grades with narrative feedback was more effective in increasing student learning than were grades by themselves.
1980s:	Researchers concluded that the person assessing students' work and giving grades was learning more than were the students receiving the grades and, therefore, students should be in assessing and evaluating each other's work.
1990s:	Alternative assessment procedures such as portfolios were recommended.

Why Give Grades

Rank the following reasons for giving grades from most important ("1") to least important "8").

______ To make students conform to the demands of the instructional program (value the goals, be involved, complete assignments, learn).

______ To provide students access to certain educational programs and careers.

______ To give students information about their level of achievement so they can (a) gauge their strengths and weaknesses, (b) better understand what is expected of them, and (c) better understand how they may improve.

______ To communicate a student's level of achievement to parents and other interested parties (such as college admission officers and potential employers).

______ To give students an extrinsic reward or incentive to learn.

______ To sort students into categories and identify students for particular educational paths or programs.

______ To evaluate an instructional program's effectiveness.

______ To punish students who do not comply with requests or obey the rules or who display a lack of effort, responsibility, civility, and respect.

Not all purposes can be accomplished with any one grade. Different teachers will use grades to accomplish different purposes and, therefore, conflicts over grading can arise in a school or district. Many primary teachers report that they give grades because the school district requires it, while many middle and high school teachers report they give grades to inform students of their progress.

Subjective Nature Of Grading

One of the criticisms of grading is that grades are too subjective. In 1912, Starch and Elliott shocked educators into a consideration of subjectivity by publishing a study in which two papers written for a first year English class in high school were sent to English teachers in 200 high schools for grading. Each teacher was asked to score the papers according to his or her school's standards. A percentage (0 to 100) scale was to be used, with 75 percent as a passing grade. Fifteen percent of the teachers gave one paper a failing mark while 12 percent gave it a score of 90 or more. The scores ranged from 64 to 98 percent, with a mean of 88.2. The other paper received a mean score of

Meaningful And Manageable Assessment Through Cooperative Learning, Interaction Book Company, 7208 Cornelia Drive, Edina, MN 55435, (612) 831-9500, FAX (612) 831-9332.

80.2 with scores ranging from 50 to 97. Some teachers graded the papers on whether it communicated its message while other teachers took into account neatness, spelling, and punctuation. Defenders of percentage grading criticized this study on the basis that judging good writing is, by its very nature, very subjective. In 1913 Starch and Elliott, therefore, repeated their study using history and geometry papers. For the geometry papers they found even greater variations, with scores on one paper ranging from 28 to 95. Some teachers took neatness, form, and spelling into account while others graded only for correct answers.

No matter what you do, grading and reporting will **always** involve some degree of **subjectivity**. Subjectivity opens the door to bias. Teachers' prejudices and expectations can influence their judgments of students' achievements and performances and certain characteristics (such as neatness of handwriting) can significantly influence a teacher's judgment. Subjectivity of grading is increased when ambiguous student behaviors are included in the grade estimates. Subjectivity can be reduced by (a) making the criteria contained in the scoring rubric specific and detailed and (b) ensuring that all teachers in the school district use the same criteria. Having each student performance evaluated by more than one teacher will also reduce subjectivity.

Types Of Grading Systems

There are two types of grading systems: Single-grade and multi-grade. Most commonly, teachers have used a single-mark system of grading in which students can receive an A, B, C, D, or F. The single mark system of grading is simple, concise, and convenient. The most common single mark system is letter grades of:

A	Excellent, Outstanding Work	Distinguished	4 Points
B	Good, Noteworthy Work	Proficient	3 Points
C	Average, Competent Work	Apprentice	2 Points
D	Poor, Minimally Acceptable Work	Novice	1 Point
F	Failing, Unacceptable Work		0 Points

In elementary school, teachers sometimes use single mark system of outstanding-satisfactory-unsatisfactory. Some secondary schools use a pass-fail or pass-no credit system.

The advantages of the single-mark system are that grades (a) provide a succinct description of achievement, (b) are generally understood, (c) predict future grades and how many years of conventional education students will attain, (d) can motivate students to expend more effort to achieve (perhaps more to avoid the consequences of low grades than to attain high grades), and (e) are positive recognition of success.

Meaningful And Manageable Assessment Through Cooperative Learning, Interaction Book Company, 7208 Cornelia Drive, Edina, MN 55435, (612) 831-9500, FAX (612) 831-9332

The disadvantages of the single-mark system are that the single grade (a) cannot give a full picture of the many facets of achievement, (b) is limited to one particular frame of reference, (c) is inherently ambiguous as to what it represents (as it is not keyed to any common standard), and (d) may discourage effort to learn by creating a ceiling for high achievers and demoralizing lower-achieving students.

There are other problems with grading. One is that a grade is essentially arbitrary. There is no way to make meaningful "break points" between the different grades. If a grade of B ranges from 80 to 89, students at both ends of that range receive the same grade even though their scores differ by nine points, but the student with a score of 79 (a one point difference) receives a grade of C). Another is that grades are often overgeneralized so that they are taken as an indication of a student's total competence and worth as an individual, rather than as a summative evaluation of the student's mastery of certain limited knowledge and skills.

A third problem is the wide diversity among teachers as to the criteria they use when assigning grades. While the criteria for awarding grades is sometimes specified by the school district, most often each teacher uses very broad guidelines in deciding what criteria to use in grading students. A teacher may be questioned if he or she gives most students As or Fs, but between these two extremes teachers have considerable leeway to assign grades on any basis they wish.

A fourth problem is that grades have little value as either incentives or feedback as they are often given infrequently, far removed from student performance, and poorly tied to student behaviors. Finally, the evidence indicates that grades are nearly useless in developing important qualities such as inventiveness, leadership, workmanship, good citizenship, personal maturity, and family happiness.

A multi-grade system may contain different grades for different aspects of learning. Grades may focus on **product criteria** (a summative evaluation of student achievement that focuses on what students know and are able to do), **process criteria** (the processes students use to learn including effort or work habits), or **progress criteria** (improvement scoring, learning gain). While a combination of the three may be used to determine grades, usually the more process and progress criteria are taken into account, the more subjective and biased grades may become. Grades have also been proposed for (a) how the student's achievement compares with other students at the same grade level or with the standards set by the district, state, or country or (b) the degree of the student's effort.

How To Grade

The power of grades to impact students' future life creates a responsibility for giving grades in a fair and impartial way. A procedure for doing so is as follows:

1. **Decide what the grade will represent**:

   a. Decide on the primary purpose of the grade. Usually, the purpose of grading is to indicate how much each student learned during the course.

   b. Decide on who the grade is intended for. Usually, the grade is primarily intended for the student.

   c. Decide on the results you are hoping to achieve with the grade. Usually, the hoped for result is to enhance students' learning.

2. **Estimate what percentage of students should receive each grade.** After grades have been awarded you compare the actual number of students who received each grade with your ideal estimate.

3. **For indices of learning in a cooperative or individualistic context, set criteria for making categorical judgments about student performance**. Seek help from the curriculum coordinator, subject matter specialists, teacher committees, the school administration, and from parents and students.

4. **For indices of learning in a competitive context**, rank the students from best to worst. The number of competitive learning situations should be nonexistent or very limited to avoid the destructive effects of introducing competition among students. For a discussion of the conditions under which competition may be used constructively, see Johnson, Johnson, and Holubec (1992).

5. **Standardize the scoring system and determine the total number of points earned by each student during the course**.

   a. At the end of the grading period, add together all the scores for each type of performance and compare the actual number of points earned with the total possible number of points. Covert each raw score to a percentage score. This initially equalizes the scores for each type of student performance.

   b. Decide how much weight each type of performance should have in the final grade. Weight the different assignments according to their accuracy in demonstrating what students have actually learned during the course.

   c. Multiple the performance score times the weight.

d. Then all the total points together to determine the grand total.

e. Look for extremely low scores on an assignment that may bias the results. Remember that the final grade should reflect what the student has actually learned and mastered. Use your judgment in discarding any extremely low scores that may have unfair influence on the final grade. Then recalculate the percentage score for that type of performance.

6. **Set the criteria on which final grades will be determined.** Students should know at the beginning of the course how many points it will take to earn an A and how each assignment will be weighted. Grades should never surprise students. Students should know how they are doing throughout a course and know how their grades will be computed.

7. **Personalize the evaluation by including notes on incidents and behaviors**, with dates, summaries of conferences with parents and other teachers, and long-term growth information. Grades should not stand alone. More comprehensive written narrative and checklist evaluations should be added to provide more information to students.

8. **Avoid practices that result in grades that misrepresent the student's level of achievement**. The key question is, "*What is the level of the student's achievement*?" Two of those practices are averaging and assigning zeros to missing or late work (Guskey, 1994).

   a. Averaging fails to provide an accurate description of what students have learned. If a student has to get a B on a comprehensive final exam to pass a course, for example, it is confusing because clearly the student has learned the assigned material at a B level. Yet many teachers would give the student a D by averaging his or her scores over the entire course.

   b. When work that is late, missed, or neglected is given a score of zero, it does not accurately reflect the level of the student's learning. The zero is usually assigned to punish students for not displaying appropriate responsibility. A zero is especially punishing when it is combined with the practice of averaging. When a student receives a single zero, chances for an A are usually eliminated because a single extreme score skews the average.

Some districts have eliminated traditional letter grades at the primary level or even through the eighth grade and replaced them with checklists and narratives. Even in some high schools and colleges, traditional letter grades are being replaced with portfolios and other alternative assessment procedures.

Checklists And Narratives

Because of the limitations of a single-mark system of grading, some schools have adopted more complex and complete summative evaluation procedures, such as checklists and narratives.

Checklists

Checklists are aimed at providing a detailed analysis of the student's strengths and weaknesses. The advantages of checklists include (a) they provide a clear description of achievement and (b) they are useful for diagnosing what students do and do not know and for prescribing what students should study next. The disadvantages of checklists include that they are (a) often too complicated to understand and (b) seldom communicate the appropriateness of progress the student is making in relation to expectations for their level.

Narratives

A narrative is a detailed, personal report written by the teacher containing all that is known about the student. The advantages of narratives are that they (a) provide a clear description of progress and achievement and (b) are useful for diagnosing what students do and do not know and prescribing what they should learn next. The disadvantages include they (a) are time-consuming for teachers to prepare, (b) may not communicate appropriateness of the student's progress, and (c) may contain standardized comments.

Narratives allow teachers the greatest latitude in personal judgment. Many teachers know their students, understand various dimensions of students' work, and have clear notions of the progress students are making. Teacher judgments may yield very accurate descriptions of what students have learned.

Giving Students Grades in Cooperative Learning

The way grades are given depends on the type of interdependence the instructor wishes to create among students. Norm-referenced grading systems place students in competition with each other. Criterion-referenced grading systems require students to either work individualistically or cooperatively. Here are a number of suggestions for giving grades in cooperative learning situations.

1. **Individual score plus bonus points based on all members reaching criterion:** Group members study together and ensure that all have mastered the assigned material. Each then takes a test individually and is awarded that score. If all group

Meaningful And Manageable Assessment Through Cooperative Learning, Interaction Book Company, 7208 Cornelia Drive, Edina, MN 55435, (612) 831-9500, FAX (612) 831-9332

members achieve over a preset criterion of excellence, each receives a bonus. An example is as follows.

Criteria	Bonus	Members	Scores	Bonus	Total
100	15 Points	Bill	100	10	110
90 - 99	10 Points	Juanita	95	10	105
80 - 89	5 Points	Sally	90	10	100

2. **Individual score plus bonus points based on lowest score:** The group members prepare each other to take an exam. Members then receive bonus points on the basis of the lowest individual score in their group. This procedure emphasizes encouraging, supporting, and assisting the low achievers in the group. The criterion for bonus points can be adjusted for each learning group, depending on the past performance of their lowest member. An example is as follows:

Criteria	Bonus	Members	Scores	Bonus	Total
90 - 100	6 Points	Bill	93	2	95
80 - 89	4 Points	Juanita	85	2	87
70 - 79	2 Points	Sally	78	2	80

3. **Individual score plus group average:** Group members prepare each other to take an exam. Each takes the examination and receives his or her individual score. The scores of the group members are then averaged. The average is added to each member's score. An example is given below.

Student	Individual Score	Group Average	Final Score
Bill	66	79	145
Juanita	89	79	168
Sally	75	79	154
Benjamin	86	79	165

Meaningful And Manageable Assessment Through Cooperative Learning, Interaction Book Company, 7208 Cornelia Drive, Edina, MN 55435, (612) 831-9500, FAX (612) 831-9332.

4. **Individual score plus bonus based on improvement scores:** Members of a cooperative group prepare each other to take an exam. Each takes the exam individually and receives his or her individual grade. In addition, bonus points are awarded on the basis of whether members percentage on the current test is higher than the average percentage on all past tests (i.e., their usual level of performance). Their percentage correct on past tests serves as their base score that they try to better. Every two tests or scores, the base score is updated. If a student scores within 4 points (above or below) his or her base score, all members of the group receive 1 bonus point. If they score 5 to 9 points above their base score, each group member receives 2 bonus points. Finally, if they score 10 points or above their base score, or score 100 percent correct, each member receives 3 bonus points.

5. **Totaling members' individual scores:** The individual scores of members are added together and all members receive the total. For example, if group members scored 90, 85, 95, and 90, each member would receive the score of 360.

6. **Averaging of members' individual scores:** The individual scores of members are added together and divided by the number of group members. Each member then receives the group average as their mark. For example, if the scores of members were 90, 95, 85, and 90, each group member would receive the score of 90.

7. **Group score on a single product:** The group works to produce a single report, essay, presentation, worksheet, or exam. The product is evaluated and all members receive the score awarded. When this method is used with worksheets, sets of problems, and examinations, group members are required to reach consensus on each question and be able to explain it to others. The discussion within the group enhances the learning considerably.

8. **Randomly selecting one member's paper to score:** Group members all complete the work individually and then check each other's papers and certify that they are perfectly correct. Since each paper is certified by the whole group to be correct, it makes little difference which paper is graded. The instructor picks one at random, grades it, and all group members receive the score.
9. **Randomly selecting one member's exam to score:** Group members prepare for an examination and certify that each member has mastered the assigned material. All members then take the examination individually. Since all members have certified that each has mastered the material being studied, it makes little difference which exam is scored. The instructor randomly picks one, scores it, and all group members receive that score.

10. **All members receive lowest member score:** Group members prepare each other to take the exam. Each takes the examination individually. All group members then receive the lowest score in the group. For example, if group members score 89, 88, 82, and 79, all members would receive 79 as their score. This procedure emphasizes

encouraging, supporting and assisting the low-achieving members of the group and often produces dramatic increases in performance by low-achieving students.

11. **Average of academic scores plus collaborative skills performance score:** Group members work together to master the assigned material. They take an examination individually and their scores are averaged. Concurrently, their work is observed and the frequency of performance of specified collaborative skills (such as leadership or trust-building actions) is recorded. The group is given a collaborative skills performance score, which is added to their academic average to determine their overall mark.

12. **Dual academic and nonacademic rewards:** Group members prepare each other for a test, take it individually, and receive an individual grade. On the basis of their group average they are awarded free-time, popcorn, extra recess time, or some other valued reward.

Summary

Teachers need to assess student learning and progress frequently, but they do not need to evaluate or give grades. Assessing involves checking on how students are doing, what they have learned, and what problems or difficulties they have experienced. Grades are symbols that represent a value judgment concerning the relative quality of a student's achievement during a specified period of instruction. Grades are necessary to give students and other interested audiences information about students' level of achievement, evaluate the success of an instructional program, provide students access to certain educational opportunities, and reward students who excel. Grading systems may involve a single grade or multi-grades. It is vital that grades are awarded fairly as they can have considerable influence on students' futures. Being fair includes using a wide variety of assignments to measure achievement. Grades may be supplemented with checklist and narratives to give a more complex and complete summative evaluation of student achievement. Having students work in cooperative groups adds further opportunity to measure aspects of students' learning and assign grades in a variety of ways.

Meaningful And Manageable Assessment Through Cooperative Learning, Interaction Book Company, 7208 Cornelia Drive, Edina, MN 55435, (612) 831-9500, FAX (612) 831-9332.

Grading And Communicating Student Learning

ANSWER EACH OF THE QUESTIONS BELOW AS HONESTLY AS YOU CAN.

1. What are your reasons for giving grades?

a. ______________________________

b. ______________________________

c. ______________________________

2. For whom is the information intended? ______________

3. What are the desired results?

a. ______________________________

b. ______________________________

4. For your classes, indicate (a) what percent of students should ideally receive each grade and (b) what percent of students receive each grade:

Grades	Your Classes	Ideally
A		
B		
C		
D		
F		

5. What assignments were structured:

a. Cooperatively (Criteria-Referenced):

b. Individualistic (Criteria-Referenced):

c. Competitively (Norm-Referenced):

Meaningful And Manageable Assessment Through Cooperative Learning, Interaction Book Company, 7208 Cornelia Drive, Edina, MN 55435, (612) 831-9500, FAX (612) 831-9332

6. **Standardize the scoring systems and determine the total number of points earned by each student during the course:**

Student: ______________________ **Date:** ______ **Course:** ______________

Performance	Percentage Points	Weight	Total
Tests, Quizzes			
Compositions			
Oral Presentations			
Projects, Experiments			
Portfolio			
On-Task, Reasoning			
Social Skills, Helping Others			
Positive Attitudes			
Learning Log, Journal			
Quality Chart			
Homework, Extra-Credit			
Attendance, Participation			
Grand Total			

7. **What are the criteria on which the final grade will be based (never assign final grades on a norm-referenced basis)?**

Grade	Points
A	
B	
C	
D	
F	

8. **How will you personalize the grade for each student?**

Meaningful And Manageable Assessment Through Cooperative Learning, Interaction Book Company, 7208 Cornelia Drive, Edina, MN 55435, (612) 831-9500, FAX (612) 831-9332.

9. What do you like most about assigning grades and using report cards?

a. ____

b. ____

c. ____

10. What do you like least about assigning grades and using report cards?

a. ____

b. ____

c. ____

Meaningful And Manageable Assessment Through Cooperative Learning, Interaction Book Company, 7208 Cornelia Drive, Edina, MN 55435, (612) 831-9500, FAX (612) 831-9332

Chapter Sixteen: Reflections

Conducting Assessments

In the time of change, learners inherit the earth, while the learned find themselves beautifully equipped to deal with a world that no longer exists.

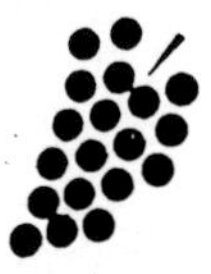

Eric Hoffer

In 1955 Edward Banfield lived for nine months in a small town in southern Italy that he called "Montegrano." What Banfield noticed most was the town's alienated citizenry, grinding poverty, and pervasive corruption. He concluded that the primary source of Montegrano's plight was the distrust, envy, and suspicion that characterized its inhabitants' relations with each other. They viewed communal life as little more than a battleground. Town members consistently refused to help one another unless it would result in material gain. Many actually tried to prevent their neighbors from succeeding, believing that others' good fortune would inevitably undercut their own. Consequently, they remained socially isolated and impoverished, unable to cooperate to solve common problems or pool their resources and talents to build viable economic enterprises.

Montegrano's citizens were not inherently more selfish or foolish than people elsewhere. But for a number of complex historical and cultural reasons, they lacked the norms, habits, attitudes, and networks that encourage people to work together for the common good. They lacked what Alexis de Tocqueville called "the habits of the heart." Habits of the heart include taking responsibility for the common good, trusting others to do the same, being honest, having self-discipline, reciprocating good deeds, and perfecting the skills necessary for cooperation and conflict management. The relationship between democracy and such habits is supported by the fact that in the United States, since the early 1960s voter turnout in national elections has fallen by a quarter and the number of citizens saying that "*most people can be trusted*" has dropped by more than a third.

There is far more to assessment than giving students grades. It is vital to assess what students know, understand, and retain over time (academic learning). It is equally important to assess (a) the quality and level of their reasoning processes and (b) their skills and competencies (such as oral and written communication skills and skills in using technology). In today's complex and every changing world, a broad view of education is needed rather than a narrow focus on the memorization of facts. More than ever, schools need to focus on teaching students appropriate work habits (such as completing work on time and striving for quality work and continuous improvement) and attitudes (such as a love of learning, desire to read good literature, commitment to democracy).

Meaningful And Manageable Assessment Through Cooperative Learning, Interaction Book Company, 7208 Cornelia Drive, Edina, MN 55435, (612) 831-9500, FAX (612) 831-9332

Your Assessment Plan

Given below are generic assessment targets and procedures. In planning your assessment program, check the targets that you wish to assess and then check the procedures you wish to use. Match the procedures with the targets so it is clear how you will assess each target.

What Is Assessed	Procedures Used To Assess
_____ Academic Learning	_____ Goal Setting Conferences
_____ Reasoning Process/Strategies	_____ Standardized Tests
_____ Skills & Competencies	_____ Teacher-Made Tests
_____ Attitudes	_____ Written Compositions
_____ Work Habits	_____ Oral Presentations
	_____ Projects
	_____ Portfolios
	_____ Observations
	_____ Questionnaires
	_____ Interviews
	_____ Learning Logs & Journals
	_____ Student Management Teams

In achieving these complex and long-term responsibilities of the school, teachers need to conduct three types of assessments: diagnostic, formative, and summative. These assessments need to focus on both the process and the outcomes of learning and instruction. Assessments need to take place in more authentic settings as well as in the classroom. The number of stakeholders in education have increased as the world economic and the interdependence among nations have increased. And the stakes of many of the assessments have increased, as students' futures are more and more determined by what they have learned and how many years of formal education they have completed. As the seriousness of educators' responsibilities have increased, so has the need to use a wider variety of assessment procedures.

Meaningful And Manageable Assessment Through Cooperative Learning, Interaction Book Company, 7208 Cornelia Drive, Edina, MN 55435, (612) 831-9500, FAX (612) 831-9332

Making Assessments Meaningful And Manageable

The two major issues educators face in conducting effective and responsible assessments are making the assessments:

1. Meaningful to the various stakeholders.

2. Manageable (so they will actually get done).

Meaningful Assessment

Involvement In Process		Use Of Outcomes	
Less Meaning	**More Meaning**	**Less Meaning**	**More Meaning**
Isolated Goals	Interdependent Goals	Individual Celebration	Joint Celebration
Work Alone	Joint Effort With Others	New Isolated Goals	New Interdependent Goals
Self-Assess Only	Assess Other's Work As Well As One's Own		
Receive Feedback Only	Both Give And Receive Feedback		

The three influences on meaningfulness are interdependence with others, involvement in the learning and assessment processes, and useful results. The more students work alone for strictly self-benefit, the less meaningful the learning and assessment. To increase the meaning, you ensure that students:

1. Are involved in setting learning goals that are interdependent with the goals of groupmates.

2. Are involved in planning how they will achieve their learning goals as part of a joint effort with groupmates.

3. Are involved in planning and conducting the assessment process by assessing the work of their groupmates as well as their own.

4. Participate in a joint celebration of their hard work and success.

5. Reflect on assessment results in ways that provide remediation for what they did not learn and a clear direction for new goals that will take them to the next sequence of learning and assessment activities.

Serious management problems arise in involving students in formulating their learning goals, choosing the paths for achieving the goals, assessing their progress and success, planning how to improve, and implementing their plan.

One teacher working by him- or herself can no longer manage the entire assessment system. The most natural sources of help for teachers are students and colleagues. Students provide the most help because they are available at all times. To be constructive participants in the assessment process, however, students need to be organized into cooperative learning groups. Students oriented toward competition or only their own individualistic efforts are not very helpful in creating a high quality and continuously improving assessment system. To provide quality assessment, students have to be as committed to classmates' learning and academic success as they are to their own. Such commitment only comes from clear positive interdependence.

Cooperative learning groups provide the setting, context, and environment in which assessment becomes part of the instructional process and students learn almost as much from assessing the quality of their own and their classmates' work as they do from participating in the instructional activities.

1. Cooperative learning allows assessment to be integrated into the learning process. **Continuous assessment requires continuous monitoring and support, which can best be done within cooperative learning groups.**

2. The new assessment practices are so labor intensive that students who are sincerely committed to each other's learning and success may need to be involved.

3. Cooperative learning groups allow more modalities to be used in the learning and assessment process while focusing on more diverse outcomes.

4. Cooperative learning groups allow groupmates to be sources of information in addition to the teacher and the curriculum materials.

5. Involving groupmates in assessment reduces possible biases resulting from the teacher being the sole source of feedback and the heavy reliance on reading and writing as assessment modalities.

6. Cooperative learning groups provide each student help in analyzing assessment data, interpreting the results, and implementing improvement plans.

It is difficult to imagine a class in which cooperative learning groups do not help make the assessment system more manageable or how a comprehensive assessment program can be managed without cooperative learning groups.

Conferences With Students

Without clear learning and instructional goals, assessment cannot take place. The goals are created and re-emphasized in three types of conferences with each student: A **goal-setting conference** is conducted to establish a contract containing the student's learning goals, **progress-assessment conferences** are conducted to review the student's progress in achieving his or her goals, and a **post-evaluation conference** is conducted in which the student's accomplishments are explained to interested parties.

Assessment begins with a goal-setting conference in which the student's learning goals and responsibilities for helping other students learn are established. The goal setting conference may be between the teacher and the student (T/S), the teacher and the cooperative learning group (T/G), the cooperative learning group and the student (G/S), and a cooperative learning group and another group (G/G). In all cases, the emphasis is on helping students set and take ownership for learning goals that meet the START criteria (specific, trackable, achievable, relevant, transferable). The goal-setting conference contains four steps: Diagnosis of current level of expertise, setting START goals, organizing support systems and resources to help each student achieve his or her goals successfully, and constructing a plan for utilizing the resources to achieve the goals and formalizing the plan into a learning contract.

Progress-assessment conferences provide wonderful opportunities for teachers to hear how students are thinking about their work. Some schools recommend that a student be interviewed at least once a month. An elementary school teacher would then have one progress-assessment conference a day while a secondary school teachers may need to have four or five conferences a day. Group interviews provide another option.

The hard truth is that most teachers do not have the time to conference with each individual student, whether it is a goal-setting conference, a progress-assessment conference, or a post-evaluation conference. This does not mean that such conferences cannot happen. Teachers can engineer and supervise such conferences through appropriate use of cooperative learning groups. Groups can regularly have progress-assessment conferences with each member while the teacher listens in or pulls one aside individual students for conferences.

Finally, post-evaluation conferences can be held with the teacher, student, and parents. These conferences are especially interesting and fruitful when the student leads them.

Assessment Procedures

Once students have formulated and agreed to their learning goals, a variety of assessment procedures can be used. The assessment procedures include tests, compositions, presentations, projects, portfolios, observations, interviews, questionnaires, and learning logs and journals.

Tests And Examinations

Both standardized and teacher-made tests may be used to assess student learning. Standardized tests are often high-stake events for which students need to be carefully prepared. Teacher-made tests are often a routine part of an instructional program to assess quickly and efficiently a broad sampling of students' knowledge. They may be multiple-choice, true-false, matching, short answers, interpretative, or essay. Although there are many effective assessment procedures, testing remains a mainstay in what teachers do. Cooperative learning groups may be used with tests through the GIG (group preparation, individual test, group test), group discussion, and Teams-Games-Tournament procedures.

Compositions And Presentations

Every educated person should be able to present what they know in written and oral form. These are difficult competencies and to become skilled writers and presenters, students need to write and present every day. This presents an assessment problem, as someone has to read each composition and listen to each presentation and provide helpful feedback. Using cooperative learning groups to assess members' performances accomplishes four goals at the same time. It allows students to engage in the performance frequently, receive immediate and detailed feedback on their efforts, observe closely the performances of others, and see what is good or lacking in others' performances, and provide the labor needed to allow students to engage in a performance frequently. Two of the most common performances assessed are compositions and presentations. In composition pairs, students are assigned to pairs, discuss and outline each other's composition in their pairs, research their topic alone, in pairs write the first paragraph of each composition, write the composition alone, edit each other's composition, rewrite the composition alone, re-edit each other's compositions, sign-off on partner's composition verifying that it is ready to be handed in, and then process the quality of the partnership. The procedure for presentations is very similar.

Individual And Group Projects

A standard part of most every course is allowing students to be creative and inventive in integrating diverse knowledge and skills. This is especially important in assessing multiple intelligences and the ability to engage in complex procedures such as scientific investigation. Projects allow students to use multiple modes of learning. The use of cooperative learning groups allows projects to be considerable more complex and elaborate than any one student could do alone.

Portfolios

Students become far more sophisticated and educated when they can organize their work into a portfolio that represents the quality of their learning in a course or school year. There is no substitute for having students collect and organize their work samples and write a rationale connecting the work samples into a complete and holistic picture of the student's achievements, growth, and development. The resulting portfolio may feature the student's "best works" or the "process" the student is using to learn. Like all other complex and challenging tasks, students need considerable help in constructing their portfolios and in presenting them to teachers, parents, and other interested stakeholders. Portfolios, therefore, may be more manageable when they are constructed within cooperative learning groups. The group can help each member select appropriate work samples and write a coherent and clear rationale. The portfolio may also include the group's assessment of the student's learning and growth.

An interesting extension of portfolios is to have the student, the teacher, and the student's cooperative learning group all independently decide of what represents the student's best work and why. They then have a conference to compare their assessments and resolve any differences.

Observing

There is a limit to the information gained by having students turn in completed tests, compositions, projects, and portfolios. Answers on a test and homework assignments handed in and tell teachers whether students can arrive at a correct answer. They cannot, however, inform teachers as to the quality of the reasoning strategies students are using, students' commitment to classmates' success and well-being, or the extent to which students' can work effectively with others. Teachers must find a way to make students' covert reasoning processes overt, demonstrate behaviorally their attitudes and work habits, and show how skillfully they can work with others. Observing students in action thus becomes one of the most important assessment procedures.

Using observation as an assessment tool requires that you understand the basis of observing, know how to prepare for observing, know how to observe, and know how to summarize the data for use by students and other stake-holders. Preparing for observing involves deciding what actions to observe, who will observe, what the sampling plan will be, constructing an observation form, and training observers to use the form. Observations may be formal or informal, structured or unstructured. In summarizing observations, the data may be displayed in bar or run charts, feedback is then given to the students or other interested parties, the recipients reflect on the feedback and set improvement goals.

One of the primary uses of observation procedures is to assess the use of social skills. The assessment of social skills consists of several steps. **First**, you review the assumptions underlying the teaching of social skills. Social skills must be learned. Every cooperative lesson is a lesson in social skills as well as academics. You must understand what social skills to teach and how to teach them. When teaching social skills be specific, start small, and emphasize overlearning. **Second**, you teach students each social skill. You show the need for the skill, define it with a t-chart, set up practice situations in which students can use the skill, ensure that students receive feedback on their use of the skill and reflect on how to improve, and ensure that students persevere in practicing the skill until it becomes automatic. **Third**, as part of teaching students social skills you structure cooperative learning situations so students can use the social skills and you can observe their doing so. **Fourth**, you intervene in the cooperative learning groups to ensure that members are using the social skills appropriately and to reinforce them for doing so. **Fifth**, you facilitate the self-diagnosis by students of the level of their mastery of the targeted social skills. Students can complete checklists or questionnaires to do so. **Sixth**, you assign students in setting improvement goals to increase their social competence. **Seventh**, you assess students' knowledge of social skills. **Finally**, you report on the level of students' social skills to interested stakeholders, such as the students, parents, and potential employers.

Interviewing

Closely related to observing students in action is interviewing students. Like observing, interviews can make the covert overt through asking students more and more detailed questions about their reasoning processes and strategies. The strengths of the interview is that it is personal and flexible. The personal nature of interviews allows you to build a more positive, supportive, and trusting relationships with each student. The flexibility of interviews allows you to interview either one or a small group of students before, during, and after a lesson and to use the interview for both assessment and teaching purposes. Socrates is an example of a teacher who used interviewing as his major instructional strategy.

Attitude Questionnaires

All learning has affective components and in many ways the attitudes students develop may be more important than their level of academic learning. Getting an "A" in math class, for example, does a student little good if he or she has learned to hate math and never wants to take a math class again. Obviously, loving math and wanting to take math courses throughout one's educational career is far more important than the level of achievement in any one math class. Attitudes largely determine whether students continue to study the subject area, become uninterested, or wish to avoid it in the future. In assessing student attitudes, you (a) decide which attitudes to measure, (b) construct a questionnaire, (c) select a standardized measure if it is appropriate, (d) give the measures near the beginning and end of each instructional unit, semester, or year, (e) analyze and organize the data for feedback to interested stakeholders, (f) give the feedback in a timely and orderly way, and (g) use the results to make decisions about improving the instructional program. In constructing a questionnaire, each question needs to be well-worded and requiring either an open-ended (fill-in-the-blank or free response) or closed-ended (dichotomous, multiple choice, ranking, or scale) response. The questions are then arranged in an appropriate sequence and given an attractive format. A standardized questionnaire, such as the Classroom Life instrument may be used to measure a broader range of student attitudes.

Learning Logs And Journals

Students often do not spend enough time reflecting on what they are learning and how it relates in a personal way to their lives. Learning logs and journals help students document and reflect on their learning experiences. **Logs** tend to emphasize short entries concerning the subject matter being studied. Logs are especially useful in conjunction with informal cooperative learning. **Journals** tend to emphasize more narrative entries concerning personal observations, feelings, and opinions in response to readings, events, and experiences. These entries often connect what is being studied in one class with other classes or with life outside of the classroom. Journals are especially useful in having students apply what they are learning to their "action theories."

Summary

Traditionally, assessment procedures have been quite limited. Teachers often notice the light in a student's eye, changes in voice inflections, the "aha" of discovery, the creative insight resulting from collaborating with others, the persistence and struggle of a student determined to understand complex material, the serendipitous use of skills and concepts beyond the context in which they were learned, and reports from parents and other teachers on the changes in a student resulting from a course of study. What has been lacking is a systematic way of collecting and reporting such evidence.

Times have changed. The diverse assessment procedures discussed in this book are quite developed and may be used effectively as part of any instructional program. Each has its strengths and its weaknesses. Each can be integrated into ongoing instructional program and managed when they are used as part of cooperative learning. Together, they allow cooperative learning groups to engage in total quality learning.

Total Quality Learning

Total quality learning begins with assigning students to teams and assigning them the task of continuously improving the quality of the processes of learning and assessment. **Continuous improvement** is the ongoing search for changes that will increase the quality of the processes of learning, instructing, and assessing. Each time students write a composition, for example, they should find at least one way to improve their writing skills. The changes do not have to be dramatic. Small, incremental changes are fine.

To improve continuously the processes of learning and assessment, students need to engage in eight steps. **First**, they must form teams. Quality learning is not possible without cooperative learning groups. **Second**, team members analyze the assignment and select a learning process for improvement. **Third**, members define the process to improve, usually by drawing a flow chart or cause-and-effect diagram. **Fourth**, team members engage in the process. **Fifth**, students gather data about the process, display the data, and analyze it. Tools to help them do so include observation forms, Pareto charts, run charts, scatter diagrams, and histograms. **Sixth**, on the basis of the analysis, team members make a plan to improve the process. **Seventh**, students implement the plan by engaging in the learning process in a modified and improved way. **Finally**, the team institutionalizes the changes that do in fact improve the quality of the learning process.

One way to enhance the use of total quality learning is through the use of student management teams. A **student management team** consists of three or four students plus the instructor who assume responsibility for the success of the class by focusing on how to improve either the instructor's teaching or the content of the course. The group members monitor the course through their own experience and the comments of classmates. There are four stages of using student management teams: forming the team by recruiting and choosing members, building a cooperative team by structuring the five basic elements, improving the instruction and content of the course, and reaping the long-term gains from the process by carrying on the improvements to the next course.

Teaching Teams And Assessment

The days are gone when a teacher, working in isolation from colleagues, could instruct, assess, and report results by him- or herself. The practices have become so labor intensive and complex that one teacher cannot expect to do them alone. Realistically, colleagial teaching teams are needed to coordinate and continuously improve the instruction, assessment, and reporting process. Teachers need to begin their instruction, assessment, and reporting efforts with forming a colleagial teaching team. This allows them to capitalize on the many ways teams enhance productivity. The team focuses its efforts on continuously improving both student learning and the quality of instruction. The team as a whole conducts the assessment and reporting process by developing rubrics, applying the rubrics effectively, and reporting results to interested audiences. The team then establishes a continuous improvement process focusing on maximizing the quality of instruction of each member. While engaging in the continuous improvement process, the team also engages in continuously retraining aimed at improving the effectiveness of their use of the assessment procedures. The use of colleagial teaching teams provides the framework for developing schoolwide criteria and standards to be used in assessment.

Giving Grades

Teachers need to assess student learning and progress frequently, but they do not need to evaluate or give grades. Assessing involves checking on how students are doing, what they have learned, and what problems or difficulties they have experienced. Grades are symbols that represent a value judgment concerning the relative quality of a student's achievement during a specified period of instruction. Grades are necessary to give students and other interested audiences information about students' level of achievement, evaluate the success of an instructional program, provide students access to certain educational opportunities, and reward students who excel. Grading systems may involve a single grade or multi-grades. It is vital that grades are awarded fairly as they can have considerable influence on students' futures. Being fair includes using a wide variety of assignments to measure achievement. Grades may be supplemented with checklist and narratives to give a more complex and complete summative evaluation of student achievement. Having students work in cooperative groups adds further opportunity to measure aspects of students' learning and assign grades in a variety of ways.

The Stars And The Ground

Aesop tells a tale of an astrologer who believed he could read the future in the stars. One evening he was walking along an open road, his eyes fixed on the stars, when he fell into a pit full of mud and water. Up to his ears in the muddy water, he clawed at the slippery sides of the pit. Unable to climb out he cried for help. As the villagers pulled him out of the mud, one of them said, *"What use is it to read the future in the stars if you can not see the present in the ground at your feet?"* What Aesop so aptly points out in this fable is that you must be able to simultaneously focus on the future vision of what you hope to achieve and see each little step required to get there. That is the dilemma of assessment. You must keep your efforts focused on the future (the goals you hope to achieve) while being aware of the present (the processes of learning and instruction that are taking place).

Sigmund Freud believed that a sense of worth came from two life-sustaining drives--the capacities to love and to work. Many educators forget that the most significant motivating forces for students are to increase their competencies in a way that benefits those they care about. Such personal meaning is created by three factors:

1. **Structuring positive interdependence among students.** It is positive interdependence that creates positive relationships among students, a commitment to each other's learning and well-being, a desire to contribute to the common good, the motivation to strive to be one's best for the sake of others as well as oneself, and the conviction that there is more to life than selfish self-interest. The influence of positive interdependence on assessment is so profound and foundational that it cannot be overemphasized.

2. **Involve students in the learning and assessment processes.** Students need to be involved in formulating their learning goals, choosing the paths for achieving the goals, assessing their progress and success, planning how to improve, and implementing their plan, serious management problems arise. This process cannot be completed alone. Each student needs an ongoing support system made up of individuals who genuinely care about him or her and are committed to his or her learning and well-being. These groupmates provide an external source of critical assessment with a framework of caring and commitment. In cooperative relationships, students will seek out critical feedback, clarify it, and use it to guide their efforts to improve and grow.

3. **Ensure assessment data is organized in a way that it may be used.** Useful results help students to seek remediation for what they misunderstood, reviews to fill in gaps in what they know, and new learning experiences to take the next steps to advance their knowledge and skills. If the external assessors are perceived to be unreliable or ill-intentioned, then the use of the assessment results is placed in question and improvement hindered. If the gap between self-assessment and the assessment of others is too great, the student and his or her groupmates need to engage in a dialogue to clarify their differences and gain a consensus as to how the work compares to the assessment criteria.

These three issues are interrelated. Cooperative learning creates the framework for the involvement. The involvement creates the ownership of the learning and assessment processes and the motivation to use the assessment results to improve one's understanding and competencies. Using the assessment results requires the help of collaborators. Together they make a gestalt that fuels continuous improvement and total quality learning.

Looking Forward

There is an old story about 12 men in a lifeboat. One of the men announced that he had decided to bore a series of holes in the bottom of the boat. "*You can't do that,*" the other eleven men cried. "*Why not?*" the man answered. "*I've divided the boat into twelve equal parts. Each of us has part of the boat. We can do anything to our part of the boat we want to. I've decided to drill holes in the bottom of my part. You do anything you want with your part. It's your right!*" While many people see the world in these terms, assessment does not work that way. Assessment is a community responsibility involving everyone in the classroom and school.

At the end of this book you may be at a new beginning. Years of experience are needed to gain real expertise in (a) integrating the assessment procedures into instruction and (b) capitalizing on the strengths of cooperative learning groups to help you do so. Involving students in the assessment process will eventually result in more sophisticated students who can help you continuously improve the assessment process. For too long adults have had the sole proprietorship assessment. The highest level of Bloom's Taxonomy (1976) is generating, holding, and applying a set of internal and external criteria. It is time that much of the responsibility for assessment is shared with students. Working jointly with students creates a learning community in which students' involvement in the assessment process will enhance all aspects of learning and instruction.

Meaningful And Manageable Assessment Through Cooperative Learning, Interaction Book Company, 7208 Cornelia Drive, Edina, MN 55435, (612) 831-9500, FAX (612) 831-9332

Glossary

Academic tournament: Objective test conducted in a game format where students study in cooperative learning group, compete in tournament triads consisting of students from three different cooperative learning groups) to determine who has learned the material the best, and take their scores back to their cooperative learning group and compute a total group score. The cooperative learning group with the highest score is recognized.

Action theory: Theory as to what actions are needed to achieve a desired consequence in a given situation.

Assessment: The collecting of information about the quality or quantity of a change in a student, group, teacher, or administrator.

Attitude: Learned disposition to respond in a favorable or unfavorable manner to a particular person, object, or idea.

Authentic assessment: Requiring students to demonstrate desired procedures and skills in "real life" contexts.

Base group: A long-term, heterogeneous cooperative learning group with stable membership.

Benchmarking: Establishing criteria based on best known practices.

Category system: The observer lists a set of categories so that every observed behavior can be recorded into one, and only one, of a series of mutually exclusive categories.

Cause-and-effect diagram: A visual diagram of the relationship between some effect and all its possible causes.

Closed-ended questions: Calls for student to indicate the alternative answer closest to his or her internal response.

Colleagial teaching teams: Two to five faculty members whose purpose is to increase teachers' instructional expertise and success by working together to implement instructional assessment, and reporting procedures with fidelity and flexibility as well as solve any implementation problems that may arise.

Competition: A social situation in which the goals of the separate participants are so linked that there is a negative correlation among their goal attainments; when one student achieves his or her goal, all others with whom he or she is competitively linked fail to achieve their goals.

Completion test item: Students are required to supply a brief answer consisting of a name, word, phrase, or symbol.

Conflict-of-interests: When the actions of one person attempting to maximize his or her needs and benefits prevent, block, interfere with, injure, or in some way make less effective the actions of another person attempting to maximize his or her needs and benefits.

Continuous improvement: Ongoing search by everyone involved for incremental changes to increase the quality of learning, instructing, and administrating processes.

Controversy: When one person's ideas, information, conclusions, theories, and opinions are incompatible with those of another, and the two seek to reach an agreement.

Cooperation: Working together to accomplish shared goals and maximize own and other's success. Individuals perceiving that they can reach their goals if and only if the other group members also do so.

Cooperative imperative: We desire and seek out opportunities to operate jointly with others to achieve mutual goals.

Cooperative learning: Students working together to accomplish shared learning goals and maximize their own and their groupmates' achievement.

Criterion: A predetermined standard.

Criteria-referenced measure: Designed to compare a student's performance to preset criteria defining excellence on learning tasks or skills.

Deutsch, Morton: Social psychologist who theorized about cooperative, competitive, and individualistic goal structures.

Diagnostic assessment: The collection of information about a student's entry level characteristics before an instruction unit, course, semester, or year.

Discrimination: When a norm-referenced measure is used, each item has to discriminate among students as high, medium and low on the skill or knowledge being measured.

Distributive justice: Rewards may be distributed according to **equity** (the person who contributes the most or scores the highest receives the greatest reward), **equality** (every person receives the same reward), and **need** (those who have the greatest need receive the greatest reward).

Egocentrism: Embeddedness in one's own viewpoint to the extent that one is unaware of other points of view and of the limitations of one's perspectives.

Essay tests: Students are required to write paragraphs or themes as responses to a question. **Short-essay items** require students to recall, explain, or apply specific information they have learned in their own words.

Evaluation: Judging the merit, value, or desirability of a measured performance.

Event sampling: The observer records a given event or category of events each time it naturally occurs.

Exhaustive categories: Every instance of observed behavior can be classified into one of the available categories.

Expertise: A person's proficiency, adroitness, competence, and skill.

Feedback: Information that allows individuals to compare their actual performance with standards of performance.

Fermenting skills: Skills needed to engage in **academic controversies** to stimulate reconceptualization of the material being studied, cognitive conflict, the search for more information, and the communication of the rationale behind one's conclusions.

Filter question: Question used to exclude a respondent from a particular sequence of questions if the questions are not relevant to him or her.

Flow chart: Visual representation showing all the steps of a process or procedure and how they relate to each other.

Focused interview: Arranges questions like a funnel so that the initial questions are broad and general and subsequent questions require the student to give more and more precise and specific answers.

Formal cooperative learning group: A learning group that may last for several minutes to several class sessions to complete a specific task or assignment (such as solving a set of problems, completing a unit, writing a theme or report, conducting an experiment, or reading and comprehending a story, play, chapter or book.

Formative assessments: The periodic collection of information to provide students feedback concerning their progress toward achieving their learning goals.

Forming skills: Management skills directed toward organizing the group and establishing minimum norms for appropriate behavior.

Formulating skills: Skills directed toward providing the mental processes needed to build deeper level understanding of the material being studied, to stimulate the use of higher quality reasoning strategies, and to maximize mastery and retention of the assigned material.

Frequency distribution: A listing of the number of people who obtain each score or fall into each range of scores on a test.

Functioning skills: Skills directed toward managing the group's efforts to complete their tasks and maintain effective working relationships among members.

Funnel sequence: Begins with broad question and then progressively narrows down the scope of the questions until very specific questions are asked at the end.

Goal: A desired place toward which people are working, a state of affairs that people value.

Goal setting conference: Conference in which each student sets personal learning goals and publicly commits him-or herself to achieve them.

Goal structure: The type of social interdependence structured among students as they strive to accomplish their learning goals.

Grades: Symbols (letters, numbers, words) that represent a value judgment concerning the relative quality of a student's achievement during a specified period of instruction.

Grade-equivalent scores: The average of the scores of all students in the norming sample at that grade level.

Group: Two or more individuals in face-to-face interaction, each aware of his or her membership in the group, each aware of the others who belong to the group, and each aware of their positive interdependence as they strive to achieve mutual goals.

Group discussion test: Students meet in their cooperative base group and discuss the content of the assigned readings to verify that all members can meet a set of criteria in their understanding of the material covered.

G-I-G test procedure: A procedure for giving tests where students prepare for the test in cooperative learning groups, take the test individually, and then retake the test in their cooperative learning groups to clarify the answer to each question and provide immediate remediation for anything the student does not know.

Group portfolio: An organized collection of group work samples accumulated over time and individual work samples of each member.

Group processing: Reflecting on a group session to (a) describe what member actions were helpful and unhelpful and (b) make decisions about what actions to continue or change.

High-performance cooperative group: A group that meets all the criteria for being a cooperative group and outperforms all reasonable expectations, given its membership.

Histogram: Shows how continuous measurement data are clustered and dispersed.

Individual accountability: The measurement of whether or not each group member has achieved the group's goal. Assessing the quality and quantity of each member's contributions and giving the results to all group members.

Individualistic goal structure: No correlation among group members' goal attainments; when group members perceive that obtaining their goal is unrelated to the goal achievement of other members. Individuals working by themselves to accomplish goals unrelated to and independent from the goals of others.

Informal cooperative learning group: A temporary, ad hoc group that lasts for only one discussion or one class period. Its purposes are to focus student attention on the material to be learned, create an expectation set and mood conducive to learning, help organize in advance the material to be covered in a class session, ensure that students cognitively process the material being taught, and provide closure to an instructional session.

Instruction: Structuring situations in ways that help students change, through learning.

Interpretive items: Students are required to study a graph, diagram, map, or descriptive paragraph and interpret what it means.

Interview: A situation in which both the interviewer and the respondent are present when the questions are asked and answered.

Kaizen: A society-wide covenant of mutual help in the process of getting better and better, day after day.

Learning: A change within a student that is brought about by instruction.

Learning goal: A desired future state of demonstrating competence or mastery in the subject area being studied, such as conceptual understanding of math processes, facility in the proper use of a language, or mastering the procedures of inquiry.

Learning journal: Self-report procedure in which students record narrative, personal entries concerning aspects of the subject matter being studied that has personal value and relevance. Entries may be personal observations, feelings, and opinions in response to readings, events, and experiences.

Learning Log: A self-report procedure in which students record short entries concerning the subject matter being studied.

Lewin, Kurt: Father of group dynamics; social psychologist who originated field theory, experimental group dynamics, and applied group dynamics.

Likert scale: A question with a response scale of anywhere from three to nine points.

Matching test-item: List of concepts and responses; students match one of the responses with each concept.

Mean: The sum of all scores divided by the number of individuals.

Median: The midpoint in the set of scores arranged in order from highest to lowest.

Motivation: A combination of the perceived likelihood of success and the perceived incentive for success. The greater the likelihood of success and the more important it is to succeed, the higher the motivation.

Multiple-choice items: Direct question or incomplete statement (called the stem) followed by two or more possible answers (called responses), only one of which is to be selected.

Multi-grade system: Contains different grades for different aspects of learning. Grades may focus on **product criteria** (a summative evaluation of student achievement that focuses on what students know and are able to do), **process criteria** (the processes students use to learn including effort or work habits), and **progress criteria** (improvement scoring, gain in learning).

Mutually exclusive categories: Categories that are precisely distinguishable and independent from each other.

Normal curve equivalent: Standard score with arange from 1 to 99 with a mean of 50 and a standard deviation of about 21.

Norm-referenced tests: Designed to test a student's performance as it compares to the performances of other students.

Objective tests: Tests whose items are easily scored and analyzed, given to large numbers of students, take very little time to administer and score, and are free of bias in scoring and in requiring unrelated skills such as writing.

Objectivity: The agreement of (a) experts on the correct answer to a test item and (b) different scorers on what score should be assigned to a test paper or questionnaire.

Meaningful And Manageable Assessment Through Cooperative Learning, Interaction Book Company, 7208 Cornelia Drive, Edina, MN 55435, (612) 831-9500, FAX (612) 831-9332

Observation checklist: A record keeping device for teachers to use to keep track of the degree to which each student has demonstrated a targeted behavior, action, skills, or procedure.

Observation form: Used to tally and count the number of times a behavior, action, or event is observed in a specified time period.

Open-ended question: Calls for students to answer by writing a statement that may vary in length.

Oral examination: Students are interviewed about what they have learned.

Pareto chart: A form of vertical bar chart that helps teams separate the vital few problems and causes from the trivial many that takes its name from the Italian economist Vilfredo Frederico Damaso Pareto (1548-1623).

Pareto principle (80/20 rule): 80 percent of the trouble comes from 10 percent of the problems.

Percentile rank: The percent of the class with scores below that obtained by the student (ranges from 0 to 100).

Performance assessment: Students are required to engage in a set of actions to demonstrate their level of skill in enacting a procedure or creating a product.

Portfolio: An organized collection of evidence accumulated over time on a student's or group's academic progress, achievements, skills, and attitudes. Two common types are best works portfolios and process portfolio.

Positive goal interdependence: When students perceive that they can achieve their learning goals if, and only if, all other members of their group also attain their goals.

Positive interdependence is the perception that you are linked with others in a way so that you cannot succeed unless they do (and vice versa), that is, their work benefits you and your work benefits them.

Post-evaluation conference: Conference in which the level of student achievement is explained by the student to interested parties.

Practicality: The cost per copy, the time it takes to administer, the ease of scoring, and other factors teachers have to take into account before deciding to use a particular measure.

Procedural learning: Learning conceptually what the skill is, when it should be used, how to engage in the skill, practicing the skill while eliminating errors, until an automated level of mastery is attained.

Process: All the tasks, organized in a sequence, that contribute to the accomplishment of one particular outcome.

Progress-assessment conference: A conference in which the student's progress toward achieving his or her goals is reviewed.

Project: An assignment aimed at having students produce something themselves on a topic related to the curriculum rather than just "reproduce" knowledge.

Promotive interaction: Actions that assist, help, encourage, and support the achievement of each other's goals.

Pseudo group: A group whose members have been assigned to work together but they have no interest in doing so. The structure promotes competition at close quarters.

Psychological health: Ability to build and maintain cooperative, interdependent relationships with other people.

Quality chart: Shows the extent to which the quality or quantity of performance is increasing or decreasing over time.

Reliability: When a student's performance remains the same on repeated measurements.

Rubric: Indicators of different levels of a criterion being used to assess a performance.

Run chart: Used to monitor a process over time to see whether or not the long-range average is changing.

Sampling plan: A course of action specifying in what order you will observe each learning group for what amount of time.

Scatter diagram: Displays the relationship between two actions, conditions, or causes.

Self-assessment: Reflection on how well a person performed academically and how often and how well a person performed the targeted social or cognitive skills.

Self-disclosure: Revealing how you are reacting to the present situation and of giving any information about the present that is relevant to an understanding of your reactions to the present.

Semantic differential question: A series of rating scales of bipolar adjective pairs referring to the concept towards which the person wishes to obtain student attitudes.

Sign system: Listing beforehand a limited number of specific kinds of behavior of interest and recording only those behaviors that fall into one of the categories.

Social competence: Extent to which a person can use interpersonal and small group skills to ensure that the consequences of his or her actions match his or her intentions.

Social skills: The interpersonal and small group skills needed to interact effectively with other people.

Social skills training: A structured intervention designed to help individuals improve their interpersonal skills.

Socratic interviewing: Procedure for using an interview to lead students to deeper and deeper insights about what they know.

Standard score: Indication of how far each student is above or below the mean in a way that allows comparison of scores from different tests, regardless of the size of the class or the number of items on the test. Found by subtracting the mean from the student's raw score and dividing by the standard deviation.

Stanine score: Standard score with mean of 5 and a standard deviation of 2.

Standardized tests: Tests prepared for nationwide use to provide accurate and meaningful information on students' levels of performance relative to others at their age or gráde information on students' levels of performance relative to others at their age or grade levels.

Structured coding system: Requires observers to categorize each group behavior into an objectively definable category.

Student-management team: Three or four students plus the instructor assume responsibility for the success of the course by focusing on how to improve either the instructor's teaching or the content of the course.

Summative assessment: The collection of information at the end of an instructional unit to judge the final quality and quantity to student achievement and/or the success of the instructional program.

Support: Communicating to another person that you recognize his or her strengths and believe he or she has the capabilities needed to productively manage the situation.

Teacher-made tests: Written or oral assessments of student achievement that are (a) not commercially produced or standardized and (b) designed specifically for the teacher's students.

Test blueprint: An analysis of a test to ensure that it covers a representative, accurate sample of what is covered in the learning unit.

Test norms: Records of the performances of groups of individuals who have previously taken the test.

T-chart: Procedure to teach social skills by specifying the nonverbal actions and verbal phrases that operationalize the skill.

Time sampling: The observer records the occurrence or nonoccurrence of selected behavior(s) within specified, uniform time limits.

Traditional learning group: A group whose members agree to work together, but see little benefit from doing so. The structure promotes individualistic work with talking.

Transfer: Person taking what he or she learned in one setting and using it in another setting

True-false test item: A fact, statement, definition, or principle followed by two responses (true or false).

Unstructured observations: The recording of significant, specific events involving students in a notebook or index cards.

Validity: Validity means that the test actually measures what it was designed to measure, all of what it was designed to measure, and nothing but what it was designed to measure.

Z-scores: Standard score with a mean of 0 and standard deviation of 1.

References

Afflerbach, P., & Sammons, R. (1991). **Report cards in literacy evaluation: Teachers' training, practices, and values.** Paper presented at the National Reading Conference, Palm Springs, California.

Astin, A. (1985). Involvement: The cornerstone of excellence. **Change**, July/August, 35-39.

Austin, S., & McCann, R. (1992). **Here's another arbitrary grade for your collection: A statewide study of grading policies**. Paper presented at the American Educational Research Association, San Francisco.

Baron, J. (1994, April). Using multi-dimensionality to capture verisimilitude: Criterion-referenced performance-based assessments and the ooze factor. Paper presented at the annual meeting of the American Educational Research Association, New Orleans.

Bennett, R., Gottesman, R., Rock, D., & Cerullo, F. (1993). Influence of behavior perceptions and gender on teachers' judgments of students' academic skill. **Journal of Educational Psychology**, **85**, 347-356.

Bloom, B. (1976). **Human characteristics and school learning**. New York: McGraw-Hill.

Brookhart, S. (1993). Teachers' grading practices: Meaning and values. **Journal of Educational Measurement, 30**(2), 123-142.

Canady, R., & Hotchkiss, P. (1989). It's a good score! Just a bad grade. **Phi Delta Kappan, 71**, 68-71.

Cangelosi, J. (1990). Grading and reporting student achievement. In **Designing tests for evaluating student achievement** (pp. 196-213). New York: Longman.

Chastain, K. (1990). Characteristics of graded and ungraded compositions. **Modern Language Journal, 74**(1), 10-14.

Connecticut State Board of Education. (1991). Common Core of Learning Assessment. Hartford, CT: Author.

Connecticut State Board of Education. (1992/1994). Connecticut Academic Performance Test. Hartford, CT: Author.

Davis, A., & Felknor, C. (1994). The demise of performance based graduation in Littleton. Educational Leadership, 51(6), 64-65.

Deutsch, M. (1949). A theory of cooperation and competition. **Human Relations, 2**, 129- 152.

Deutsch, M. (1962). Cooperation and trust: Some theoretical notes. In M. R. Jones (Ed.), **Nebraska symposium on motivation** (pp. 275-319). Lincoln, NE: University of Nebraska Press.

Deutsch, M. (1985). **Distributive justice**. New Haven: Yale University Press.

Deutsch, M. (1979). Education and distributive justice: Some reflections on grading systems. **American Psychologist, 34**, 391-401.

Meaningful And Manageable Assessment Through Cooperative Learning, Interaction Book Company, 7208 Cornelia Drive, Edina, MN 55435, (612) 831-9500, FAX (612) 831-9332

DeVries, D. & Edwards, K. (1974). Student teams and learning games: Their effects on cross-race and cross-sex interaction. **Journal of Educational Psychology, 66**, 741-749.

Ebel, R. (1979). **Essentials of educational measurement** (3rd ed.). Englewood Cliffs, NJ: Prentice-Hall.

Feldmesser, R. (1971). **The positive functions of grades**. Paper presented at the American Educational Research Association Convention, New York.

Frary, R., Cross, L., & Weber, J. (1993). Testing and grading practices for instruction and measurement. Educational Measurement: **Issues and Practices, 12**(3), 23-30.

Frisbie, D., & Waltman, K. (1992). Developing a personal grading plan. **Educational Measurement: Issues and Practices, 11**(3), 35-42.

Guskey, T. (1994). Making the grade: what benefits students? **Educational Leadership, 52**(2), 14-20.

Gronlund, N. (1988). **How to construct achievement tests** (4th ed.). New York: Macmillan.

Hills, J. (1991). Apathy concerning grading and testing. **Phi Delta Kappan, 72**(2), 540-545.

Johnson, D. W. (1970). **Social psychology of education**. New York: Holt, Rinehart, & Windston.

Johnson, D. W. (1991). **Human relations and your career** (3rd Edition). Englewood Cliffs, NJ: Prentice Hall.

Johnson, D. W. (1996). **Reaching out: interpersonal effectiveness and self-actualization** (6th Ed.) Englewood Cliffs, NJ: Prentice Hall.

Johnson, D. W., & Johnson, F. (1996). **Joining together: group theory and group skills** (6th Ed). Englewood Cliffs, NJ: Prentice Hall.

Johnson, D. W., & Johnson, R. (1983). Social interdependence and perceived academic and personal support in the classroom. **Journal of Social Psychology, 120**, 77-82.

Johnson, D. W., & Johnson, R. (1985). Impact of classroom organization and instructional methods on the effectiveness of mainstreaming. In C. Meisel (Ed.), **Mainstreamed handicapped children: Outcomes, controversies, and new directions** (pp. 215-250). New York: Lawrence Erlbaum.

Johnson, D. W., & Johnson, R. (1989a). **Cooperation and competition: theory and research**. Edina, MN: Interaction Book Company.

Johnson, D. W., & Johnson, R. (1991a). Cooperative learning and classroom and school climate. In B. Fraser & H. Walberg (Eds.), Educational environments: Evaluation, antecedents and consequences. New York: Pergamon.

Johnson, D. W., & Johnson, R. (1991b). What cooperative learning has to offer the gifted. Cooperative Learning, 11(3), 24-27.

Johnson, D. W., & Johnson, R. (1994). **Leading the cooperative school** (2nd Ed). Edina, MN: Interaction Book Company.

Johnson, D. W., & Johnson, R. (1995a). **Teaching students to be peacemakers**. Edina, MN: Interaction Book Company.

Johnson, D. W., & Johnson R. (1995b). **My mediation notebook**. Edina, MN: Interaction Book Company.

Johnson, D. W., & Johnson, R. (1995c). **Creative controversy: Intellectual challenge in the classroom**. Edina, MN: Interaction Book Company.

Johnson, D. W., Johnson, R., & Anderson, D. (1983). Social interdependence and classroom climate. **Journal of Psychology, 114**, 135-142.

Johnson, D. W., Johnson, R., & Holubec, E. (1993). **Circles of learning: Cooperation in the classroom** (4th Ed.). Edina, MN: Interaction Book Company.

Johnson, D. W., Johnson, R., & Holubec, E. (1993). **Cooperation in the classroom** (5th Ed.). Edina, MN: Interaction Book Company.

Johnson, D. W., Johnson, R., & Holubec, E. (1992). **Advanced cooperative learning** (2nd Ed.). Edina, MN: Interaction Book Company.

Johnson, D. W., Johnson, R., & Holubec, E. (1995). **The nuts and bolts of cooperative learning**. Edina, MN: Interaction Book Company.

Johnson, D. W., Johnson, R., & Smith, K. (1991). **Active learning: Cooperation in the college classroom**. Edina, MN: Interaction Book Company.

Miles, M. (Ed.). (1964). **Innovation in education**. New York: Teachers College Press.

Middleton, W. (1933). Some general trends in grading procedure. **Education, 54**(1), 5-10.

Nava, F., & Loyd, B. (1992). **An investigation of achievement and nonachievement criteria in elementary and secondary school grading**. Paper presented at the American Educational Research Association, San Francisco.

O'Donnell, A., & Woolfolk, A. (1991). **Elementary and secondary teachers' beliefs about testing and grading**. Paper presented at the American Psychological Association Convention, San Francisco.

Ornstein, A. (1994). Grading practices and policies: An overview and some suggestions. **NASSP Bulletin, 78,** 55-64.

Osgood, C., Suci, C., & Tannenbaum, P. (1957). **The measurement of meaning**. Urbana: University of Illinois Press.

Page, E. (1958). Teacher comments and student performance: A seventy-four classroom experiment in school motivation. **Journal of Educational Psychology, 49**, 173-181.

Peters, T., & Waterman, R. (1982). **In search of excellence**. New York: Harper & Row.

Schwartz, R. (1996). Student management teams. **ASEE Prism**, January, 19-23.

Selby, D., & Murphy, S. (1992). Graded or degraded: Perceptions of letter-grading for mainstreamed learning disabled students. **British Columbia Journal of Special Education, 16**(1), 92-104.

Shavelson, R., Gao, X., & Baxter, G. (1991). Design theory and psychometrics for complex performance assessment: Transfer and generalizability. Los Angeles: University of California, Center for Research on Evaluation, Standards, and Student Testing.

Starch, D., & Elliott, E. (1912). Reliability of the grading of high school work in English. **School Review, 20**, 442-459.

Starch, D., & Elliott, E. (1913). Reliability of the grading of high school work in mathematics. **School Review, 21**, 254-259.

Stiggins, R. (1994). Communicating with report card grades. In R. Stiggins, **Student-centered classrooom assessment** (pp. 363-396). New York: Macmillan.

Stiggins, R. (January 1988). Revitalizing classroom assessment: The highest instructional priority. Phi Delta Kappan, 363-368.

Stiggins, R., & Duke, D. (1991). **District grading policies and their potential impact on at-risk students**. Paper presented at the American Educational Research Association, Chicago.

Stiggins, R., Frisbie, D., & Griswold, P. (1989). Inside high school grading practices: Building a research agenda. **Educational Measurement: Issues and Practice, 8**(2), 5-14.

Sweedler-Brown, C. (1992). The effect of training on the appearance bias of holistic essay graders. **Journal of Research and Development in Education, 26**(1), 24-29.

Watson, G., & Johnson, D. W. (1972). **Social psychology: Issues and insights** (2nd Ed.). Philadelphia: Lippincott.

White, N., Blythe, T., & Gardner, H. (1992). Multiple intelligences theory: Creating the thoughtful classroom. In A. Costa, J. Bellanca, & R. Fogarty (Eds.), **If minds matter: A foreword to the future**, Volume II (pp. 127-134). Palatine, IL: IRI/Skylight Publishing.